Welcome to
THE
EVERYTHING
Family Guides

THESE HANDY, PORTABLE BOOKS are designed to be the perfect traveling companions. Whether you're traveling within a tight family budget or feeling the urge to splurge, you will find all you need to create a memorable family vacation.

Use these books to plan your trips, and then take them along with you for easy reference. Does Jimmy want to go sailing? Or maybe Jane wants to go to the local hobby shop. *The Everything® Family Guides* offer many ways to entertain kids of all ages while also ensuring you get the most out of your time away from home.

Review this book cover to cover to give you great ideas before you travel, and stick it in your backpack or diaper bag to use as a quick reference guide for the activities, attractions, and excursions you want to experience. Let *The Everything® Family Guides* help you travel the world, and you'll discover that vacationing with the whole family can be filled with fun and exciting adventures.

 FACT

Important sound bytes of information

 ESSENTIAL

Quick handy tips

 ALERT!

Urgent warnings

D1365236

 QUESTION?

Solutions to common problems

THE
EVERYTHING®
— Family Guides —

Dear Reader,

Prepare yourself for a family trip to remember. Whether you own an RV or are considering renting or purchasing one, this book can help you make your trip worry free and full of wonderful memories. My family has been RV traveling for more than fifteen years, starting from the time my eldest child was just a toddler. We have found it to be a fun, economical, and memorable way to travel. From the beaches of southern and central California, to the cornfields of Iowa, we have traveled throughout the United States and Canada. I'll share with you all of my tips and checklists for planning and enjoying any RV trip, whether close to home or farther afield. You'll have the chance to get close to nature, or to see your favorite theme park from an entirely new angle.

Having traveled in several different RVs over the years, from a fold-down trailer to a large motorhome, I'll help you plan for your individual needs, both now and in the future. From budget travel to luxury accommodations, today's RVs have it all. So sit back, and let me help you get started on your best family vacation ever!

Marian Eure

THE

EVERYTHING®

FAMILY GUIDE TO

RV TRAVEL
AND
CAMPGROUNDS

From choosing the right vehicle
to planning your trip—all you need
for your adventure on wheels

Marian Eure

Adams Media
Avon, Massachusetts

*This book is dedicated to my husband, Robert, and children,
Bobby and Jeanne, with whom I have shared many wonderful days and
nights of travel. Thanks so much for the support and encouragement.*

Publishing Director: Gary M. Krebs
Managing Editor: Kate McBride
Copy Chief: Laura M. Daly
Acquisitions Editor: Gina Marzilli
Development Editor: Larry Shea
Production Editor: Jamie Wielgus

Production Director: Susan Beale
Production Manager: Michelle Roy Kelly
Series Designer: Daria Perreault
Cover Design: Paul Beatrice, Matt LeBlanc
Layout and Graphics: Colleen Cunningham,
Rachael Eiben, Michelle Roy Kelly,
John Paulhus, Daria Perreault, Erin Ring

An Everything® Series Book.
Everything® and everything.com® are registered trademarks of F+W Publications, Inc.

Published by Adams Media, an F+W Publications Company
57 Littlefield Street, Avon, MA 02322 U.S.A.
www.adamsmedia.com

ISBN: 1-59337-301-5
Printed in Canada.
J I H G F E D C B A

Library of Congress Cataloging-in-Publication Data
Eure, Marian.
The everything family guide to RV travel and campgrounds / Marian Eure.
p.   cm.
ISBN 1-59337-301-5
1. Recreational vehicle camping–United States. 2. Family recreation–United States.
3. Campsites, facilities, etc.–United States–Directories. 4. Recreational vehicles–Purchasing.
I. Title. II. Series: Everything series.

GV198.6.E87 2005
796.7'9–dc22

2004026019

This publication is designed to provide accurate and authoritative information with regard to the subject matter covered. It is sold with the understanding that the publisher is not engaged in rendering legal, accounting, or other professional advice. If legal advice or other expert assistance is required, the services of a competent professional person should be sought.
    —From a *Declaration of Principles* jointly adopted by a Committee of the American Bar Association and a Committee of Publishers and Associations

Many of the designations used by manufacturers and sellers to distinguish their products are claimed as trademarks. Where those designations appear in this book and Adams Media was aware of a trademark claim, the designations have been printed with initial capital letters.

Interior illustrations by Eric Andrews / Cartography by Map Resources
This book is available at quantity discounts for bulk purchases.
For information, call 1-800-872-5627.

Contents

Top Ten Advantages of Traveling by RV

1. Traveling by RV can save you lots of money over the cost of airplane tickets and hotel room rates.

2. You get to sleep in familiar surroundings, in your own bed, every night.

3. Kids can take along more activities to keep them occupied, and they'll be less likely to get bored and whiny during long trips.

4. Even during peak travel season, when nearly every motel and hotel is posting a "No Vacancy" sign, you will always have a place to sleep.

5. No more dealing with grimy service station restrooms— you've brought your own portable restroom with you.

6. Your pet can usually travel with you, saving money on boarding fees and eliminating heartache and anxiety for you and your pet.

7. By cooking in your own kitchen and on your own grill, you will save money you'd otherwise spend eating out.

8. You'll get closer to nature; most natural parks have camp grounds that let you enjoy the natural world up close and personal.

9. You can set your own schedule, and you won't be tied down by airline schedules or held up by time-consuming security requirements.

10. You meet some of the nicest people when traveling by RV.

Acknowledgments

Thank you to Bob and Fay Eure and to Keith and Regi Gross for sharing the knowledge they have picked up from their many years of RV travel.

Thanks also to the staff of the Recreation Vehicle Industry Association for their prompt responses to inquiries. They provide excellent support for all RV owners.

Introduction

From the early days of this country, the desire to travel has been an important part of the American character. For years, RVs have been a part of that wanderlust, especially as roads have improved and more leisure time has become possible.

RVs have become more affordable and larger over the years. As advances in automotive technology have changed the automotive industry, so, too, has the RV industry been transformed.

Some skeptical travelers may be leery of jumping into RV travel. If you are an old movie buff, you may remember the 1954 movie starring Lucille Ball and Desi Arnaz titled *The Long, Long Trailer*. This comedy follows a newlywed couple as they buy a 30-foot travel trailer and set off on a cross-country trip to their new home and his new job. Their misadventures make for a funny and entertaining movie, but they don't really show the true side of RV travel. In fact, this movie should be mandatory viewing for all RV travelers as a guide to what *not* to do in an RV.

In these days of long lines at airports due to increased security requirements, RV travel is becoming more appealing to those who prefer not to be tied down to any schedule other than their own. For the most part, you can come and go as you please and see parts of the United States and the rest of North America that few others will ever see. With an RV, you can get close to nature on the beach or in the mountains, or you can play tourist in the middle of the big city. There are few places you can't go in an RV.

Traveling in an RV is the perfect way to see the country and appreciate the beauty we are surrounded by. Rather than just flying over the Grand Canyon, you can spend your time seeing it up close and in person.

RV travel is also the perfect way to reconnect with your family. Families with children find that the hours they spend on the road are the perfect time to talk, something that is often overlooked in our stressful, busy lives. Single travelers find it a great way to see the country on their own terms and without a lot of pressure. Older families and empty nesters find RV travel a great way to fill the time that is freed up when children grow up and move away. It is also a great way to visit far-flung children without intruding too much on their space—after all, you're bringing your space with you.

RV travel is affordable for most, and an RV is available to fill almost any need and desire. Even in times of increased fuel costs, RV travel remains very affordable when you compare it to most other ways of traveling.

If you're still not sure RV travel is right for you, rent one for a weekend or a week and give it a trial run.

CHAPTER 1

Welcome to RV Travel!

ACCORDING TO the Recreational Vehicle Industry Association, nearly one in twelve U.S. households that owns a vehicle also owns an RV. That accounts for nearly 7 million households that are RV owners. In a University of Michigan study, the "typical" RV owner is forty-nine years old and married. Of Americans over the age of fifty-five, a full 10 percent are RV owners, while the largest group of RV owners by far is the baby boomers (35–54 years of age). As the baby boomers age, the percentage of RV owners who are over fifty-five, and the total number of RVs on the road, should increase substantially. Older owners typically have more disposable income and time to travel.

Finding Your Travel Style

What is your travel style? Do you crave luxury or love roughing it? Are you trying to get closer to nature, or to just get away? Do you like sleeping on a comfortable bed every night but get tired of eating in restaurants for every meal? If you answered yes to the last question, then RV travel will be a great fit. A closer look at different travel styles will help you find the perfect rig for your family.

Back to Nature

If your idea of the perfect vacation is getting away from civilization and communing with nature, then RV travel is ideal for you. A foldup trailer is compact enough for most wilderness areas. You achieve the closeness to nature of sleeping in a tent without having to sleep on the hard ground or worry about heavy rain forming a river through the middle of your tent. You will be able to keep your clothing and food sanitary, dry, and out of the elements. With the additional storage your trailer provides, you will be able to extend your vacation or spend less time restocking in the middle. You will also have room for all the fishing, hunting, or hiking equipment you need.

If the great outdoors is not your cup of tea, RV travel is still a great way to travel. Most large cities have suburban RV parks that are no wilder than your own backyard. Your RV becomes your home base for exploring museums, sightseeing, or even just escaping the weather.

Pursuing Your Passions

Are you a bird-watcher? Is square dancing your passion? Are you a big NASCAR fan? Using your RV to combine your vacation and your pursuit of these interests is a perfect fit. An RV will get you close to the action. If that rare species of bird can only be found in the hour before the sun comes up, you will often only have to step out the door to greet nature.

Square dancers are able to merge their love of travel and dance by planning group events, meeting in RV parks that provide places to dance. Many areas of the country have "Camping Squares" square dance clubs that plan outings on a monthly basis, combining an RV getaway with dancing and providing fellowship with others who share your interests. Many privately owned parks have a clubhouse or recreation hall that can accommodate several squares at once. Some groups even own portable dance surfaces that they can transport to events.

Some people who travel a lot for their jobs have found RVs to be the perfect home/office on wheels. Rather than dealing with uncertain comfort and cleanliness of strange motel rooms, they can sleep more comfortably and work more productively.

The Road to Adventure

RVs can take you from the mountaintops to the seashore and almost everywhere between. An RV specially outfitted for cold-weather camping can take you on ski trips to some of the finest ski areas in the country. A smaller truck camper can take you into some of the more remote wilderness areas. Just make sure you have your fishing equipment ready, and be prepared to be awed by the splendor of Mother Nature.

For those who are adventurous—but only up to a point—there are several companies that offer guided RV tours to some exotic locations. These types of tours are great for exploring Mexico, for example. The guide leading each tour will be on hand to keep you safe and, in case of problems, to get any help needed. Breakdowns in a foreign country, especially when you don't speak the language, can be a frustrating and expensive experience. Being part of a group can help prevent problems.

Living in Luxury

The wonderful thing about RV travel is that it can appeal to almost anyone's travel style. If you only want to travel in luxury, you can find RVs that will fit your need. On the high end of price and appointments, there are luxury motorcoaches that give the feel of a fine hotel suite.

These upper-end vehicles can rage from $250,000 to $500,000 and even more. Most are custom-built on a bus platform and feature wood trim and upgraded carpet and tile. Three to four slide-outs provide them with an exceptionally roomy feel. Kitchens are fully equipped for serious cooking, and these rigs come with loads of storage underneath. Many people who own such luxury RVs also pull a trailer that holds an additional vehicle for transportation while they are at their destination.

Some RV parks and campgrounds cater especially to these upscale travelers. They provide resort-style amenities that may include spas and extra-large paved sites. The fees at these resorts are high to encourage the upscale traveler and to discourage families with children.

 FACT

> RV is short for *recreational vehicle* and is used interchangeably for all types, from foldup campers to luxury bus conversions. Many RV owners refer to their RV as a *rig*. Some even give them names, but that is a personal preference.

The RV Lifestyle

The RV lifestyle can be anything you want it to be. You can travel full-time, explore the wilderness, visit family, escape harsh weather, or even work your way around the country. Once you become an RVer, you will find that you have joined a club populated by very diverse group of people who all have one thing in common—they like to travel.

Another great thing about RVing is that you can pick your own schedule. If you want to stay in one place for a week (and you have the time from work), you can. If you stay one day and decide to move on, nothing is holding you back.

Learn the Lingo

As with most hobbies or lifestyles, RVing has its own language. Listen in on a group of experienced RV travelers and you may feel as though you have just gone to a foreign country. Don't worry; you will pick it up readily, as most RV owners are more than willing to share their experiences with you. Ask a question and you will get an answer. Try to attend at least one RV show. Pick up all the literature and information offered. If any classes or seminars are offered, take them if possible. Talk with the dealers, and don't be afraid to ask questions—the more knowledgeable you are, the more enjoyable your RV travels will be.

ESSENTIAL

RV owners have a language of their own, and a new RV owner may find it confusing at first. Most RVers are very friendly and more than willing to share their experiences with you. Take any advice that sounds unsafe with a grain of salt, and check with an expert before trying it.

A Front Porch Neighborhood

Do you miss the days when everyone in the neighborhood spent more time out on the porch visiting with the neighbors than inside watching TV? RV travel naturally lends itself to getting outside and socializing. Space limitations inside the RV can make the outdoors more appealing. In any RV park or campground you visit, you will be living with a group of people who share your interests and values. It is not unusual to see RVers out socializing around a campfire and sharing stories of travels or tips to make travel better. Campgrounds that welcome families with children usually have a playground and often have a pool. Many RVers have found long-lasting friendships and treasured traveling companions along the road.

The Joy of the Open Road

No matter what the initial reason for choosing RV travel is, in the end it usually comes down to a love of independence and a dislike of being at the mercy of others and their schedules. With RVs, you can avoid the long lines and waits in airports. You don't have to worry that you have accidentally packed some contraband that will set off the security detectors. When you travel in an RV, you will not spend precious time searching for a clean restroom or a decent restaurant. It will be easier to stick to a special diet if it is needed. Every night you will get to climb into a familiar bed rather than a hotel room bed of questionable comfort or cleanliness. You can eat when you want, where you want, and you can eat at your leisure.

If you find you don't like the area you're in, or you are not pleased with the campground, you can just pack up and go. You won't have to live out of a suitcase, feeling frumpy in perpetually wrinkled clothing. You will have to make your own bed, but you won't have to worry about hiding your valuables from housekeeping staff who may be less than honest.

You can choose to visit wilderness areas and commune with nature or spend your time in the big city. If you spend time shopping, you will be able to carry a lot more souvenirs in your home on wheels than you would in your suitcase, and you will be able to get them home with fewer hassles than you would on an airplane.

 FACT

The Internet has become a great tool for RV owners trying to find groups of RV owners who share their interests. Just search on the term "RV" or "RV Travel," and your search will yield hundreds of links to sites with information for RVers all over the world.

RV travel can help foster family togetherness and bonding. It can be an effective method for getting your children out from in front of the television or computer screen. It is a great way to visit family without wearing out your welcome or being relegated to sleeping on the floor or the lumpy sleeper sofa.

Rent or Borrow for a Trial Run

You have decided that RV travel is for you. Great—but then another dilemma arises. How do you decide which RV or RV type is the one that will best meet your needs? Would a motorized RV be right for your family, or would the best choice be an RV that you can tow behind a vehicle? How big of an RV do you want? How many beds will you need? Buying an RV is a major investment, and you will want to avoid buyer's regret. While careful and informed shopping is important, actually taking a trial run in an RV will give you great insight into your family's needs when it comes to RV travel.

If you have a willing friend or family member, you may be able to borrow their RV for a short weekend trip. Ask them what they like best about their rig and what they would change if they had the opportunity.

Borrowing an RV may not always be possible. The next best option would be to rent an RV. The RV rental business has exploded over the past few years as families have found it to be a great way to take a fun and hassle-free family vacation without the initial large or ongoing financial outlay of buying an RV. RV rental is also a great option for people who have limited time to travel and don't feel they want to buy an RV when they may only use it two weeks out of the year. You may also want to consider renting if storage is an issue. In some crowded urban areas, RV storage fees may be prohibitive.

Renting an RV is almost as easy as renting a car. There are more than 500 national chain outlets that specialize in RV rentals. Additionally, many local dealers offer RV rentals as a part of their services. Another fairly recent addition to the RV rental market is rental RV fly-and-camp vacation packages.

Most rental companies carry a wide variety of motorized RVs for rental. Overall, motorized RVs are the most popular recreational vehicle to rent. Some also rent towable RVs such as foldup trailers, travel trailers, and fifth-wheel trailers. When you rent a towable trailer, you will be responsible for providing the tow vehicle (it will need to be rated for towing). If it is not equipped with a tow hitch or the larger mirrors that are needed for towing, you will have that additional expense of making your vehicle tow ready.

Most RV rental companies can also provide a package that provides the necessities for your vacation, including dishes, pots and pans, and toilet chemicals. You will be responsible for providing linens, and—of course—food and snacks will be your responsibility. Be prepared for the cost of fuel; RVs do not get the same type of gas mileage as your family car.

Challenges for Families

Families like RVs come in every shape, form, and size. Families with young children will have much different needs than families with older children or teenagers. Families with school-aged children will often be limited in travel opportunities by school and activity schedules. (On the other hand, some families with children travel on a full-time basis by homeschooling their children.) Reservations for camping spots close to popular family attractions may be difficult to get during peak travel times around school breaks. Unfortunately, many RV park operators also raise their rates during these popular travel times.

Not all RV resorts welcome children, nor do all your fellow RV travelers. Though RV parks cannot specifically refuse to take campers with children, they will often make it less than desirable if they prefer adult patrons only. Look for those parks with amenities such as playgrounds, lifeguard-supervised pools, and activities specifically geared to the younger set. Parks with these features listed usually welcome children. Additional features you will probably find appealing when traveling with children are onsite laundry facilities and game rooms. The weather is never guaranteed, and children usually hate to be cooped up. For the sake of your sanity, it is nice for them to have a place that offers rainy-day diversions.

Space is always an issue in RVs, and this is especially true when traveling with small children. Babies always seem to come with a lot of stuff: cribs, high chairs, strollers, diapers, and toys. While you cannot bring every baby item you would normally have at home, you can try to keep things under control.

If you are traveling with a baby, a car seat is a necessity and a stroller is very desirable. Try to find a combination stroller/car seat. The bottom wheeled portion folds up compactly while you are traveling with the baby in the car seat. When you get to your destination, the car seat attaches to the wheeled portion and becomes a stroller.

Another concern with a very small child is sleeping accommodations. A full-size crib is not practical in an RV because of space considerations. In the never-ending line of baby accessories, you should be able to find a foldup travel bed that will accommodate your little one until she is big enough for a real bed.

 ALERT

When shopping for a bunkhouse floor plan in a travel trailer, pay particular attention to the weight ratings for the bunks. They can vary from 100 to 200 pounds, depending on the manufacturer. Bunks that are rated for 100 pounds may not meet your future needs with a growing family.

If you have older children when you get your first RV, or if you are looking to move up to a larger trailer, there are many RV floor plans that are great for families. One very popular innovation over the past few years has been the introduction of the bunkhouse floor plan to travel trailers. Most travel trailer manufacturers have at least one model with bunkbeds. Depending on the length of the trailer, there may be two, three, or four bunks. In most floor plans, the bunks are on the opposite end of the trailer from the "master" bedroom, if there is one. This layout provides additional privacy for the parents.

If you are traveling with very young children, safety can be a big concern. You will not have a fenced yard to prevent them from wandering out into traffic. While most speed limits in parks are less than 10 miles per hour, RVs are large vehicles with some sight limitations, especially when backing up. You will need to keep a close watch on young ones to prevent injury. If you are camping in wilderness areas, a young child could wander off in a few moments and run into danger.

You will need to childproof the inside of your RV in much the same way you would a home. Install safety latches on all cabinets. Turn down the temperature on your water heater to prevent scalding. Move any dangerous chemicals and medications to high areas that the child cannot reach. Install covers over electric plugs to prevent electrical shock and keep electric heaters out of reach of small fingers that can poke through the grill.

Traveling in a motorhome is no different than traveling in a car. All passengers need to follow seat belt laws for their own safety. Children under four years of age should travel in an approved car seat and should never be allowed to wander unrestrained in a moving vehicle. While one of the great appeals of motorhome travel is that a passenger can use the restroom or prepare a snack while traveling down the freeway, that is never advisable. Motorhomes come equipped with seat belts on not only the front driver and passenger seats but also on some living or dining area seating. If additional seat belts are needed for passengers, the dealer can add them on request.

Children who are old enough to understand and handle them correctly should be taught the location of fire extinguishers and how to use them in the event of a fire. They also need to be shown how to use the emergency exits. A fire drill should be a part of every family vacation. If you were taking a cruise, you would have a lifeboat drill before you set sail. Make fire drills a habit, and if you have a real emergency, everyone will be prepared.

In an RVIA study of RV owners, respondents said that bringing the family closer together, having new experiences, and teaching respect for nature were some of the important benefits of family camping.

Challenges for Special Needs

With the popularity of RV travel increasing, especially among people over the age of sixty-five, it is inevitable that some travelers will be physically disabled in some fashion. While a physical disability may increase the challenges and in many cases the cost for these groups of travelers, many disabled travelers are finding that RV travel is a wonderful option for their needs.

With a specially adapted recreational vehicle, most disabled travelers will find it as easy to get out on the open road as other travelers. Disabled travelers often find they have more travel options with their own specially equipped RV than with other methods of transportation and that travel is more comfortable. For one thing, they will be able to eliminate most worries about nonaccessible bathroom facilities; they have their own traveling bathroom. They have the reliability of a comfortable bed adapted for their needs and the storage space to bring along any necessary adaptive aids. Disabled travelers who depend on wheelchairs for mobility are severely limited when traveling by air. They are at the mercy of airport and rented wheelchairs at their destination. If they need a motorized chair, their options are even more limited. The cost of transporting or renting a motorized chair can be prohibitive.

 FACT

The Handicapped Travel Club was formed in 1973 to help support and encourage RV travel for people with a wide range of disabilities. They hold rallies and get-togethers in various parts of the county, and they also publish a newsletter listing RV campgrounds with accessible facilities.

For travelers who require oxygen for health reasons, air travel is again very difficult. They will not be able to carry their own tanks on the plane (due to federal safety regulations), and they will have to purchase or rent equipment at their final destination. Most insurance plans do not pay for medical equipment for travel. Most medical equipment causes difficulties for air travelers, especially with the heightened security regulations that are in effect. For many travelers with disabilities or chronic medical conditions, travel has just become too difficult. Travel in a specially adapted RV could be just the thing to keep them on the road. According to the RVIA, besides the ordinary amenities, additional modifications that can be made to RVs can include the following:

- Wheelchair lifts or ramps
- Lower kitchen counter and cabinets
- Wider entrances
- Roll-in showers
- Conveniently located controls
- Longer faucet handles
- Roll-under sinks
- Brighter lighting

By traveling in an accessible vehicle that also provides accessible living space, the disabled traveler is able to focus on the trip rather than the disability and the need to find accessible accommodations.

Many RV campgrounds have adapted their facilities to meet the needs of disabled travelers. Accessible campsites will have wide, flat, and paved sites. This type of site makes it much easier to use a wheelchair lift, wheelchair, scooter, or walker. Many campgrounds also have made laundry facilities, restrooms, showers, and camp stores completely accessible.

There are several RV manufacturers and after-market companies that can make the modifications that are needed to make an RV handicapped accessible. Play-Mor Corp. is presently the only RV manufacturer that builds RVs for the physically challenged from the ground up.

Staying in Touch

You might ask, why do I need to stay in touch? I just want to get away from it all. Even so, there will be times when you will need to communicate with the world outside your RV, and with today's technology it is easier than ever.

Most campgrounds and RV resorts will have at least a pay phone. That may be all you need if you are just calling home to check messages. If, however, someone needs to get in touch with you for a personal or work-related emergency, a pay phone would not meet your needs.

Some private RV parks offer telephone service along with the standard hookups for water, power, and sewer. Your RV will need to be wired for phone service to use this service. This can also be a very expensive options as there may be an initial fee for hookup with high daily fees and long-distance rates.

Fortunately, in this age of advanced technology, it is much easier to stay connected. Cell phones seemed to be made to order for RV travelers. Cellular service now covers all but the most remote areas of the United States, plus Canada and Mexico. If you are planning on spending much time in more remote areas, satellite phone service is another option, though a much more expensive one. Some plans offer a tiered service, where you are only charged satellite rates if cellular is not available. Once you are back in a cellular service area, you are automatically switched back to the lower priced service.

The monthly service charge for nationwide cell phone coverage is fairly reasonable. Most offer free nights and weekends, so if you time your calls well you should not have to worry about going over your "minutes" and incurring per-minute charges.

Having a cell phone can also help you get online, though the connection speed will probably be much slower than other methods of connecting to the Internet.

Connecting Online

If you are not online yet, you are now in the minority, as more than 50 percent of the U.S. population is able connect to the Internet. Computers and RVs seem to be made for each other, especially for keeping in touch.

Computers

You will need a computer. Desktop models are not really practical for an RV because of their size and weight. Laptop computers, on the other hand, are ideal. They are compact and portable. You can use one while parked to surf and download e-mail, and while traveling (passengers only, not drivers!) to read and respond to e-mail (offline), utilize mapping software, read e-books, and even watch DVDs. Over the past few years, laptops have become much more affordable as well as more powerful and compact. Shop around and you will find the ideal laptop for your needs. Be sure that it has a modem installed that will enable it to connect to the Internet.

 ESSENTIAL

If the campsite you are in does not have a phone line, don't despair. More and more RV resorts offer limited access for campers. Common areas such as activity rooms, laundry rooms, and offices are all possible areas where a phone jack may be available for you to connect. Be courteous and limit your time online. Read and respond to your e-mail offline, then connect to send.

CHAPTER 2

What's in Your Budget?

BEFORE YOU START TO LOOK AT RVS, you first need to look at your budget. Can you pay cash for an RV, or if you are borrowing, how much can you afford to pay monthly? If you start shopping armed with those numbers, you can then narrow down the options that are available in your price range. You should have a down payment of at least 10 percent of the cost of the rig in cash. And you will also need to factor in some additional costs that will be added to the actual sales price.

Financing an RV

RV loans are easy to find, but it still pays to shop around. Most RV buyers are considered good risks because they tend to be older with higher incomes and very often they are purchasing an RV as a second home.

Most RV dealers offer some type of financing, and these are worth looking into. You may find special rates and rebates not available through institutional lenders. When considering dealer financing, watch out for unexpected fees, such as extended warranties or loan insurance. You can say no to these fees. If they are overly pushy, just get up and walk out—that will usually change their tune. Read the loan paperwork carefully for prepayment clauses. If you should sell or trade in the RV before the loan is paid off, you may be hit with an unexpected fee.

Check also with your bank or credit union for financing, as interest rates may be slightly lower for established customers. Loans from these institutions normally do not have prepayment fees or require loan insurance.

 ALERT

With the wide availability of home equity loans and lower interest rates over the past few years, many people are using the equity they have built in their homes to purchase an RV. If you are looking into this financing option, remember that equity is based on the difference between the amount you still owe on the primary mortgage and the assumed resale value. If the housing market declines, you may find yourself with a negative equity on your home.

Costs of RVs

RVs can range in price from under $5,000 for a basic foldup trailer to more than $500,000 for the most luxurious Class C motorhome. Within each class of RV, you'll find wide variations in price. The final price will depend on a variety of factors, including:

Size of RV: Travel trailers can range in size from 12 to 35 feet. In general; the longer the trailer, the higher the price.

Manufacturer: Some manufacturers build for the luxury market, and some build for the budget market. The differences are usually found in the type and grade of carpeting, quality of cabinets and woodwork, and standard amenities. Products by higher-end manufacturers, such as Airstream, hold their value well and will depreciate less.

Number of slideouts: Slideouts add additional living space, but they also add to the cost of construction due to the added weight and electronics needed for the slide mechanism. It is not uncommon to see up to three slideouts on the bigger trailers and motorhomes.

Options: Every year, RV manufacturers come out with more options for their products. From satellite dishes to washer/dryer combinations, an almost endless list of options is available. While they may be tempting, they can quickly add up and put the final price out of your budget.

Appliance upgrades: Many manufacturers will offer appliance upgrades, such as the addition of an icemaker to the standard refrigerator freezer, or a convection oven rather than the standard oven. Once again, this is something you will need to consider. Look back at your travel style. If you plan on cooking outdoors most of the time, an upgraded oven may be unnecessary.

Optional floor plans: Most manufacturers provide a wide selection of floor plans in their most popular sizes of trailer and motorhome. If you are a family with more than one child, you should look at models that feature a bunkhouse sleeping arrangement. You get more sleeping space in less floor space, saving on length, weight, and price.

 ALERT

Besides driving up the price of your RV, optional accessories can drive up its weight. Excess weight reduces fuel economy, increases engine and tire wear, and can even be downright unsafe. Choose optional equipment carefully and leave off anything you really don't need.

Quality of construction: It usually goes without saying that quality will come with a higher cost. Shop around and look at all the RVs in your price range, and buy the best-quality RV you can afford. Check the consumer reports, the RV magazines, and the Web sites for RV enthusiasts for reviews. Don't be afraid to crawl underneath the vehicle to look for signs of shoddy construction.

Tow vehicle: If you do not have a vehicle capable of towing the travel trailer you purchase, you will need to add the cost of a new vehicle to the final price of the trailer. Depending on the price of the tow vehicle, you may decide that a motorized RV (motorhome) would meet your needs.

Model year: RV manufacturers, just like automobile manufacturers, bring out new models every year. When the new models come into the showrooms, the unsold rigs from the previous year are often reduced in price to help them move out. Find out when the new model year arrives and look for your RV then. You may save yourself a lot of money by buying last year's model.

 FACT

If you own a small or compact car that you plan on using as a tow vehicle, you will probably be limited to looking at a foldup trailer. Don't be discouraged: Foldup trailers are great for the beginning RV owner. They are generally easy to sell when you are ready to move up to a larger rig, and they hold their resale value if well cared for.

Dealer: Buying an RV is a lot like buying a car: It pays to shop around. If you live in an area with several RV dealerships, you can comparison-shop over a few days to get the best price on what you want. If you have some time and access to the Internet, you can comparison-shop online. It may be worth your while in savings to order an RV from a dealer in another city and travel there to pick it up. You may also be able to use a lower quote from an out-of-town dealer as a bargaining chip with your local dealer. Most RV dealers are willing to negotiate the price. Getting the initial sale can mean a customer for service, after-market purchases, and future upgrades.

Factory buying: Some RV buyers have bypassed the dealer completely and bought directly from the manufacturer. Savings are impressive, but not all manufacturers offer this option. The one downside is that you will have to go to the factory to pick it up yourself and financing options may not be available. For cash buyers, this could be either a windfall or an opportunity to upgrade and stay within their budget.

Tax Advantages

If you decide to finance the purchase of an RV, you may be able to deduct some or all of the interest payment for the loan on your federal income tax return. Under IRS regulations, you can deduct your home mortgage interest payment on your main home or your second home. They define a home as a house, condominium, mobile home, house trailer, boat, or similar property that has sleeping, cooking, and toilet facilities. To qualify for the interest deduction, the debt must be secured. A secured debt is defined as one in which you sign an instrument (such as a mortgage, deed of trust, or land contract) in which the home is put up as collateral.

Your main home is the home where you ordinarily live most of the time. You could then treat your RV as a second home, as long as it is not rented out during the year. You do not have to use the home during the year to designate it as your second home for tax purposes.

Depending on the amount of the loan, this can be a fairly sizable deduction. The rates of RV loans are not based on home mortgage rates but are more closely tied to the rates you would get on a manufactured home. The interest rate is generally higher and for a period of ten to fifteen years instead of the typical thirty-year note for a site-built home and land.

Remember that, unlike a home, an RV will depreciate in value over the time you own it. Much like a car, it will begin depreciating the minute you take delivery of it from the dealer. In all likelihood, the amount of interest you are able to deduct from income tax will not offset the amount that your RV will depreciate. Don't purchase an RV as an investment; purchase it for the enjoyment it will give you.

 ALERT

For more information on your eligibility for deducting the interest on your RV loan, check with the Internal Revenue Service and ask for a copy of IRS Publication 936, "Home Mortgage Interest Deduction," and Publication 523, "Selling Your Home." Both are available by calling the IRS at ✎1-800-829-3676 or by going online at ✎*www.irs.gov*.

New or Used?

One of the decisions you will need to make when buying an RV is whether you should buy new or used. There are advantages and disadvantages to both that you should be aware of.

The first consideration is price. A new RV will cost more. A new RV will depreciate quickly over the first couple of years, much like a new automobile. A two-year-old motorhome could save you 30 to 40 percent over a similar new model. A travel trailer of the same age could help you realize savings of 20 to 25 percent.

Buying a used RV does mean that you will not have a choice of floor plans, accessories, or color schemes. Although, with careful shopping, you may find a used RV that is very close to your ideal.

When buying used, you may be at the mercy of the previous owner's lack of maintenance, so it is in your best interest to look over a used RV very closely. If you are considering a motorized RV, it is not unreasonable to ask to have a mechanic you trust look the vehicle over. While it is illegal, there are still reports of finding used vehicles where the odometer has been tampered with. An experienced mechanic can usually detect this kind of chicanery. If you are friendly with an RV technician, then you will have another advantage. An RV technician will be able to check out the RV systems that are not related to the drivetrain. It is very disheartening to take your first outing in your new (to you, at least) used RV and find that you need to replace the air conditioner or that you have serious plumbing leaks. If you are lucky, you may be able to get some type of warranty on a used RV, but it most likely will not be of the scope of a warranty on a new RV.

 FACT

A motorized RV will depreciate at a faster pace than a towable RV due to the wear and tear on the engine. A motorized RV with a diesel engine can be expected to get more miles from its engine, so it would most likely hold its value for a longer time than a gasoline-powered RV.

Places to Look for Used RVs

There are many places you can find used RVs, some better than others. Check out several to get a better idea of prices and conditions of the various rigs available.

RV Dealers

Most RV dealers take trade-ins on new RV sales. This is good business for the RV dealer who is looking for another stream of revenue. One advantage of buying from an RV dealer is that the rig should have been checked out mechanically and structurally before being put out on the lot for sale. This is one of the few places you may have a possibility of getting even a limited warranty.

Bankruptcy Sales

When an RV dealership files for bankruptcy, the units left on the lot are often put up for sale at a bankruptcy auction. All RVs in inventory, both new and used, are usually included in the auction. This type of auction can be a hit-or-miss event for the prospective RV buyer. Prices may be very good, but if bidding is active, prices may be higher than the units are actually worth. Don't bid on an RV unless you have done your homework and you know the average selling price of a similar used RV from a dealer. Avoid auctions where you are not allowed to physically inspect the RV prior to the start of bidding. Auctions are best for the more experienced RV buyer and not for the novice.

Estate Auctions

Estate auctions are very different from bankruptcy auctions. Estate auctions are generally held when a family member dies or when an older adult is downsizing to move to some type of assisted living or retirement home. Very often, these older adults are no longer able to use their RVs and have no family members who care to take them on. You may find a good deal on a barely used RV at one of these sales. Professionals in the field who take a percentage of the overall sale as their commission run most estate sales. They are well versed in how to price items to sell. Check your local newspaper for announcements of any estate sales; often the ads will highlight the availability of items like RVs. As with any used RV, be sure to check it out completely, and if possible, have an RV mechanic or technician look at it before you buy.

Online Auctions

You can buy almost anything on eBay, and that includes RVs. Online auctions are very popular, but for a high-priced item such as a motorhome you should be very careful when dealing with this or any online auction site. With an online auction, you will not be able to see, touch, or test-drive the RV until the auction is over. If you have buyer's remorse, you generally have very little recourse. Buying an RV through an online auction is similar to buying from an individual. You may get a great price but no warranties. Do your homework before you bid on any RV from an online auction.

Repossessions

You may find a good deal in an RV that has been repossessed by the bank or finance company. Check out the newspaper for announcements of sales of repossessed goods. You can also contact banks and financing organizations that may specialize in RVs and let them know you are interested in learning about RVs if they become available.

Classifieds

Your local newspaper will often have RVs listed for sale. The RVs for sale by private sellers are often much more of a bargain than those from a dealership. The private seller does not have to pay a commission. If the owner has taken good care of the RV and is good about keeping records, you may get a better record of maintenance through a private sale than with any other type of sale.

Former Rental RVs

Companies that rent RVs replace their fleets on a regular basis and, as a consequence, sell the used RVs. Some rental companies will provide a warranty when they sell these RVs. Purchasing a used RV from a rental company can be risky for the buyer. These units have been driven by many different people and may have been very abused during their time as rentals. Most rental companies will provide routine maintenance while they own the vehicles (you don't make money if it is in the shop), but the rigs are still at the mercy of the customers who drive them.

How Much Is Enough?

Visit any RV show and you will usually find the biggest crowds and most excitement around the "luxury" RVs. Built on a bus chassis by companies like Monaco, Newell, Bluebird, Marathon, and Provost, they are the mansions of RV travel. You will find glove leather seating, Italian marble baths, and the most up-to-date accessories you will find outside of a luxury hotel. Unfortunately, their price tag also matches that of many mansions. Unless you are lucky enough to be born rich, to inherit a fortune, or to win the lottery (with a very large payoff), these RVs are fun to look at but not for the average family traveler.

Find the most suitable RV for your price range and camping style and you will enjoy your travel experiences much more. If you buy more RV than you can afford, you may find you don't have the money to use it. If you buy an RV that is too big, you may find that you are limited to camping in higher-priced RV parks and cannot stay in some national and state parks that get you closer to nature for a bargain price.

 ALERT

Slideouts that have become very popular in motorhomes, travel trailers, and even foldup campers can be difficult in some campgrounds with narrow sites. Do you want to pay extra for a wider site, or even pay for two sites? These are all things to consider as you shop for your RV.

Cost Savings of RV Travel

Family RV travel will save you money over almost any other form of travel, while providing the comfort, versatility, and adventure you crave. Even factoring in the initial cost outlay of the RV, a family of four can realize savings of 50 percent or more over other types of vacation travel.

A budget cruise for a family of four can run $3,500 to $4,000 for a week. Add spending money, tips, and costs of getting to and from port to that, and you are going to spend some serious cash for a week of fun. No doubt about it, cruises are great, but for ongoing fun that you can experience every weekend if you like, nothing beats RV travel.

Ways to Save Money

There are many things you can do after you buy your RV to keep your costs down.

Maintenance

A well-maintained RV runs better and cheaper. RVs are big and weigh a lot, and consequently gas mileage suffers. It is not unusual to get fewer than 5 miles per gallon of gas. If a motorhome engine or tow vehicle engine is not well maintained, gas mileage can suffer even more. You should be sure that this maintenance includes tire and tire pressure checks before every trip, especially when traveling in extremely hot or cold weather. According to information from the Bridgestone/Firestone North American Tire and Recreational Vehicle Safety Education Foundation, four out of five RVs in one survey had at least one underinflated tire. Nearly 40 percent of RV users say they go six months or more without checking their tires, even though tires in good condition can lose between 1 and 2 pounds of inflation pressure per month. Besides being a safety hazard, improper tire inflation can severely affect fuel economy.

Campgrounds

You can save money if you choose your campground carefully. A campground off the beaten track with fewer "extras" can help keep costs down. If you are on a cross-country trip, you might consider some low-cost or free camping options for your overnight stays until you get to your final destination. If the only thing you need is a place to park your RV for sleep, paying for a full night in an RV park does not make much sense. Many places allow overnight parking, including rest stops, grocery and department store lots, some municipal parks, and some government-run parks. When parking on private property, always ask for permission, especially as some municipalities have ordinances against overnight parking of RVs. Your best bet may be to try to find this type of overnight parking place outside the big city. Small towns and rural areas often have fewer restrictions.

Planning for High Fuel Prices

The combination of few miles per gallon and high fuel prices can be a killer. To save some money, try to travel during off-peak times. Fuel prices always seem to rise just before Memorial Day and drop off again after Labor Day, so planning a trip during other times of the year can cut down your fuel bill. If your travel times are governed by the schedules of school-age children, you still have some options. Certain areas such as Texas traditionally have lower gasoline prices (due to lower fuel taxes). Keeping your vehicle well maintained will also help keep fuel economy at its peak.

If you are pulling a high-profile trailer with a car or van, you might want to invest in an air deflector for your vehicle. These deflectors can help ease the wind resistance you encounter while driving down the highway.

When it is time to fill up, lower prices can often be found off the beaten track. Travel centers on major highways often charge more—especially if they are the only game in the neighborhood open twenty-four hours a day. One consideration is that you may be able to park overnight at these travel centers (along with the truckers) with better security.

Unexpected Costs

The sticker price on that new or used RV is only the beginning of the money you will spend to become an RV traveler. There will always be some unexpected costs you will encounter when purchasing an RV. Be prepared for these and it will help prevent buyer's regret and allow you to fully enjoy your purchase.

The first expenses you will have are the fees for taxes and title. Just as with automobile purchases, these fees will vary depending on the state you live in. Even if you buy your RV in a state with lower taxes, you will still need to pay the fees required by the state you claim residence in. Property (your home) is usually the standard by which residence is gauged, so you won't be able to register your RV in another state just because the fees are lower.

Insurance is also a necessity for your RV. Shop around for rates. Many companies will give you a discount if you give them all your business (home, auto, etc.), but be sure you are getting the specialized coverage an RV needs. Standard automobile insurance usually excludes living in a vehicle, and you could end up with a very expensive surprise if you have to file a claim. Certain companies specialize in RV insurance coverage, and they will be able to provide insurance that is adequate for your needs.

 ESSENTIAL

If you plan on traveling out of the country (such as to Mexico or Canada) or into the United States from those places, check with your insurance agent. You will probably need to purchase special insurance for your vehicle that covers you while you are in another country.

If you have never owned an RV before, your first gasoline fill-up may cause palpitations. Most RVs are equipped with a much larger gas tank than your family car. Be sure your vacation budget includes fuel for a vehicle that gets less than 10 miles per gallon

If you are a do-it-yourselfer, you may be able to take care of much of the maintenance on your rig. If you do need repairs that you cannot do yourself, you will have to pay an RV mechanic. Most dealerships have specially trained technicians who can work on all the different RV systems. They are not inexpensive. When buying new, you may want to consider an extended warranty. Read the fine print, as some of these after-market warranties promise the moon and deliver almost nothing because of high deductibles.

If you do break down on the road, towing charges to a service center may be very expensive. There are RV or auto clubs that cover towing, and some insurance policies may offer roadside assistance with towing service as well. Look into these clubs; they may be worth their weight in gold. If your RV does break down, you may also have to find a place to stay for a night or two to wait for repairs to be finished, if the service department is backed up or if parts are not in stock. Figure in the cost of an emergency fund when looking at the cost of your RV, especially if you are buying a used RV.

CHAPTER 3

Start Small

RECREATIONAL VEHICLES COME IN MANY DIFFERENT sizes and styles. The smaller RV types include conversion vans, truck bed campers, and foldup campers (also known as "pop-up" campers). Determining the correct size for your needs depends on many factors including available budget, storage space, travel destinations, and the number of family members. A small RV can be a good "starter" for a family with a limited budget, limited space, and limited time to devote to RV travel.

Advantages

Smaller RV units may not have the glamour of some of the larger and more luxurious rigs, but they do have their charms. Some RV owners who move to larger vehicles often regret the move.

Some advantages include the following:

- Less expensive
- Easier to store
- Lighter weight
- Towable type (foldup) can be towed by a wider range of vehicles
- Lower operating costs
- Lower insurance costs

- Generally will not require the driver to have anything more than standard operating licenses
- Affords more access to some remote or wilderness campsites
- Easier handling for inexperienced drivers

Disadvantages

Along with their advantages, smaller RVs do have some disadvantages, such as:

- More time and labor required to set up at camping site
- Limited cold weather use
- Canvas sides prone to mold and rot if not conditioned, dried, and stored properly
- Limited sleeping options
- Limited storage
- Can feel cramped or claustrophobic to some
- Truck campers require an appropriate pickup truck
- Truck campers more difficult to store
- High profile of truck campers may decrease fuel economy and decrease stability in windy areas

Van Conversions

Conversion vehicles fall into a category somewhat closer to the family car than to an RV, but they do offer some features that make them useful for family RV travel. While the most common conversion is usually a full-size van, full-size SUVs (the Chevrolet Suburban is a good example), and full-size pickup trucks are also now in this category. They generally only offer sleeping space for two with a rear bench seat that folds down into a bed. They do not provide cooking or bathroom facilities. They do, however, make excellent tow vehicles.

Conversion vehicles usually begin their life as a vehicle made by Ford, Chrysler, or General Motors. Conversion companies take basic vehicle shells and modify them into luxury conversions. They typically have plush seating, upgraded carpet, and custom window and wall treatments along with the latest consumer electronics. A van conversion can make getting there half the fun. Many come equipped with extra features like video game systems for the kids and headphone-equipped rear stereo systems for the parents. Extended roofs can provide more headroom.

When towing a foldup or small travel trailer, a conversion vehicle with a rear bed can provide overflow bed space.

Truck Campers

For pickup truck owners who want to get into RV travel, a truck camper is a logical first step. This specially built unit is loaded into the bed of a pickup truck and fastened in place with tie-downs attached to the vehicle's chassis. The tailgate of the truck is removed while the camper is in place in order to allow entry into the camper through its rear door. The camper can be set up on its own jacks at home for storage or at the campsite, freeing the truck for separate use. When not being used for camping, the pickup truck can make an excellent primary or secondary family vehicle. Truck camper units range in length from 18 to 25 feet. The unit size will depend on the size of the pickup truck. Depending on the model, truck campers can sleep up to six campers.

Truck campers have traditionally been built to make the most efficient use of limited space. Most are self-contained with sleeping, cooking, and bathroom facilities onboard. Truck camper manufacturers offer a wide range of sizes and floor plans, with some maximizing living and sleeping space with extended cabovers.

Adding a truck camper to your pickup truck will affect the handling and gas mileage. A truck camper may add more than 36 inches to the overall height of the vehicle. They often appear top-heavy, leaving the driver with the feeling that the vehicle is going to roll over at any minute. In fact, rollover-type accidents involving these vehicles do occasionally occur. High-wind areas, tight curves, sudden swerving, wet or slippery conditions, and uneven roads all require an experienced, capable driver behind the wheel. Talk with both your RV dealer and your vehicle mechanic to be sure that your truck can handle the camper you are considering.

TRUCK CAMPER

Some truck campers combine features of campers with foldup trailers. While traveling, the camper is a very low-profile truck camper. When set up with the roof raised, the necessary headroom is provided by canvas that extends the sidewall to the dimensions of a conventional truck camper. This type of configuration has some advantages in reducing the overall weight of the camper and in improving stability when driving. You may also find that it improves fuel economy due to reduced wind resistance. Make sure your tires are in good condition and properly inflated to handle the load. That way, you won't feel like a turtle about to be flipped over on its back.

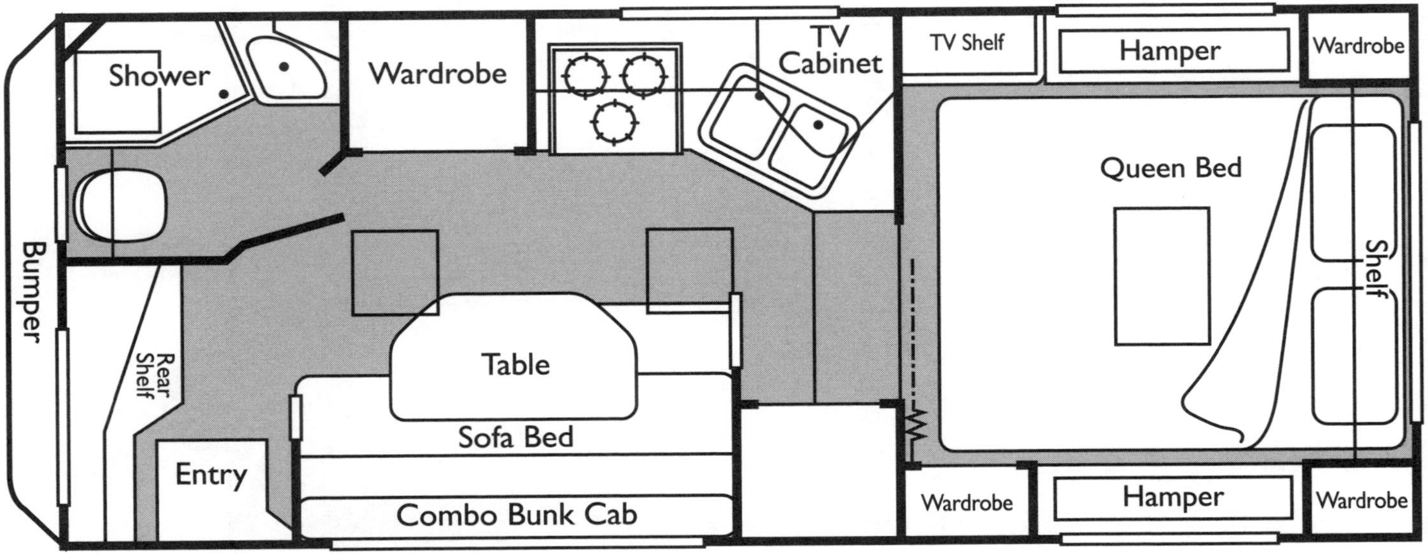

TRUCK CAMPER FLOOR PLAN

Wardrobe

Shelf

Wardrobe

Hamper

Queen Bed

Hamper

TV Shelf

Wardrobe

TV Cabinet

Wardrobe

Table

Sofa Bed

Combo Bunk Cab

Shower

Entry

Rear Shelf

Bumper

Truck campers can range in price from $3,800 to $24,000, with the average price around $15,000. This does not include the price of the pickup truck that will carry the camper.

The smaller size of the truck camper makes it especially suitable for people who want to camp in remote wilderness areas accessible only by back roads. Pickup truck campers can go places that are sometimes unsuitable for any other type of RV. A vehicle with four-wheel drive capability will make the combo even more versatile on difficult roads.

Fold-Down Trailers

Also popularly known as pop-up campers, or tent trailers, these versatile units are an excellent choice for an entry-level RV. They are suitable for couples or for a family with young children who don't mind sharing a bed. They are lightweight, with a hard top and sides that collapse for towing and storage. They range in weight from 1,500 to 4,000 pounds and can be towed easily by most SUVs, minivans, pickup trucks, or larger sedans.

FOLD-DOWN CAMPER

Fold-down trailers are easy to tow, inexpensive to operate and maintain, and easy to set up and store. These RVs offer much of the charm and adventure of tent camping with much more protection from the elements. With the collapsible side generally made of heavyweight canvas, you will be able to listen to the sounds of the great outdoors while lying in your bed. Mosquito-netting mesh windows—just like those found in traditional tents—provide light and ventilation. Heavy vinyl or canvas tieback panels provide privacy and shelter from the elements. Most fold-down trailers provide two double beds formed by the sides that fold out, plus a dinette that can be converted into a double bed. They also often feature a small icebox or mini-refrigerator, a two- or three-burner range, and storage areas. More expensive trailers can come equipped with RV toilet and shower facilities (shower facilities may be inside or outside) and a water heater. In the past few years, some manufacturers have even been offering models with slideout rooms that greatly increase the amount of living space as well as more extensive cooking features. Some units come standard with an RV furnace for cool-weather camping. You can also opt for an air-conditioning unit (which may be a highly desired feature, depending on the time of year you will be traveling and the area of the country you will travel to).

 ALERT

Before you start looking at any pop-up trailer, you need to determine if the vehicle you intend to tow it with is up to the job. Not all vehicles are rated to tow a trailer, even a small one. Check your owner's manual or ask your dealer or the manufacturer. Improper towing could void the warranty.

Among other features, an awning over the entrance is wonderful for keeping out the sun and rain. Screened rooms may even be available to attach to the front of the trailer. These can provide additional storage and living space while protecting you from insects and the elements. Folded down for towing or storage, these RVs become a low-profile rectangular box trailer that hooks onto a standard trailer hitch.

Foldup campers are not suitable for winter camping, as they do not provide insulation from the cold, even with a furnace. While they are stable, their lightweight design makes them more vulnerable during hazardous weather, especially during high winds. Stay alert for weather warnings; even a small tornado could turn a foldup trailer into an airship.

Upkeep and Maintenance

You will need to perform some basic maintenance on your RV to keep it in top shape between trips. Much of the basic upkeep chores can be done by the RV owner. Some will need the expertise of an informed do-it-yourselfer or of an experienced RV technician.

Proper Storage

One of the advantages of the smaller trailers is ease of storage. In most cases you can store them (foldup campers and truck campers) in a single-car garage. If you have the room in your garage, use it to protect your investment if you need to store it for a time. Storing your pop-up or truck camper in a sheltered garage should eliminate extensive winterizing preparations. Full sun and weather extremes are very hard on even these small trailers. At a typical base weight, many of these trailers can be guided into the storage space by hand. Most truck campers are low profile enough when not mounted on the truck to store in a garage also. You will need to be sure you have sufficient clearance up top and on the sides to prevent damage.

Foldup Trailers

Keeping any type of RV clean and dry in storage is one of the most important steps you can take in maintaining your RV for years of enjoyment. Never store a foldup trailer wet, as mold and mildew can lead to rotting canvas and upholstery. The smell of mildew is extremely difficult to remove from fabrics; it may end up affecting your travel enjoyment now and your ability to sell the RV in the future. Mold can be a health hazard, especially for anyone with a respiratory condition such as asthma or severe allergies.

Foldup trailers have canvas sides that are made from the same material as many tents. This canvas has been specialty treated to make it waterproof. Check your owner's manual for information on cleaning and treatment of tears. Improper use of cleaners or of chemicals not recommended for use on the canvas may void or otherwise affect your warranty.

Check the exterior and the hardtop roof for leaks. Seams in the canvas are especially vulnerable places. Foldup trailers stored outside may be subject to roof damage by things such as falling tree limbs.

Interior cleaning is also recommended for any periods when the trailer is not being used for travel. Cleaning out food storage, cooking, and eating areas will make the trailer much less inviting to critters looking for a new home. There is nothing worse than opening up your trailer to pack for a trip and finding a family of mice or hoards of ants marching through your vacation home on wheels. Baits and traps can help with unwanted guests, but use them carefully when there are children and pets around. Also remove all chemicals or items that could leak or explode—this includes all spray cans. Another step in proper maintenance is to lubricate the lift system and any other moving parts such as locks, bed slides, and hitches twice yearly.

The tires your foldup trailer rides on also deserve a lot of attention. Tires can be one of the biggest safety hazards on any vehicle. Check your tire pressure frequently with a gauge, not by just looking at them. Replace any worn or old tires as needed—ten-year-old tires on your trailer are nothing to brag about. Repack the wheel bearings annually.

Another area of maintenance you may need to be concerned about is your trailer brake. Legal requirements for trailer brakes on pop-ups vary from state to state. There are some that require aux-iliary brakes on any trailer weighing as little as 1,000 pounds. Two types of trailer brakes are available: surge and electric. They require little in the way of maintenance other than checking to see that they work properly and that the brakes are adjusted properly. Refer to the manufacturer's manual for information on properly adjusting brakes.

If you need to store your trailer outside:

- Seal any holes (waterline openings) on the underside of the pop-up.
- Remove the battery, store it in a warmer place inside, and keep it charged.
- Cover any vent openings to keep moisture, bugs, and crit-ters out.
- Lower the end where the tongue is to allow for better drainage of rain and snow, instead of letting it accumulate on the roof.
- Cover the tires to protect them from the sun.
- You can buy covers for your tent trailer (similar to car covers). Refer to your owner's manual to see if covering the unit during storage is recommended.

Truck Campers

Maintenance for your truck camper is very similar to that for most other campers. If it is being stored over the winter, it should be stored in a covered garage if one is available. While you may not have tires to worry about with a truck camper, there are other challenges. Truck campers have jacks that elevate them to the proper height for loading on the truck bed. You can store the camper on the jacks, but you should always have additional sup-port under the camper for stability. This support can be anything from a custom-made box to a couple of 50-gallon drums.

You should check and lubricate all moving parts on the camper at least twice yearly. Check the tiedowns for structural integrity. You really don't want the camper sliding off the back of your pickup if you have to stop suddenly. RV system maintenance will depend on the type of camper you have—fully loaded or stripped down.

One important area not to overlook is your roof. Check your roof for leaks. It is a good idea to re-seal or re-caulk all roof seams and around roof vents and openings. This will help prevent future leaks.

The vehicle that carries your camper should not be overlooked when it comes to maintenance. Check your tires frequently and replace them when needed. They will be carrying a lot of weight with a fully loaded camper, and you do not want them to fail. Check all tires (including the spare) frequently to be sure they are properly inflated. Most full-sized, loaded pickup trucks come standard with a full-sized spare. Some smaller or low-end trucks may come with only a temporary or space-saver spare. While these spares are great for day-to-day driving to get you a short distance to a tire shop, they are not appropriate for driving a truck with a truck camper for any distance. They are not rated to carry that additional weight and can be very dangerous.

Preparing for the Weather

When traveling, you will run into many different climates and weather situations. Some of these weather situations can be dangerous or unhealthy for travelers.

Winter Camping

Of the smaller towable RVs, the truck camper is the only one that is practical for winter camping. Your foldup camper may have a furnace, but it will generally only cut the chill and not keep you warm in subfreezing temperatures. Depending on the type of truck, the terrain, the amount of snow, and the condition of the roads, the truck camper may be the only RV—towable or motorized—that can access some winter camping areas. With a truck camper, you may also be able to pull a small trailer carrying your snowmobiles or other toys to play in the snow with.

Winter camping can be a great experience, but it does come with some added safety considerations. This is not the time to camp alone. Winter camping is great for a group of at least three or more families to camp. Winter weather can make for treacherous traveling conditions. Very cold weather can drain batteries more quickly than more moderate temperatures. If an individual or family has problems or needs some kind of emergency help, having traveling companions can mean the difference between life and death.

Before you set out for a winter trip, you will need to take care of some maintenance details. There are also some supplies that will be needed only for winter camping.

Your truck needs to be in top condition for the cold weather. Have the oil changed, making sure to use the appropriate oil weight recommended in your owner's manual for winter weather. Check the fluid levels in your engine and battery to prevent freezing. Check that your tires are in good shape and tires are inflated correctly. Get tire chains and use them if you are on slippery roads.

Make sure you have sufficient fuel to run the heater, stove, and water heater. These run very efficiently on propane, but only if the tanks are filled.

Take along enough dry clothing to last the entire trip. Even in subzero weather, you will sweat when doing something physically exerting. That sweat can later cause hypothermia, a very dangerous condition. Warm and dry clothing in layers is the best defense against the cold.

Setting Up Camp

When you are shopping for RVs, some salesperson will try to steer you away from a smaller towable RV and into a larger, more expensive travel trailer or motorhome. Be prepared to hear how inconvenient a foldup trailer is, how much of your valuable travel time will be wasted setting it up and then packing it up again when it is time to go home. They will tell you how much you will regret buying a truck camper when you realize how little storage space (and space in general) they have.

It is always wise to remember that RV salespeople work on commission. They earn more on the sale of a 30-foot fifth-wheel trailer than they do on a basic foldup trailer. Stick to your guns. Foldup trailers and truck campers are wonderful ways to travel, and if they fit your lifestyle, then they are what you should have.

Every RV will have some setup time once you get to your campground. Setting up your foldup camper may take you a few minutes longer than the travel trailer in the next space, or you may be lighting the grill for dinner while your neighbor is still struggling to get his rig leveled.

Foldup Trailer Setup

First of all, walk around your site before you pull in. Where are the electric and water hookups? The location will dictate the direction your trailer faces and which part of the site you can use for the trailer. Look up! Is that just a nice, friendly shade tree, or is it a menacing threat to your trailer, with dead branches and limbs that may come crashing down on your home in a slight breeze?

The next step is to put your trailer in the spot where you will set it up. If you are lucky, you will have a pull-through site and can just drive it in. Otherwise you will generally have to back it in. Lightweight foldup trailers can be challenging to back up for the inexperienced. Their low profile makes them more difficult to see and their light weight means that small bumps and changes in grade can send them in their own direction. Fortunately, because they are lightweight, many foldup trailers can be maneuvered the last few feet into the right position by hand.

Once in the right spot, level the trailer from side to side, put up the stabilizer jacks, and unhitch it from the tow vehicle. You should also use tire chocks to prevent it from rolling.

When the trailer is level and stabilized, it is time to open it up. Each trailer from a different manufacturer will open up in a slightly different manner. Usually it involves unhooking the latches from the top and then using a lever to crank up the top. Once the top is up, the platforms that form the beds on either end are pulled out. They will be braced underneath the extension. The extensions for the beds will have some type of pole or brace to keep them fully extended. The door can then be put in place, and the awning rolled out.

Once you are set up, the water and electricity can be hooked up. You will then be ready to get the grill going and enjoy your vacation.

Small Can Be Beautiful

Here's a story that demonstrates how having a small trailer does not necessarily limit the fun you can get out of your RV experience: One couple with two young children aged three and five traveled from southern California to southern Ontario in Canada and back over a three-week period. They towed a small pop-up trailer behind their six-cylinder Chevy Astro van. The majority of time they stayed only a night or two in one location, and it was a memorable trip for the fun and togetherness they experienced. They had a set routine with both adults having their part in getting the trailer set up. They were able to get everything set up in about twenty minutes by the end of the trip, they said. They both felt that this was one of the best vacations they'd had; they saw a lot of the country, met some wonderful people along the road, and were able to do it without breaking the bank.

For the small family on a budget, the traveler who wants to be closer to nature with a little more comfort, or the traveler who is not comfortable pulling a larger trailer, the small towables are great.

CHAPTER 4

Upgrading Your RV

AT SOME POINT IN YOUR TRAVELS, you may get the urge to get a bigger, better, or newer RV. For many RVers, a visit to an RV show seems to pass this fever along. Seeing all those bright, shiny, new RVs with the latest and greatest accessories and options, you may easily start to dream of replacing the RV you own now with a new one.

Outgrowing Your RV

If you enjoy visiting RV shows, it may be hard to resist the temptation to trade in your present RV and replace it with the latest and greatest in RV technology. Just as with cars and computers, the RV industry is continually improving and refining their product. Veteran RV travelers can attest to the innovations that have been made over the years. In the early days of RVs, the appliances were more or less just home appliances stuck into an RV shell. These days, appliances and equipment are made specifically for RVs and take into account the space and weight limitations required.

As with many aspects of RV travel, size and weight can be important considerations in your decision to get a new or newer RV. Compare a twenty-year-old RV of the same length with approximately the same options, and you will likely find that the newer RV weighs much less. They are also more efficient in terms of floor layout and storage options. Newer building materials have produced well-built rigs on very lightweight frames.

Fuel efficiency is another factor that may encourage you to look at buying a new RV. Vehicle fuel efficiency has improved approximately 30 percent from 1970 rates. An older motorhome will run hotter, which decreases fuel efficiency and increases maintenance costs. Improving fuel economy by even three miles per gallon can save significant money over the time you own an RV.

Perhaps you have a small RV, along with a growing family. Popular in the last few years are RVs (especially travel trailers) with "bunkhouse" floor layouts. These sleeping arrangements can make RV travel much more enjoyable by keeping sleeping children separated from parents.

 ALERT

When purchasing a travel trailer with a bunkhouse option, look for the weight limits on the bunks. This information should be listed on a sticker in the bunk area. Many upper bunks have a limit of 100 pounds, making them unsuitable for older children.

If you are an empty-nest couple, you may find that the RV you used for the family has become too big for just the two of you, or that the vehicle you used to tow the travel trailer has finally worn out. You may be thinking that a self-contained motorhome would be a better option for your travel needs. These are all good reasons for looking for a new RV.

RVs depreciate in value just as cars do (though travel trailers depreciate at a slower pace than other RVs do). If the repair bills on your RV are adding up to more than it's worth, it may be time to move on to a new one, unless you are a truly dedicated do-it-yourselfer. Most people would rather spend their time with their RV out on the road instead of in the garage.

Look at your repair bills and bankbook. Does it make sense to pay for repairs, or should you take on payments for a newer RV?

Getting the Best Price

If you are replacing an older or smaller RV with a newer RV, you will need to decide how you want to get rid of the old one. You will have several options for selling or trading, but first you will want to set a price.

You will get the best price if you have a good product to sell. If you have neglected proper maintenance and upkeep over the time you've owned the vehicle, you should not expect to get a premium price.

Preparing Your Vehicle to Sell

What do you need to do in order to impress buyers? First, take a look at the automotive engine:

- The engine should be clean and dry, and it should not have any leaks.
- It should perform smoothly and quietly.
- It should be quite powerful, and it should not have any delays while accelerating.
- There should be no smoke coming from the engine.
- The engine oil level, coolant level, and any other fluids should all be at normal levels.

Next, you should look at the interior and address any easily and inexpensively corrected problems:

- Clean and polish the exterior, paying special attention to small scratches.
- Check for any corrosion, and fix small areas with a wire brush and spray paint.
- Check the tire pressure and fill tires with air if necessary.

Finally, tackle the interior of the RV:

- Vacuum and clean the carpet and upholstery. If they are very soiled, you might consider having an auto detailer do this.
- Clean the refrigerator and oven. Place an open box of baking soda (not baking powder) in the refrigerator to absorb odors.
- Clean the bathroom, and repair any leaky faucets or other plumbing problems. Clean and deodorize the toilet.
- Clean and deodorize holding tanks.
- Make up beds with attractive coverings (indicate in your listing if they come with the RV).
- Vacuum the dust from all curtains.
- Keep batteries fully charged.
- Keep some water in the freshwater holding tank.
- Fill propane tanks if necessary.

 ESSENTIAL

Instead of baking soda, you could try using coffee in your refrigerator. Leave an open container with ground coffee in the refrigerator to absorb odors and moisture and also leave a pleasant smell in the RV. Throw out coffee after it loses its scent. Flavored coffees are good choices.

Establishing the Right Price

Once you have improved the appearance of your RV, you can then decide on the price you wish to get.

The first place to check for the correct selling price is the *NADA Used RV Prices Guide.* Similar to the "Blue Book" for autos, this guide will give you average selling prices for every RV made for years going back to 1986. You will get a range of prices, but your final selling price will depend on the condition of your RV.

If you are buying new, look at the resale prices for older models of the brands you are looking at. The resale prices can give you a good idea of which brands and models are more favored in the resale market. Go to a dealer or resale dealer and look at the condition of various brands. While the condition may vary because of usage patterns of individual owners, manufacturing quality can keep units in good condition despite poor maintenance.

 QUESTION?

Which RV holds its value best?
Generally, a travel trailer (including fifth-wheel trailers) will depreciate at a slower pace. Motorhomes, being part truck and part trailer, depreciate at much the same rate as cars and trucks. Generally the higher-priced motorhomes with diesel engines hold their values better than lower-priced units with gasoline engines.

Planning for Growth and Change

Life is always a series of changes. As your age and health, your family, and your travel needs change, so will your personal requirements in an RV.

If you have a young family, sleeping space is often of prime importance. Bunkhouse floor plans are popular with families with children as they can then have a separate bed for each child. This can be important in settling children down to sleep at night. Those children will grow and gain weight. Many upper bunks have weight limits of 100 pounds, making them useless for some children as young as seven or eight years of age. It can be discouraging to outgrow your RV just because your child has had a growth spurt.

Older RV owners may find that health problems turn their dream RV into a nightmare. Look at your purchase with a critical eye, especially if you are over the age of sixty-five. Will you be able to get up and down stairs in five years, set up a foldup trailer by yourself, or will you need modifications made for a wheelchair or scooter? While you may not have health problems at the present time, you are at an age where the risks are higher.

Many older RV owners downsize, both at home and in their RV. Opting to buy a smaller RV can be prudent. Older drivers have slower reflexes, and a shorter, lighter RV may be better in matters of road safety such as stopping distances and backing up.

 FACT

> You can plan ahead and add some things to your RV to make it better suited to older users right now. Grab bars are easily added to bathrooms both in the tub and by the toilet. For adults with balance problems or lower-extremity weakness, these can be a lifesaver.

Be sure that there are at least two drivers available for the RV. If the driver becomes ill, everyone will be stuck if there is not a second driver. Plan your needs in an RV around all potential travelers.

Trade or Sell?

If you are buying a new RV, should you sell your current one, or should you negotiate with the dealer on a trade-in? This question is one that every RV owner will face when upgrading or changing. There are several factors that you will need to consider when making your decision.

Selling

Selling your present RV privately is very appealing to many people. In general, you will get a higher price for your RV than you would from a dealership as a trade-in. When you trade in your RV, the dealer becomes a middleman of sorts in its resale. By eliminating the intermediary, you can often give your buyer a better price than he or she would see on a dealer lot, and you also may come away with more money in your pocket.

Many RV buyers prefer to deal firsthand with the previous owner; with a big purchase, it is good to meet the owner and get a feel for the type of care the RV was given. The owners who keep good maintenance records and maintain their RVs well will have a much better product to sell and may command a higher selling price than a dealer could.

On the downside, you will have to spend some time making the sale. Readying the RV for sale and maintaining it in top condition can be time-consuming. You will have to place ads, take phone calls and inquiries, and show the RV to prospective buyers. It can be frustrating to receive calls about an ad, to set up appointments to show the RV, and then to wait for prospective buyers who never show up.

 ALERT

When you make the sale, insist that your buyer pays with cash or a certified check. While your buyer may seem to be the nicest person in the world, this is not the time for trust, except in the case of a close friend or family member. Even then, some RV owners have been burned by family and friends, so be as careful as you can be.

Trade-Ins

Most RV dealers will willingly take your present RV as a trade-in. Don't be afraid to negotiate the best deal you can get for your RV. Do some research on resale prices and go armed with this information when it comes time to bargain. Do what you need to get your RV into the best condition you can without spending more money than you can recoup in the sale or trade value.

Be alert for the sneaky salesperson who may try to increase the sale price of the new RV you are considering while giving you the RV trade-in price you want. He or she will come out ahead every time. If possible, keep the possibility of a trade-in allowance out of the mix until you've settled on a final sale price for the RV. Don't be afraid to comparison-shop. Look at comparable RVs from different dealers and get offers in writing. Use these offers to negotiate your best price.

Safety Inspections

Before you purchase any RV—especially a used one—a safety inspection is recommended. Although the RV may look fine on the outside, serious safety hazards may lie just beneath the surface.

Look for work done by the do-it-yourselfer. While many RV owners are competent to undertake minor repairs, most are not trained in the complexities of RV systems. As one visitor to the forum at RV.net notes, "The biggest problems are the things that someone else put his hands on." If the RV you are considering has had modifications from the standard, ask for details on installation and maintenance.

Driving Safety

If you are considering a self-propelled motorhome, road safety is the first item to consider. Approach buying a motorhome as you would approach buying a car. These items should be in good condition:

Tires: Look for any cuts, holes, or defects in the sides or any part of the rubber. Check for any "cracking" or splits on the sides between the treads or at the valve stem. Any sign of uneven wear or "balding" on the treads may indicate a problem with alignment, or it could indicate chronic overloading of the RV during its years of use.

Brakes: If you can hear any squeaking, squealing, or grinding sounds as you apply the brakes, it is a sign that they may need to be serviced or repaired. In particular, a squeaking sound usually indicates that brake service is needed. Grinding sounds can be caused by completely worn brake pads and should always be inspected. Also check that the brake lights work properly. Check brake fluid; it should be to the full mark on the reservoir. Low brake fluid may cause your brakes to operate improperly.

Lights: Turn on all lights and flashers. Do emergency flashers work properly? In case of a breakdown, they may help to prevent a crash. Check that turn signal lights (blinkers) work properly. Turn on headlights and check both high beams and low beams for function. Check the alignment and inspect lenses for cracks that may permit water to leak in.

Exhaust system: Check the exhaust system for leaks and ensure that the body is intact to prevent leakage of exhaust gases into the passenger compartment.

Living Area Safety

In a motorhome or travel trailer, you will also want to check for any issues that could pose safety problems for you or your family.

Vents: Make sure that all gas appliances are vented to the outside properly. Watch for any "add-ons" that may cause blockage of these vents. This included luggage carriers and awnings.

Wiring: Look for exposed wires that may cause shocks or fires. All electrical appliances should be properly grounded.

Fire extinguishers and smoke detectors: Look at expiration dates on extinguishers; they should be replaced as needed. Use the check button on smoke and gas detectors to check that they are functional.

Doors and latches: Check all cupboard, cabinet, and refrigerator doors, and make sure they latch securely. If latches fail during a sudden stop in a motorhome, passengers may be injured by flying objects.

CHAPTER 5

Towable RVs

TRAVEL TRAILERS AND FIFTH-WHEEL TRAILERS are towable RVs that fall into the same category as foldup trailers and truck campers. They can towed by a car, van, or pickup by means of a bumper or frame hitch. They are larger and heavier than foldup trailers and will require a tow vehicle that is rated to tow its weight. These types of trailers are popular choices in the RV world because of the variety of floor plans available, which makes them suitable for families with children from toddlers to teenagers. When you arrive at your destination, you can unhook the trailer from your tow vehicle and have transportation to all the sights in the area, with a comfortable bed to sleep in at night.

Travel Trailers

Travel trailers can range in length from 12 to 35 feet. Prices of travel trailers range from $10,000 to $66,000; according to RVIA, the average retail price runs around $16,000. These trailers are self-contained units with sleeping space for up to eight, fully equipped kitchens, and eating areas. Many have spaces with furniture for relaxing and entertainment after a long day of sightseeing. Most trailers come equipped with a television antenna, at the least, and many include a satellite dish as an option. Built close to the ground, travel trailers will have an overall height that is lower than that of a motorhome, but the interior height will be comparable.

TRAVEL TRAILER

When towing anything but the smallest of these trailers, the tow vehicle will need to be outfitted with a special load-distributing hitch and special sway-control devices. Because the entire load of the trailer is concentrated behind the tow vehicle, it is very prone to swaying and instability, especially in situations with high winds or on roads with steep grades.

In their eagerness to close the sale, some less-than-reputable RV salespeople will downplay the importance of adding these antisway controls to large travel trailers. When you see a travel trailer on the highway slithering and swaying like a snake after an eighteen-wheeler has passed, it is very likely that trailer has no sway control in place.

Feeling like you have lost control of both the tow vehicle and the trailer can be a frightening experience, especially for a new RV traveler. These stability problems can lead to major accidents and injury. Many new RV owners, thinking the trailer is defective, have gone back to their RV dealers demanding a refund. Some home-work, training, and working with a reputable salesperson can help prevent these situations.

Nightstand

Queen Bed

Nightstand

Entertainment Center

Sofa Bed

Stools

Dinette

Pantry

Upper/Lower Bunk Beds

Upper/Lower Bunk Beds

Ward

TRAVEL TRAILER FLOOR PLAN WITH BUNK

Lightweight Travel Trailers

Improvements in technology and in construction materials and techniques have made most travel trailers much lighter, more efficient, and more aerodynamic. In recent years, several manufacturers have introduced ultralightweight models. These trailers are typically less than 26 feet in length and weigh less than 4,000 pounds. Weight is also reduced by the use of lighter-weight construction materials. The newer trailers are also much more aerodynamic in order to reduce wind resistance and drag. These lighter trailers are popular because many six-cylinder family vehicles are able to tow them.

 FACT

The stated length of your trailer is its measurement from its rear bumper to the tip of the tongue hitch. Your actual living area will be about 3 feet less than the length on its sticker. You will have to account for this when planning your trips.

Advantages

Travel trailers are much less expensive than motorhomes and have a longer life span. Even older trailers can be spruced up and remodeled to give additional years of service. Maintenance costs are generally less because there is no motor and drive train. They are a great home base for vacationers. Once you have arrived at your destination and set up, you have a vehicle for sightseeing in. Travel trailer floor plans are the most flexible available. There is also some flexibility in the choice of tow vehicle as long as it is rated to tow the required amount of weight. While full-size pickup trucks can tow travel trailers, you are not limited to a specific tow vehicle.

Disadvantages

The longer and heavier a trailer is, the harder it will be to manage in windy conditions and on steep grades. When the

National Weather Service issues a wind advisory for high-profile vehicles, travel trailers (including fifth-wheels) and motorhomes are advised to proceed with caution or pull over until conditions improve. Such an unexpected stop could affect your travel plans.

You will need to spend an additional $200 to $600 to equip your tow vehicle with the appropriate hitch for a travel trailer. Your vehicle may also need more extensive suspension modifications to work for towing.

Currently, no travel trailers are equipped with internal generators. This will mean that you would need to have a standalone generator to run some appliances when shore power is not available.

Fifth-Wheel Trailers

Another very popular large towable trailer is the fifth-wheel trailer. While technically still travel trailers, they differ in their exterior shape with a raised front that extends over the bed of the truck. Fifth-wheel trailers can only be towed by a specially equipped, full-size truck or by a custom-built tow vehicle.

 FACT

Fifth-wheels have an extension on the front of the trailer box that extends over the tow vehicle and a horizontal plate that looks like a wheel that rests on the tow vehicle for support. The name "fifth-wheel" comes from this wheel-like plate.

The hitch arrangement needed puts the load in the center of the tow vehicle instead of behind. This large, broad mount is similar to the hitch used by tractor-trailers. Most people feel this type of towing arrangement allows for greater stability in the ride of the truck. The driver should feel less push by the trailer on the truck, especially in situations when the trailer is buffeted by high winds.

FIFTH-WHEEL TRAILER

Fifth-wheel trailers can range in length from 21 to more than 40 feet measured from front extension to rear bumper. Their features are similar to those of larger travel trailers. Manufacturers of fifth-wheels offer a large variety of floor plans and options. In most, you will see the front of the trailer portion that extends over the truck bed functioning as the master bedroom. There are generally three to five stairs needed to get up to the bedroom; this may limit its use by physically challenged travelers. This front living space turns fifth-wheels into a very high-profile trailer.

Because full-size trucks must pull these trailers, the trailer can often be quite large. It is not uncommon to see two, three, or even four slideouts on some models. They are generally very roomy and spacious. As with most RVs, you will find trailers with prices from reasonable to expensive. Some of the higher-end models include washer-dryer combinations and kitchens equipped with dishwashers and trash compactors.

These trailers are self-contained and many come equipped with a generator. Storage space is usually very generous.

Advantages

With no engine or transmission to wear out, fifth-wheel RVs can have a long lifespan. They are ideal for the full-time RVer, or the

RVer who takes extended trips, because of the amount of storage and living space. If you have a trailer pulled by a tow vehicle, you will have transportation when you get to your destination.

Disadvantages

The fifth-wheel type of RV requires a full-size pickup truck with a very powerful engine. If you don't already own a truck, you will need to buy one. A comfortably equipped truck suitable for towing this RV can cost upward of $40,000. The hitch adds about $900 to the price. Another modification you may want to make is to replace the truck tailgate with a mesh-type tailgate unit that will cut down on wind resistance. This will be an additional expense, but it can help improve gas mileage and handling when high winds are a problem.

Because these trailers are generally so high-profile, storage and parking can be a problem. Low-hanging tree branches, for example, could damage the exterior finish.

How Much Trailer Do You Need?

Shopping for a travel trailer or fifth-wheel trailer can be a confusing and sometimes frustrating affair. Before you go near an RV dealership, sit down with a pen and paper and figure out what you need, what you already have in the way of tow vehicles, and what you want now and for the future.

Sleeping Space

How many people will be sleeping in the trailer? The typical family of four (mother, father, and two children) can often get by with a smaller travel trailer with a floor plan that meets their needs. A popular floor plan is one with a bedroom with a large double or queen bed on one end and bunk beds on the other end of the trailer. The bathroom is often situated on the same end as the bunks, with the kitchen and any living space in the middle portion of the trailer. This floor plan works well in even shorter trailers by limiting the amount of living space. A smaller trailer can work well for those families who treat their trailer as a traveling hotel room, one that is used for eating and sleeping after seeing the nearby attractions.

Toy Haulers

Many people use their trailers for living space while pursuing their passions or competitive spirit. More and more RV manufacturers are offering travel trailers and fifth-wheel trailers that contain both living space and a "traveling garage." The garage is accessed through the rear of the trailer, with the rear wall swinging down to form a ramp. All kind of fun vehicles are carried in these specialty trailers, from ATVs to motorcycles to dune buggies. These trailers are usually specially ordered to the buyer's specifications and needs. They will either come with equipment to stabilize the vehicle being carried, or such equipment will need to be added. The entire trailer can be used for living and sleeping space when the "toys" are driven outside at your destination. With features such as rollup carpets and pull-down-from-the-ceiling beds, the garage disappears and a very large trailer appears. These "toy haulers" combine the best of all worlds. Pulling a trailer, you will have a vehicle that can be unhooked for sightseeing. You are also not limited to having a motorhome with a tow vehicle for the toys, but no transportation while you are at the campground.

Tow Vehicle Limitations

The tow vehicle you presently own will limit your choice of trailers. Compact family cars are not capable of towing a travel trailer. If you own a van or SUV, you may be able to tow a travel trailer, but a fifth-wheel is out of the question.

Tow Vehicles

Mating the tow vehicle to the trailer is the most important factor in towing safety and enjoyment. If the vehicles are not matched correctly, stability becomes a factor and can lead to loss of control. The tow vehicle has to be rated to tow the weight of the loaded trailer, and it needs enough power to be able to pull it up a hill and control it while on the downgrade.

A large travel trailer will require the towing power of a rear-wheel-drive V-8 equipped truck, SUV, or full-size sedan. You will also find some heavy-duty diesel trucks made specifically for towing fifth-wheel or travel trailers. They look like the trucks that pull eighteen-wheel trailers and run from $40,000 to $100,000 or more.

Towed Weight Limits

When evaluating your vehicle as a tow vehicle, you will need to know the vehicle tow weight. Look in your owner's manual for the maximum weight (GVW) the vehicle can tow. The next thing you need to find in the manual is the gross combined weight rating (GCWR). The GCWR is the maximum combined weight of the tow vehicle and the load you will pull. This is the most important towing weight specification you will need to know. You can also contact the manufacturer directly for that information.

 ESSENTIAL

Weight is calculated by adding the dry weight of both the tow vehicle and the trailer being towed. Then add in the weight of all fluids, foods, clothing, and other supplies that will be in the trailer. Add to this the weight of the passengers in a tow vehicle fully fueled and ready to go. Add a bit more for good measure. If this number does not exceed the GCWR of the tow vehicle, you are in good shape.

Based on the size and number of cylinders you give them along with the model, manufacturers can tell you the towed weight limits. Many reputable RV dealers will also be able to provide you with this information. The RV dealer who wants to keep you as a life-long customer will give you honest information and not try to sell you more trailer than you can safely pull.

Towing Packages

If you are buying a vehicle to use as a tow vehicle, be sure to ask about trailer towing packages. These optional packages come from the factory or are added on at the dealer and will increase the rated load of the vehicle. These towing packages can also be added on "after-market" to the vehicle you own already. A towing package will include upgrades to the vehicle suspension, radiator, and alternator. The flashers will need to be upgraded to support the trailer lights in addition to the cars. Another important area that will need attention is an upgraded cooling system for the engine and transmission that includes an oversized radiator and transmission oil cooler. Towing a trailer is hard work, and an engine and transmission will overheat without these additions. Towing a trailer without a tow package or modifications could also void the vehicle warranty.

Special Driving Challenges

Towing a trailer behind a vehicle is a challenge for most people. Even if you are an experienced travel-trailer owner, you should give any new or used vehicle you are considering buying a test drive. Every trailer–tow vehicle combination will have its own idiosyncrasies.

If you are a new RV owner, you may want to take some lessons. If your RV dealer does not offer this type of class, ask them why not. This is a great way to build a loyal base of repeat RV buyers.

 ALERT

Some roads will be off-limits to large trucks or extra-long trailers. When planning your trip, pay attention to the map markings and plan for alternate routes to account for roads that may not be passable.

Many driving schools offer classes for RV drivers, both new and experienced. These classes are well worth the expense in relieving the anxiety that many new RV owners experience. Most of these classes cover the most common situations that can occur while traveling, including dealing with grades and backing up. All licensed drivers who will be traveling should learn how to drive the tow vehicle and trailer. Even in the best of circumstances, illness and injury can happen and a passenger may be stranded or have to leave a trailer behind.

Mountain travel can be dangerous with very long trailers and fifth-wheel trailers. Some mountain roads are very narrow with hairpin turns. Many roads will be marked restricting long loads; if in doubt, check with the highway patrol.

STEEP GRADE SIGN

Trailer Brakes

Any travel trailer of more than 1,000 pounds should have independent wheel braking on the trailer. Depending on the state, this may be legally required, but it is foolhardy in any case to tow a trailer of that weight without trailer brakes.

There are two general types of trailer brakes: surge and electric. Surge brakes work by the "push" of the trailer toward the tow vehicle during deceleration, which automatically synchronizes the brakes of the trailer with those of the tow vehicle. Basically, as you apply the brakes or lessen the pressure on your gas pedal, the tow vehicle will slow and the trailer will push up against it (the tongue of the trailer against the tow ball on the hitch). This brings into play the hydraulic brake lines, with pressure to the master cylinder of the trailer brakes, then activating the brakes.

Electric braking units activate the trailer brakes by detecting pressure when the brake pedal is pressed. The tow vehicle is wired for electricity. Many do-it-yourselfers are tempted to wire the tow vehicle themselves and many do a fine job, but when in doubt have this done by a professional. Trailer brakes are one of the most important safety features you have, and they need to perform correctly. There is a controller mounted to the dashboard of the tow vehicle that can control the brakes independently. Most trailer brakes (and this may be required by law in some places) have a "breakaway" feature. This automatically activates the brakes if the trailer becomes totally disconnected from the tow vehicle.

Sway Controls

Sway controls are controls that are attached to the hitch and tow vehicle. They help prevent or reduce the swaying motion of the trailer that occurs when an eighteen-wheeler passes at 70 miles per hour. There are two basic types of sway control: the friction sway control and the dual-cam sway control.

Friction sway control uses friction to resist pivotal movement and works against the induced sway that results from the airflow of the passing truck. As the sway begins, the coupling between the tow vehicle and trailer stiffens. The degree of stiffening is adjusted for the trailer weight and towing conditions. It does not prevent sway from happening, but it does lessen its affect.

Dual-cam sway control works to keep sway from happening in the first place. It only works when needed. When towing in a straight line, there is basically a ridged connection between the tow vehicle and trailer. This ridged connection helps the travel trailer–tow vehicle combination act more like a motorhome or a single vehicle, and it minimizes the effects of high crosswinds and passing vehicles. To allow for turning the cams on the sway control, they need to be slid out of the locked position.

Sway often causes inexperienced drivers to overcorrect and lose control. Although sway controls are not required, they are inexpensive and highly recommended.

Setting Up

Setting up a travel trailer is usually a fairly simple affair once the trailer is backed into the correct place. Look at your parking space and find the spot that provides a level surface and is convenient for hooking up to the utilities. Some trailers come equipped with automatic leveling jacks and others have to be leveled by cranking up jacks. Be sure to chock the tires as soon as you get it into the right place to prevent the trailer from rolling.

 ESSENTIAL

Use lightweight outdoor carpeting for your entranceway or some other lightweight material that can be hosed off and dries quickly. Household carpet is very heavy, especially when wet, and it does not dry quickly.

Level the trailer from side to side first. Place the jacks or lower them at the rear of the trailer; then unhook the trailer from the tow vehicle by raising the tongue to disengage the tongue from the ball of the hitch. Once the trailer is loose, it can be leveled front to back. The trailer is then hooked up to utilities (if available), and you are all set to go.

Most people like to put out the awning and put down some kind of rug or carpet under the area shaded by the awning. This will help keep dirt and mud out of the trailer if it should rain. This covered area is also a nice place to set up your lawn chairs.

Storage

Most travel trailers and fifth-wheels are too tall for conventional home garages. Some people do build extra-large garages for their trailers. This is the best way to store your rig between trips and prevent freezing in all but the harshest of winters. If your storage garage is wired, you can use an electric heater. This will eliminate the need for prepping the stored vehicle for freezing temperatures.

The next best thing to a garage is an extra-tall, covered carport for your trailer. While it may not prevent freezing, it will keep the sun damage down.

If these options are not available, you can still take steps to protect your investment while it is not in use:

- Empty, clean, and sanitize the holding tanks (fresh water, gray water, and black water) before storage.
- Remove all perishable foods. Remove canned foods if there is danger of freezing.
- Turn off the refrigerator and make sure the interior light is off to prevent drain on the battery.
- Prop the refrigerator door open slightly and place an open box of baking soda or a few charcoal briquettes inside to remove odors.
- Close window shades to prevent sun damage to upholstery.
- If the trailer has a rain cover, allow for ventilation.
- Turn off propane tanks.
- Cover the tires to reduce sun exposure.
- Turn off circuit breakers to prevent battery drainage.

CHAPTER 6

Motorhomes

MOTORHOMES ARE AMONG THE MOST POPULAR of all the recreational vehicles available. You can find them in a wide variety of lengths and with options and floor plans to meet almost any need. They are a one-piece home on wheels, with the driver sharing the same space as the passengers in the living area. For the novice RV traveler, motorhomes are generally easier to drive and to set up at camp. Passengers can eat, drink, use the bathroom, and sleep while traveling—although, for safety reasons, this is not recommended.

Motorhome Specifics

Motorhomes can range in length from less than 18 feet to 40 feet, and from budget to luxury. They are divided into classes that are based on the type of chassis they are built on. The smaller rigs will have a gasoline engine, while many of the larger coaches will have a diesel engine mounted in the rear of the motorhome. Buying a motorhome is an all-in-one purchase without any worry about incompatibilities between tow vehicle and trailer. Motorhomes are great when you are traveling and stop in rest stops or parking lots for a few hours' sleep. Travelers feel more secure when stopping in these types of places because they do not have to get out of a vehicle to go to the sleeping quarters. If they feel that the place they have stopped in is not safe, they don't have to get out of the sleeping quarters into a potentially dangerous situation in order to leave; they just get in the driver's seat and go.

One thing to remember is that with a motorhome you will lose living space due to the driver's space that is included in the overall length. It is usually wasted space for anything but storage when you are set up in camp.

If you want to have convenient transportation for sightseeing, shopping, etc., when you reach your destination, you will need to tow a vehicle behind.

 ALERT

Motorhomes lose resale value rapidly and at a much higher rate than a comparably equipped travel trailer or fifth-wheel trailer. Wear and tear on the drive train is the biggest factor that affects the potential resale value. High-mileage RVs may be as difficult to sell as high-mileage used cars.

Class A Motorhomes

Class A motorhomes are among the largest and most expensive of the three classes of motorhomes. They are only eclipsed by the luxury bus conversions. Class A motorhomes range in size from 28 to 45 feet in length and weigh from 13,000 to 30,000 pounds gross vehicle weight (GVW). These are tall vehicles ranging from 9 to 10 feet in height. Many have one to three slideouts that increase living space. They are usually built on truck chassis that range from 3 to 10 tons or else on custom-designed chassis, depending on the manufacturer.

Larger Class A rigs will come equipped with a queen-size bed, a spacious bathroom (compared to most other RVs), and a fully equipped kitchen. Depending on their length, they may come equipped with two air conditioners for cooling efficiency.

Storage is generous in these units, in part due to the platform they are built on. Many feature "basement storage" located below the floor of the motorhome.

CLASS A MOTORHOME

Options found on Class A motorhomes range from basic to luxurious and not every manufacturer offers all of them. They will come equipped with extra-large fuel tanks that can help limit refueling stops, though you may suffer from some sticker shock when you fill up. These large, heavy vehicles are not especially fuel efficient, with many getting much less than 10 miles per gallon. Good-quality diesel engines can get somewhat better fuel economy, and diesel engines usually have a much longer life span.

 FACT

Basement storage, a common feature on larger motorhomes, is accessed from outside doors, similar to where luggage is stored on a Greyhound bus. Some motorhomes have "pass-through" basement storage, meaning that it goes from one side of the RV to the other with no dividers. This permits storage of large, bulky items that can be accessed easily from either side of the rig.

Once RV owners get used to the size of their motorhomes, they usually find they are the easiest of the full-size rigs to drive. A quality Class A motorhome, properly loaded, will generally handle much better than any trailer or fifth-wheel trailer equivalent.

Large Class A motorhomes are not permitted in some national parks, and some private parks may have limited spaces available for longer motorhomes. Due to their length and high profile, storage and parking can be an issue. Low-hanging tree branches and gas pump canopies can be hazardous. While some RV manufacturers offer extra-wide models (more than 96 inches), be cautious when considering these rigs. Some states have officially banned these RVs from their roads. Check with the highway patrol of the states you plan on visiting for their regulations. With that information in hand, you can either decide on a model that is within regulations, or plan on traveling in states that do not ban extra-wide RVs.

If you want to sightsee after reaching your destination, you will need to bring along alternative transportation. You can tow a small car, van, or SUV behind your motorhome with comparative ease. Bicycles or motorbikes are other options that can be carried on racks attached to the back of the rig or on a small trailer towed behind the RV.

 ALERT

Getting your rig as level as is possible is very important. Your refrigerator will run more efficiently, your wastewater tanks will empty more fully, and your doors will close properly. If your rig is not self-leveling, be sure you always carry a carpenter's level in the rig or in your toolbox.

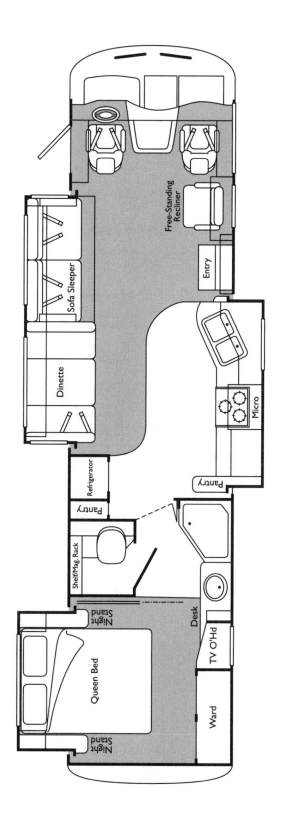

CLASS A MOTORHOME FLOOR PLAN

Free-Standing Recliner

Entry

Sofa Sleeper

Dinette

Micro

Refrigerator

Pantry

Pantry

Shelf/Mag. Rack

Night Stand

Night Stand

Queen Bed

Desk

TV O'Hd

Ward

71

Class B Motorhomes

The term "Class B" is a fairly recent name for an RV type that had been around for many years. Commonly referred to as "van campers" or "van conversions," these are the smallest of the fully enclosed self-contained motorhomes. They are built on a standard van chassis. They offer an elevated roof to provide standing head-room in the interior. They may be somewhat longer than a regular passenger van, but this is usually a minor difference, with the usual length ranging from 7 to 9 feet. They typically weigh in the 6,000- to 8,000-pound range.

CLASS B MOTORHOME

They tend to drive like a fully loaded van and are comparatively easy to handle for inexperienced RV owners. They are much easier to maneuver on crowded city streets. Parking and storage is less of an issue than with the larger motorhome cousins, as a Class B will usually fit easily into a standard parking spot. Standard home garages and parking garages can still pose a problem because of the ele-vated roofline. Most parking garages are unable to accommodate vehicles over 6 feet and 8 or 9 inches in height. Most Class B motorhomes start at a height of 7 feet, going up to 9 feet depending on the model.

Most Class B motorhomes are self-contained (though some may lack a shower), and while the salesperson or sales brochures state they sleep four, they are more comfortable for one or two. Before you set out on a cross-country trip in one of these rigs, be sure you can really spend that much "together" time with your traveling companions. While this is good advice for any family contemplating RV travel, it is especially vital when buying a Class B. You should understand that up close and personal will be the daily routine, with little or no "alone" time.

Because of the compact size of Class B motorhomes, their living space will serve multiple purposes. A dinette or couch used for eating or relaxation during the day may have to be converted to a sleeping space at night. This can be a real downside if you just want to get up and go when on vacation.

 ESSENTIAL

Class B motorhomes will force you to pack lightly and efficiently. There will be minimal storage space for clothing, cooking equipment, and food. Making friends with a backpacker should yield you a lot of information on minimalist travel.

Class B motorhomes are very expensive for the square footage of vehicle you are buying. Shop carefully, and consider looking at smaller Class C motorhomes or small travel trailers with a tow vehicle as an alternative. You may find a vehicle that meets your needs at a lower price than the Class B you have looked at. Because of their compactness, most of the appliances and furnishings in Class B motorhomes have to be miniaturized for the limited space. Not having the option of using standard RV fixtures will add to the overall cost.

Many people find the Class B to be the perfect combination of RV and second vehicle. Some use them as daily drivers besides using them as RVs. Be prepared for your Class B van conversion to depreciate rapidly and significantly when you try to resell it or trade it in.

Class C Motorhomes

The Class C motorhome is a self-contained motorhome built on an automotive-manufactured van frame. Look at the driver's portion of most Class Cs and you will see the front portion of a full-size van from one of the big three Detroit automakers. The living area is built behind and above the cab. The living quarters are basically a large box added behind the cab of the vehicle. The "box" extends over the cab of the van and is referred to as the cabover section. In most Class C floor plans, the cabover section functions as an overhead sleeping area. In some smaller Class Cs, this may be the main sleeping area, or in a larger rig with a bedroom it can function as additional sleeping space or storage. Some Class Cs forgo the sleeping space in the cabovers and opt to put in an entertainment center, closed storage, or some other use. If you are buying a new rig and don't mind waiting a bit, you should be able to get the configuration you want special-ordered if the perfect rig is not on the lot. Just be sure you take future circumstances into consideration—you may want to take grandchildren with you at some points and they will need a place to sleep.

Because it is an all-in-one motorhome, a Class C vehicle allows the passenger to move from the passenger seat into the living area, though this can be somewhat more difficult than in a Class A. In a Class C, the passenger will have to maneuver around the hump where the engine protrudes between the front seats. Depending on the vehicle make, there may also be a step up from the passenger seat to the living area, and there will be the obstacle of lower headroom in the van's cab.

CLASS C MOTORHOME

Class C motorhomes range in size from 20 to 28 feet on average, though you can find some that are shorter and some that are much longer. One or more slideouts are common on the higher priced RVs, with the most popular being two (one for the living area and one for the bedroom).

As with most of the all-in-one motorhomes, the Class C is generally easy to drive, especially if you have ever owned and driven a van or small truck. While you may be tempted to buy one of the longer Class C motorhomes, one over 28 to 30 feet in length may prove to be very unstable on the highway.

While it is very tempting to try to pack one of these rigs for a month on the road without restocking, that is not practical and can be dangerous. One of the most common causes of accidents is loss of control due to an overloaded RV. Don't be fooled by the amount of space you have available; follow the manufacturer's guidelines for weight-carrying capacities. Be sure to also follow the owner's manual for properly loading the RV, keeping the load evenly distributed.

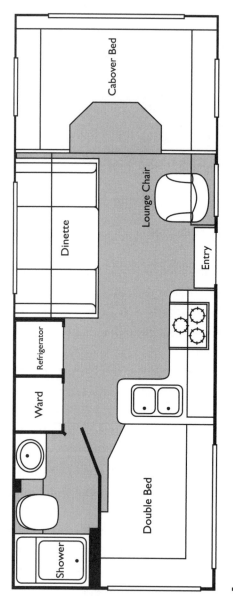
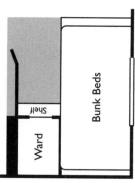

CLASS C MOTORHOME FLOOR PLAN

 **ALERT**

You can tow a small car behind a Class C motorhome with the proper towing equipment, as long as you stay within the recommended weight requirements. Do not be tempted to use the towed vehicle as additional storage space if it will put you over the weight limit. Overloading a towed car is just as dangerous as overloading the motorhome itself.

Bus Conversions

Some Class A motorhomes are mistakenly called "bus motorhomes" because of their size and shape, but they are distinctly different vehicles. While some hobbyists and do-it-yourselfers have converted used public transit buses into motorhomes (and some have been done quite well), the bus-conversion motorhomes discussed here are new units, built as motorhomes.

These are the most luxurious motor coaches (coach sounds so much more expensive) you can buy—and the most costly with prices ranging up to $1,000,000 (yes, there are six zeroes) or more. They are the longest RVs available, running 45 to 45 feet in length. With a slideout or two, the interior living space is spacious and open. These RVs are equipped with the most up-to-date, upscale appliances and options. Worried about backing into a camping space? A closed-circuit camera on the wall gives the driver a clear view of the space behind to get it backed into the correct place. Furnished with glove leather, real wood trim, and Italian marble baths, they are more expensive and more luxurious than most houses. If you want to spend extended time in a place with no electric or water hookups, these RVs are truly self-contained, with gas-powered generators and large water tanks.

Bus-conversion RVs are diesel-powered and seemingly last forever. Of all the motorized RVs, these will hold their value best, though a used bus conversion looks like a real bargain when pricing a new one.

As big as they are, they are surprisingly easy to drive; they handle well and offer a very comfortable ride. They can tow even large cars and SUVs with little effort. You could probably even tow your yacht with it.

As with other large motorhomes, the size of these rigs may limit their entry into some national parks and some private campgrounds. There are, however, some RV campgrounds that cater to these upscale motor coaches. For a very expensive fee (when compared to average RV park fees), you will have an RV space with lots of room for your rig, along with a resort setting. When you own one of these RVs, you can live á la *Lifestyles of the Rich and Famous* on the road.

 ESSENTIAL

You will often see these bus-size RVs towing a vehicle for "transportation at their destination" in a separate trailer (painted to match the RV, of course). While this adds towing weight, it is much easier on the vehicle, especially the transmission and tires. Only a large bus-conversion RV could tow the amount of weight involved.

Motorhome Maintenance

Keeping your motorhome in good shape will help ensure that you enjoy your travels on the road or in the great outdoors. Sitting in a repair shop is never fun, especially when it is in a shop far from home.

Fluids

Here are the regular steps you should take for maintenance of fluids in your motorhome:

Check all fluids at least monthly when the motorhome is sitting and weekly when you are on the road. Top off any fluids that are low.

Change the oil and filter at the intervals the owner's manual advises or even slightly sooner. Use the weight and type of oil the manufacturer advises. Always change the filter at the same time as the oil, as a dirty, blocked oil filter can cause overheating problems.

Check the level of brake fluid without removing the top of the tank. It is rare that you will need to add fluid, but a loss of brake fluid can signal problems.

Check your coolant when the engine is cold and top off as recommended by the manufacturer. This is one fluid you should carry with you, especially if traveling in very warm climates with steep grades. You can also use tap water in an emergency, if your engine boils over before you can get to a service station.

Have the cooling system drained, flushed, and refilled yearly or as recommended by your dealer.

Transmission fluid should be changed yearly in a newer motorhome. Check with an expert at a transmission shop if you have an older RV; it may be better to rebuild the transmission rather than just change the fluids.

Power steering fluid should not have to be changed or added unless there is a leak or a problem with the power steering system.

Change the fuel filter every two or three months. This can help your engine run more effectively and be more fuel-efficient.

Air Intakes

Change the air filters every 2,000 miles, or more often if you are traveling in dusty areas.

Air Conditioning

Check the temperature of the air the air conditioner is blowing out every three to six months. You can get a thermometer at an auto parts store for a few dollars. On max, the reading should be between 45 and 55 degrees. If the temperature is over 55, the air-conditioning units need to be serviced by an auto air-conditioning shop.

Tires

Tires should be checked regularly, including the air pressure. Looks for cracks, embedded nails, evidence of tread separation, or uneven wear. These are all indications that you need to have the tire repaired, replaced, or rebalanced. Check that the lug nuts are tight. Be sure to check your spare tire at the same time.

Brakes

Unless you change the oil yourself, you should have your mechanic check your brakes at the same time you have the oil changed.

Body

Look over the outside of your RV for any signs of leaks or rust. The best thing you can do for the outside of your rig is to keep it clean. If you have traveled in northern areas where they use salt on the roads, or have camped near the ocean, keep your RV rinsed off to prevent rust and corrosion. Be sure to get underneath. You might want to find a truck wash to do a good cleaning.

Gas or Diesel?

Motorhomes will have either a gasoline or a diesel engine. The type and price of the RV you decide on will usually dictate the type of engine you get. Class B and Class C motorhomes will almost always have gasoline engines, as they are based on the chassis of gasoline-powered vans.

A mid-price Class A motorhome will probably have a gasoline-powered engine, though you may be able to spend more and get a diesel engine. If you are buying a large, heavy motorhome and intend to use it for many long-distance trips, diesel makes sense. Diesels will cost more initially but are usually cheaper to operate and have fewer maintenance problems. Quality-built diesel engines can rack up an impressive number of miles before needing a major overhaul. Diesel fuel is about the same price as regular gasoline, but you will get more miles to the gallon. Another factor is fuel availability. There is usually a gas station on every corner, but most sell gasoline only. The easiest place to find diesel fuel is at large truck stops and at gas stations just off major highways. As large RVs are more suited to major highways, finding fuel should not be a problem. Most of the large bus conversions have gas tanks that hold almost enough fuel to get you hundreds of miles; the chances of running dry are very slim.

ESSENTIAL

One of the handiest gadgets an RV owner can take along is a GPS unit and mapping program. Most mapping software includes information on travel centers with diesel fuel, places to eat, campgrounds, etc. These are particularly great for travelers with no sense of direction who hate to stop and ask for help.

Driving Challenges

A well-built properly loaded motorhome will handle better than a trailer being pulled by a car or truck. You will still feel that momentary pull on the rig when passed by an eighteen-wheeler going 70 miles per hour, but a motorhome will recover its stability much faster. The laws of physics are at play, and one single vehicle will always win at that game when compared to two separate vehicles weighing several thousand pounds each attached by a hitch. With a trailer moving one way and a tow vehicle moving the other way after being buffeted by a cross-wind, the time to recover stability will be much longer with a trailer as compared to a motorhome.

One of the greatest challenges of motorhome driving is the overall size of the vehicle. If you can, try to avoid big cities with heavy traffic. If your travels do take you through larger cities, try to travel through the city at night when traffic is lighter. Adapt your schedule or route to avoid frustrating waits in rush-hour traffic jams. The commuters going to work have to be there, but you are on vacation—why put yourself into that mess if you can avoid it?

Another big challenge for motorhomes is mountainous areas. If you see a sign prohibiting trucks, or limiting trucks and trailers on certain routes, you may not be able to drive your RV on that road either. Your motorhome may be too long to navigate tight or hairpin turns. There may also be limitations on weight on some narrow mountain roads after rainstorms or earthquakes that may have undermined the road's foundation. If in doubt about a route you are unfamiliar with, check with the local police or highway patrol. They should be able to tell you if you will be able to safely traverse a route.

Motorhomes are especially vulnerable to high winds and slick roads. The sheer weight of a motorhome means that it will take that much longer and farther to stop.

Mountain roads are always a challenge to motorhomes. You will need to learn how to shift correctly to climb a grade without over-heating the engine and transmission while still maintaining enough power to get to the top. Every RV is different so even if you are a veteran, you should always try out a new (to you) RV on some smaller grades and work your way up to larger grades. Steep down-hill grades can overheat brakes and lead to brake failure, especially if you have a tow vehicle behind you.

Backing up a motorhome is another challenge that causes stress to most new owners. Unless you can always find a pull-through campsite, you will eventually have to back into a site and do it fairly precisely. You may only have a narrow strip of campsite that is level enough for your rig. Find a mall or department store parking lot that is fairly empty (Sunday morning is usually a good time) and practice backing up and parking your rig. Mark out a typical space (about 22 to 24 feet by 50 feet) with some object that you will be able to see with your mirrors, but one that you won't mind running over a few times. Agree on the hand signals that will help guide you before you start your practice. Many people utilize walkie-talkies for this task. This is sometimes easier as they can use voice directions rather than hand signals that may be misinterpreted in a rearview mirror. Walkie-talkies also work better when you arrive late and are trying to park in the dark.

 ALERT

If you decide to use walkie-talkies to help with backing up a motorhome, be sure to buy a good set with good range. They can be used to communicate in places like amusement parks and when hiking. Be sure to carry enough of the right type of batteries with you, and to store them in the same place so they will be easy to find, even in the dark.

Some larger Class A motorhomes have a backup camera installed (either standard or as an option). This camera gives the driver a view of the area behind the motorhome and can help the single traveler back in and park without additional help.

Always be aware of the weather. If you are in the mountains and a winter weather advisory is issued, you may want to shorten your vacation plans and get down to more moderate climes. If it blows through without notice, you should probably stay put to avoid driving in dangerous conditions and hope that your water lines don't freeze. High wind warnings may be another condition where you will want to pull over until conditions improve.

Setting Up

The thing that attracts most people to the all-in-one motorhome is the ease in setting up once you reach your destination. If you are pulling a car behind your RV, it is usually much easier to unhook it before you try backing into a space. Once you have backed or driven into your space, you just have a couple of things to hook up and then you are ready to relax or have fun. Put together a checklist of the things you need to do to set up your RV for camping.

The first and often most important thing is to get your rig as level as possible.

If you are staying in a campground with full hookups, you will hook up the electric power, hook up the fresh water, and set up the wastewater drainage hoses.

CHAPTER 7

Tow Vehicles, and Vehicles You Tow

IF YOU DON'T HAVE A MOTORIZED RV, you will need to have a tow vehicle that is able to pull your RV to your destination. If you do have a motorized RV, it is always nice to be able to tow a smaller vehicle behind it. When you arrive at your campsite, you can then unhook this vehicle and use it for transportation while your RV stays at the site. The most important consideration when evaluating any potential tow or towed vehicle is to make sure it's the right one for the job it needs to do.

Do You Have Enough Power?

Your tow vehicle needs to have enough power to pull the weight of your trailer down the road and over any hills along the way. How much power that may be depends on the combination of a number of factors, such as the weight of the vehicle when loaded and the size of the engine and transmission.

Even if an engine is capable of pulling a load—at least for a while—doing so can affect your vehicle condition and longevity. On a road with a level grade, your compact family car may be able to drag a travel trailer for a few hundred miles, but that distance might add several thousand miles' worth of wear and tear to the engine. If you encounter any serious hills on your route, you may lose your transmission—and eventually even the entire engine—before you reach the top. When you overload a tow vehicle, you reduce its braking capability and put greater stress on its components. The result is often a shortened service life or immediate failure. Towing a trailer that is too heavy is not only foolish in terms of safety, but it will also be costly—unless you are prepared to replace your engine and transmission every few weeks. Towing loads greater than is recommended by the manufacturer also runs the risk of voiding your vehicle's warranty. You may be an enthusiastic gambler at your weekly poker game, but this can be a very expensive risk to take.

Before you buy a motorhome, trailer, or tow vehicle you need to do your homework and learn:

- How to determine any vehicle's (even a motorhome's) weight rating, tow rating, and net carrying capacity.
- The maximum and the recommended load carrying and towing capacities of your car or truck.
- How to evaluate the various methods and devices available for towing a vehicle.
- How to evaluate the vehicle you plan on towing—is it suitable for towing, or is towing even recommended by the manufacturer? Not all vehicles can be towed.
- How to evaluate trailer hitches, including classifications and limitations.

 ALERT

Protect your investment by keeping excellent records. Don't depend on a verbal confirmation of weight capacities from your vehicle dealer or manufacturer. Get it in writing. If you have any problems later on, you will have something to back you up if your dealer or the manufacturer tries to tell you that your transmission failure is not covered by your warranty.

How Much Can You Pull?

The first place to look for information on a vehicle's towing capacity is in the owner's manual. Look in the index for a listing about "towing" or "towing a trailer." The manual should tell you if your vehicle could tow a trailer at all. If you read that towing a trailer is not recommended, then close the manual and start looking for another tow vehicle.

 FACT

> If you have lost the owner's manual or you have a vehicle you bought used without an owner's manual, you can go directly to the manufacturer for the information you need. Look for the VIN (Vehicle Identification Number) on the vehicle (along with the make and model year), and a call to the manufacturer should give you the information you need.

Maximum Loads

All RVs (both trailers and motorhomes) have two weight ratings. These ratings (numbers) are very important, and it is vital that you know and understand the significance of these ratings when you buy your RV and when you load your belongings and loved ones in them for travel.

GCWR (gross combined weight rating) is the weight of the vehicle when it is completely empty—that means no fuel, no luggage or gear, no food or drinks, and no driver or passengers. GVWR (gross vehicle weight rating) is the maximum weight that the vehicle can carry when fully loaded. The difference between these two numbers is the amount of weight you will be able to load into the rig for travel. You need to figure in everything you will be putting into the RV, and that includes the people, pets, and food you will want to take on your trip and the fuel that you need to power you. If you are tempted to add too many items or baggage to your rig, you are risking handling problems that could prove dangerous on some roads. You will find that your suspension, brakes, and tires may wear out much sooner than you expected. The damage that causes can be costly, not only in replacing parts that have worn prematurely, but also in the future when you are trying to trade the RV in on a newer rig.

 FACT

> You will usually find the GCWR and the GVWR on a metal plate located inside the door of a trailer for easy accessibility. You should also be able to find them in at least one other location, such as in the engine compartment of a motorhome. A serial number for the unit is likely to be in the same place; this can be useful for verifying with the chassis builder that the weight ratings are correct.

Some RV manufacturers will list GCWR as the weight before optional equipment is added. Air-conditioning units and microwaves will add a significant amount of weight. If the sales brochure lists these items as "optional," you will need to find out their weights and add them to the GCWR before you can figure out the weight you have available for your gear. If possible, you should try to weigh the vehicle before you purchase it and verify that the ratings are correct. If you are able to get the rig weighed and have to take it to a truck weigh station, remember to figure in the weight of the fuel in the gas tanks (about 6.15 pounds per gallon for gasoline).

Once you have an accurate number for the cargo-carrying capacity of your rig, you will then need to determine the weight of the cargo (you, your passengers, and all the stuff you need) that you plan to carry on your travels. If you want to be safe, you should write down these weights (and weigh things—yes, including yourself—to be accurate). If you find that you are over your weight limit, you will need to start eliminating things.

A smart traveler can pack well within the weight limit of his RV. If your travels will take you though populated areas, don't pack food for more than a day or two and shop along the way. With water, just keep enough in the tank to flush the toilet and carry a small amount in water bottles to drink, restocking as you run out.

Adding a Towing Package

If your tow vehicle did not come with a factory-installed towing package, you will need to have that work done before you will be able to tow your trailer. Luckily, most full-size trucks (and many smaller trucks also) come equipped with a towing package as standard equipment.

The first place to look for information about towing packages is your vehicle owner's manual. Look under "towing" in the index for information on weight limits and tow equipment recommendations. If the first thing you see says "towing not recommended with this vehicle" or something similar, then proceed no further. If you try to tow a trailer, you will void the warranty and most likely ruin your car.

If you are able to tow with the car or truck you own, you will need to add several items to the vehicle to make it tow-worthy. There are some things that a weekend mechanic can add, but for the most part this is a job for professionals. Your regular automobile mechanic can do much of the work needed, but you will also need to have work done by a hitch specialist.

To make your vehicle tow-worthy, you will need to add:

- A weight-equalizing hitch
- Trailer brakes
- Safety chains
- Fender-mounted mirrors

- A heavy-duty wiring package for turn signal flashers
- A coolant recovery system
- Engine oil cooler
- Air adjustable shock absorbers
- A flex or clutch fan

These basic upgrades will make your vehicle tow-worthy, but you can make your ride even better with a few other after-market additions.

High-tech towing systems can help eliminate the sway that trailers are so famous for and make the driving experience much more enjoyable. Another area that could benefit from improvement is shock absorption. You can upgrade the shock absorbers to help improve the ride and handling. Gas-pressurized shocks are more expensive but well worth the extra cost for the improved ride.

There are also options that can improve the trailer brake performance, though you need to be sure they will work with the towing package you have. These systems can help prevent brakes from locking up in stop-and-go traffic.

 FACT

Adding a towing package to your present vehicle will generally be more expensive than the comparable factory-installed towing package. With a factory-installed package, you also have some assurance that the tow vehicle will be covered under the warranty. You may find that a new vehicle with a towing package installed will serve you better over the long run.

Tow Bars

If you own a motorhome, you can tow just about anything with wheels or on wheels behind your motorhome (and some people do). Most travelers with a motorized RV soon come to realize that towing an auxiliary vehicle is almost a necessity when traveling. Without a separate vehicle, travelers who plan on staying in a campground for more than a night or two would need to unhook their motorhome to drive to attractions or for supplies.

Some travelers opt to bring bicycles or motorbikes along, but for more than two people that is not really practical.

 FACT

> Towed vehicles (or boats or even airplanes) are called by two different names that are interchangeable. You will hear them referred to as a "dinghy" or alternately as a "toad."

Which Vehicles Can You Tow?

Just because you have a motorhome and can tow vehicles behind it does not mean that every vehicle can be towed. Check the owner's manual of the vehicle you are considering towing to see if the manufacturer recommends towing, or if there are special towing requirements that are needed so as to not void the warranty. Even if towing of the vehicle is an approved use, there may be some restrictions that need to be followed to prevent voiding the warranty. The restrictions may include the distance and speed at which the vehicle can be towed, or they may define the manner in which it can be towed.

Some cars can be towed with all four wheels on the ground. These vehicles can be towed using the simplest and least expensive towing apparatus: a tow bar. Depending on the vehicle being towed, you may also need a device to disconnect the car's drive shaft, an axle lock, or a pump to lubricate the car's transmission.

Varieties of Tow Bars

There are two types of commonly used tow bars. The most basic variety is the rigid A-frame tow bar. They are simple, lightweight, and dependable for towing vehicles. They are also the least expensive of tow bars. They can be more difficult to hook up to the car because they do not adjust or collapse. If you plan on towing only on an infrequent basis, the A-frame may be the best choice for your budget. Because they are rigid and not adjustable, you will need to have your towed vehicle in exactly the correct position for hookup.

The more common type of tow bar you are likely to see is the collapsible tow bar. Motorhome owners who travel frequently when towing a vehicle find these to be the easiest to hook up. The arms are adjustable, allowing you to hook up the vehicle even it is not perfectly centered for the hitch. The tow bar adjusts itself as the RV is driven away; the arms extend, self-center, and lock in place to tow the vehicle correctly.

There are two different types of collapsible tow bar. Traditionally, these tow bars have been mounted on the vehicle being towed. When the vehicle is not under tow, the tow bar folds back over the front of the vehicle for storage. As it is easier to use and operate, this type of tow bar is very popular.

Motorhome-mounted tow bars fold away on the rear of the RV for storage. They will never have to be lifted off the front of the car. The RV-mounted tow bar also eliminates major modifications to the car body or frame, a consideration for resale value.

With either type of towing system, you will also need safety chains or safety cable in case of tow bar failure. These must be rated for the weight of the vehicle you are towing. Vinyl-coated cables are a good choice for towing cars as they are lighter in weight and less likely to cause wear on the front of the car (particularly on the paint job) or on the tow bars themselves.

Whether you are using chains or cable, you will always affix one end to the mounting bracket of the towed vehicle and the other end to the receiver of the motorhome. They are then loosely crossed beneath the coupler. This forms a cradle that supports the tow bars in the event of a failure. They must be slack enough for cornering but should not be so loose that they drag.

When towing a vehicle behind your motorhome, you will also need to have wiring hookups from the motorhome to the towed vehicle for the turn signals and brake lights. Many motorhomes come equipped with this equipment installed.

Tow Dollies

Some vehicles cannot be towed with four wheels on the ground. For these vehicles, a tow dolly may permit them to be towed with the drive wheels off the ground. The restriction against towing wheels-down may occur with both rear wheel and rear wheel–drive vehicles. If in doubt, check with your manufacturer for information—do not risk voiding the warranty with improper towing.

The costs for tow dollies and towing wheels-down are usually comparable due to the additional modifications that need to be made for either towing option.

 FACT

In the RV world, you will find those who feel their way of towing a dinghy is the best way and can't be persuaded to change their minds. Look at both options—wheels-down and dollies—and make your own decisions as to which meets your present and future needs.

Tow dollies do have some disadvantages compared to tow bars. Tow dollies will require more space for storage; this can be a concern if you have limited space at home in a garage or yard, or while you are on the road. Some RV campgrounds may have sites that are long enough for the tow dolly to stay hooked up while you are camping, but you should always check when you are making reservations to see if you will need to unhook, and, if you do, if there is space available to store the dolly while you are there. If the dolly has to be removed, that is one more thing you will need to hook up when it is time to move on. Tow bars generally just fold up after the toad is removed for easy storage.

Tow dollies are basically ramps attached to a towing hitch that is attached to the RV using a standard hitch configuration. The toad has to be driven onto the ramps and then secured using chains or heavy-duty webbing tie-downs. Many people find getting the vehicle properly situated on the tow dolly ramps very challenging. If this is not done properly, the car could roll off or could drive over the ramps, causing damage to the undercarriage. The tie-down apparatus can also cause damage to the vehicle if not attached properly. More challenging is loading rear wheel–drive vehicles that must be backed onto the tow dolly.

Tow-Vehicle Trailers

If you are planning on towing anything other than a car or small truck behind your trailer, you have no other option than to carry it on a trailer. Many people also prefer to carry their auxiliary vehicle on a trailer to reduce the wear and tear on the tires, suspension, and transmission. The weight of the towed vehicle plus the towing equipment, plus the loaded weight of the motorhome cannot exceed the gross combined whole weight rating of the motorhome. This is why you will generally not see anything smaller than a large Class C motorhome pulling a trailer.

You may see enclosed trailers being towed behind larger Class A and luxury bus-conversion RVs as another (though expensive) option for towing. Once again, weight becomes an issue. An enclosed trailer will weigh more than a flatbed trailer. Cargo carried on or in the trailer will need to be secured to keep it in place while traveling. Enclosed trailers will help protect expensive vehicles from damage caused by road hazards such as rocks and other debris.

These flatbed trailers and enclosed trailers have a rear door that folds down to provide a ramp to drive your vehicle into the trailer. It still requires some driving skill to center the vehicle properly in the trailer.

If you are considering towing a flatbed or enclosed trailer behind your motorhome, be sure to get one that meets your present and future needs. Will that trailer that your BMW sports car travels comfortably in be the right size for your SUV if you need more passenger room on your next trip?

 FACT

If you are one of those lucky RV owners who can afford those large luxury bus-conversion rigs, you might want to think about color coordinating your entire setup. You can have your enclosed trailer and your vehicle painted and detailed to match your rig. It also makes a nice package when the time comes to sell your equipment.

Checklist for Towing

If you are going to tow an auxiliary vehicle, tow the lightest vehicle you can that meets your needs. Look at your travel patterns and plans. If you use your motorhome as a home base for sightseeing, you'll find that an auxiliary vehicle is necessary. If you are going for a few days of wilderness hiking, you might not need a vehicle.

If you are towing, you will make your life much easier if you have a checklist that you use every time you travel. While you may be able to do everything in your sleep, a checklist used properly is an insurance policy in case of illness or other events that may be distracting.

Before you get on the road, be sure to check on the following things to be sure that you are ready to leave with your vehicle properly anchored to your RV. Checking these things every time will prevent damage to your RV, to your towed vehicle, or to any other vehicle or object you encounter on your travels.

- Is the tow bar connected in the proper way? Are the pins and clips secured?
- Check for any signs of damage to the tow bar or brackets that may weaken it.
- Check all nuts and bolts to be sure they are properly tightened (and be sure to keep your toolkit out to tighten any that need attention).
- Check that the safety cables are hooked up properly. They should be crossed under the coupler and properly attached to the towed vehicle and motorhome with the correct amount of slack.
- Is the electrical wiring connected properly? Check that all lights including turn signals and brake lights are working properly and are not burned out.
- Check that the transmission on the towed vehicle is in the correct gear for towing as specified by your owner's manual.
- Check that the drive shaft on the towed vehicle is disengaged, if necessary.
- Check that the parking brake on the towed vehicle is released.
- Unlock the steering wheel by turning the ignition to the first on or auxiliary position to allow the steering wheel to turn freely.

ALERT

Towing a vehicle wheels-down will put a drain on the tow-vehicle battery because you will have the ignition turned to the first position whenever the vehicle is in tow. You may want to consider electrical wiring that includes a six-wire system that will keep the car battery charged by the motorhome alternator while you are traveling.

- If the towed vehicle or trailer is equipped with an auxiliary braking system, check that it is connected properly and is functioning correctly.
- Lock the doors on the towed vehicle before you leave to prevent access by unwanted intruders (or stowaways). Make sure you have a spare key in the motorhome.

 FACT

Print out your checklists from your computer and then slip them into a clear plastic sleeve. Keep them on a clipboard with an erasable marker. Check off items as they are completed before you get on the road. Once all items are checked off, you can wipe the marker off and stow the checklist for the next stop.

Staying Safe

To meet legal and safety standards in all fifty states and Canada, the brake lights, tail lights, and turn signals of the towed vehicle must operate in sync with the motorhome. The towed vehicle will often block the warning lights on the motorhome and limit visibility. There are a wide variety of wiring solutions you can choose from to meet your individual needs.

1. You can purchase brake and signal light accessory kits that strap on or are magnetically connected to the rear of the towed vehicle. The wires from this light kit are routed to a junction box that taps into the motorhome's main wiring harness. You will need to be careful when you affix or remove the light array in order to avoid damaging the finish of the towed vehicle. A magnetic attachment system is not an option if you have a vehicle with a fiberglass body. Keep this in mind if you have more than one vehicle you plan to tow.

2. You may prefer a more permanent lighting system. With these systems, you directly connect the lights of the towed vehicle to the wiring system of the coach. The most common way to do this is to connect a wiring socket near the front of the towed vehicle and to install a wiring harness "bridge" with matching plugs at each end.

3. Another option is to permanently install an independent lighting system in the towed vehicle. You can hard-wire this system directly to the coach by installing automotive bulb sockets attached to wiring pigtails (one hot, one ground) placed inside the towed vehicle's taillight housing with a hot-lead pigtail that runs to the tail-light circuits of the coach. You will need to have ample clearance inside the taillight housing to use this option.

When towing a vehicle behind your motorhome, you also may want to consider adding a supplemental braking system. In most states, if the vehicle you are towing is over a certain weight (including tow bars, dolly, or trailer), you are required by law to have a supplemental braking system. They can also make your travels much safer and easier, especially if you are driving in a lot of stop-and-go traffic or on long downhill grades. Another braking system can also help reduce the wear and tear on the motorhome brakes. Some motorhome manufacturers actually specify that supplemental braking is necessary for towing loads that exceed a certain weight. If you tow a vehicle in this situation without a supplemental braking system, you could be in danger of voiding your warranty.

 FACT

While it does not affect safety, you may want to consider traveling with a cover over your towed vehicle or at least a front rock shield or bra. Your RV will throw a lot of road debris and dirt (especially if you have a diesel pusher) up behind it, and this can cause a lot of damage to the finish.

CHAPTER 8

Features and Amenities

RVS ARE TRULY YOUR HOME ON WHEELS. Most will
provide the conveniences you find in your own home. You will
have running water (though not always a water heater), electricity,
and gas for cooking and heating. You may also have cable or satellite television. Unlike home, you will have to hook things up when
you get to your campsite and unhook them when you get ready to
leave. Adding to the challenge is that these systems are located on
a vehicle that is sometimes traveling at 60 miles per hour, and at
other times sitting in storage in subfreezing temperatures. You need
to be able to perform minor repairs and routine maintenance, so
perhaps you could give yourself the title "RV Technician."

Power

Your RV has two different electrical systems onboard (or three
counting the automotive electrical system in your motorhome or
tow vehicle). The 120-volt alternating current system (AC) will be
familiar to you, because it is the one that most closely resembles
the electrical system in your home. The electricity is supplied by
an external source that you "plug" into, at an RV park or in your
own driveway. You will also hear this referred to as "shore" power
by veteran RV owners.

The motorhome or trailer also has a 12-volt direct current electrical system powered by batteries you carry onboard. This system lets you operate lights and 12-volt appliances in the RV.

The automotive power system is obtained from a gas-powered engine that drives an electricity-producing alternator. It runs the fans, headlights, and radio, and it also charges the automotive batteries that provide power to the ignition.

 FACT

If you are a dedicated do-it-yourselfer and experienced in working on electrical systems, you may want to add additional outlets to your rig. You should be able to obtain a wiring diagram from the manufacturer or dealer. Just remember that any modifications you make may void a warranty.

AC Power

When you stay in a campground with hookups, one of the first things you will do is plug into the outlet located at your campsite. This electrical current charges the RV batteries and powers all electrical devices on the RV, including the air conditioning. The amount of electricity your RV is drawing cannot exceed the amount that is available or you will have problems. Overloading your RV circuit can damage your equipment and wiring along with the power outlet and power meter for the entire campground. To increase your chances of having an enjoyable stay, you will need to understand how much power you have available and also how much power your RV draws.

All electrical appliances and devices in your RV have a rating of the amount of power they are drawing. These numbers should be in your owner's manual for devices that came with your RV and will also be on a label on the actual device itself. Don't forget "add-on" things that run on electricity like personal computers, electric shavers, and hairdryers. You might also add in two or three amps for good measure.

You will also need to know a campground's power limit (how much you can draw). Campgrounds with electric hookups will have one or more levels of electric current available: 15-, 20-, 30-, or 50-amp service are the options. Some newer or upgraded campgrounds will provide more than one level of amperage, while older or public campgrounds are more likely to have only 15- or 20-amp service available.

Each type of service requires a unique plug in order for you to hook up. Camping supply stores carry adapters that will enable you to use the service that is available. Some campgrounds will also "lend" them to you for your stay for either a price or a deposit. While these adapters allow you to draw amperage, they do nothing to increase the amount of service you have. Plugging into 15-amp service gives you 15 amps; if you are running appliances that are trying to pull 20 amps, you will have problems. You may need to ration the use of appliances in a camp where only 15-amp service is available. You should be able to run the air conditioner with 15 amps, but it should be shut off when using another high-draw appliance like the microwave. Fifteen-amp, 115-volt power sources take standard three-prong plugs (the same plug you will see on standard home appliances). Twenty-amp outlets are very similar to 15-amp outlets. If you have this type of outlet available, you can use either a 15-amp plug or a 20-amp plug in the outlet. The extra 5 amps adds a little more power to help prevent brownouts. You will still need to ration use of high-power-use devices when hooked up to 20 amps.

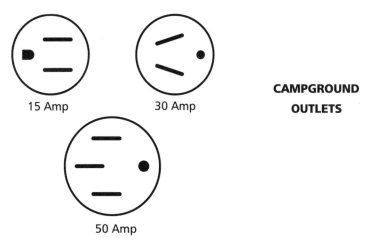

15 Amp

30 Amp

50 Amp

CAMPGROUND OUTLETS

Most new RVs are equipped with 115-volt, 30-amp service. Newer and updated campgrounds will also usually have this type of service. A 30-amp plug is round with two flat prongs in a V-shape and one round grounding prong in the middle toward the top. With this service available, you should be able to run your microwave while the air conditioner is on, but you should still be careful. If you try running too many devices, you will pop circuit breakers and fuses.

 ESSENTIAL

If you need to use an extension cord to hook up to the campground power source (this happens), make sure you are using one that is adequate for the electric load. Get one rated for outdoor use and 5 more amps higher than the power your RV will draw. They are more expensive but worth it.

Fifty-amp service is usually found in only the most expensive rigs, such as top-end Class A motorhomes and bus conversions. With this much power, you can run one or more air conditioners along with a microwave, TV, and computer all at the same time without any brownouts. It can be difficult to find RV parks that have 50-amp service and when you find one you will pay a premium price for it. The exclusive camps that cater to the RV owner with a bus conversion are most likely to provide 50-amp service. They may bill for this power separately, over and above the space rental charge. The plug for 50-amp service is round and the same size as a 30-amp plug. It will have three flat prongs and a round grounding prong. If you own one of the ultra-expensive RVs with 50-amp power and decide to slum it, you should carry adapters for either 30- or 15-amp power.

DC Power

The 12-volt power in an RV comes from a deep-cycle battery, also known as the house battery. A motorized RV will also have an automotive battery. These batteries are different from one another and have different functions and should not be interchanged.

Deep-cycle batteries discharge slowly and deeply and can be recharged many times. Smaller RVs, including foldup trailers, will usually have only one house battery, while larger RVs will often have two. The large bus conversions will have up to eight batteries. Different deep-cycle batteries are used, and each carries a group designation; Group 24 and Group 27 are the most common ones you will see in RVs. The group designations indicate amp-hour capacity and reserve capacity—basically, an indication of how long they will provide power. For most RVers, the most important thing they need to know about these different groups is which one fits their rig. Group 27 batteries are larger and may not fit the battery case.

The batteries are charged while driving through a connection to the vehicle alternator in both motorized RVs and in trailers. The connection is either permanent in motorized units or temporary when the trailer is hitch to the tow vehicle.

Batteries are useful when not connected to AC power or when there is no AC hookup available. Running a high-power air conditioner or microwave is usually not practical, but you will have enough power for your basic needs for at least a short period.

Converter-Charger

The other important component of your RV electrical system is the converter-charger. Most RVs will have this device. It is activated when you plug into shore power and basically converts AC power for use by 12-volt devices, thus eliminating draw on the battery. At the same time, it recharges the house batteries.

Heating

All but the most basic foldup trailer will have a furnace to provide warmth. For the most part, such furnaces will keep an RV comfortable in all but the coldest temperatures. RV owners who plan on doing a lot of winter camping in colder climates may opt to purchase an upgrade winter package for their RV. This package will provide better insulation in the RV, helping the furnace work more efficiently to keep you comfortable.

The most common heating system found in newer RVs is a propane-powered, forced-air furnace. It works in the same manner as the furnaces found in many homes. Propane is burned to heat the air in the furnace, and a fan then blows the heated air into the interior of the RV through vents placed throughout the RV. Most often, these systems are thermostatically controlled.

This type of heater does require both propane (for the heat) and some electricity (for the fan). Before going starting out on a winter trip, check that your propane tanks are full.

 ALERT

> If you smell gas or if your gas-powered devices are not working properly (they should burn with a blue flame), shut them off and check for leaks. Mix a solution of very soapy water and apply it to all gas fittings (connections); if you see a bubble forming there is a gas leak. Turn off the gas from the propane tanks and get the rig to your RV service center ASAP.

Try to be conservative in your use of propane to avoid running out before the trip is over. Propane will also be used for cooking and water heating. If you are not camping with hookups, the furnace fans will be running off the RV battery. You may find your battery runs down quickly if you have the temperature up too high and the fan is running often. Layering with warm clothing, sealing any leaks that may cause drafts, and adding extra insulation to the window coverings can help conserve energy. If you are winter camping, try to camp in a spot that is open and not shaded. Let the sun provide free solar energy for heat, rather than using up your propane and batteries.

Modern RV heaters are very efficient and safe. They are vented to the outside air, keeping them safe and free of problems from carbon monoxide. Part of your routine maintenance should include checking to see that all vents are free of debris for proper venting of deadly gases.

Additional heating sources can be used in your RV, but use them with caution. Electric strip heaters and ceramic strip heaters are safe if not knocked over or allowed to touch flammable items like curtains and bedding. These heaters use electricity that will quickly deplete batteries if you are not hooked up to shore power.

 ALERT

Never use gas or catalytic heaters in your RV. They are very dangerous in a closed environment, as they produce large amounts of deadly carbon monoxide that can sicken and kill quietly and quickly. The potential for fire is also much higher with these heaters, even if there is proper ventilation.

Cooling

For year-round RV travel, you will want to have at least one air-conditioning unit on your rig, and, depending on the size, you may want to have two—one aft and one rear. If you have an extra-long RV, you may even have three AC units for maximum efficiency. You will find these air-conditioning units in the roof of the RV (making it stand even taller). If you have a motorhome, these would be in addition to the engine air conditioning that blows into the driver's area when you are traveling. While you can find older RVs without air conditioning, it is rare to see a newer unit without this option, with the exception of some of the lower-priced foldup trailers.

RV air-conditioning units are generally very reliable and maintenance free. You can check how efficient they are running with a thermometer that you can purchase at a heating or air-conditioner shop. Use the thermometer by placing it in the AC vent on a warm day. If the air blowing out of the vent is in the range of 45 degrees, the unit is working correctly.

You can help your AC unit(s) work more efficiently. During the summer heat, try to park your RV in a spot with shade. Thermal heat from the sun is a blessing in cold weather but will turn your rig into an oven in the summer. Plan your travels to avoid trips to the desert Southwest or other extremely hot areas during the summer months.

RV windows are the most energy-inefficient part of your RV. Having the windows tinted and using insulated, light-colored window coverings will reduce the amount of thermal heating from the outside. Awnings will also help keep the sun and its heat out of your RV. Most RVs come with at least one awning on the right passenger side of the rig. It will unroll like a window blind and roll back and be secured against the RV when traveling. Some more expensive RVs will have awnings over each window. These can be added on to increase AC efficiency.

Plumbing

Your RV has a water system that supplies clean water for cooking, bathing, and all those other activities that require fresh, clean water. You have three tanks on your RV: a freshwater tank, a gray water holding tank, and a black water holding tank.

 ALERT

Plumbing leaks are common in RVs due to the constant movement when on the road and the use of poor insulation in an attempt to keep weight down. Check your plumbing lines and fittings frequently as leaks can lead to mold and rot in the floors and walls of your rig.

Fresh Water

Your fresh water is supplied either by the water you carry on board in the freshwater tank in your RV or from the public water supply you are hooked up to in your campground (or in your driveway). If you are using your onboard water supply, an electric pump will get it to the faucet. The public water supply is based on water pressure and will not use a pump. Carry your own freshwater hose with you for hooking up to the public water supply. Buy one that is designed to carry drinking water—an ordinary garden hose should not be used. Make sure you have a good length of hose, as some water spigots are shared and it may be a distance to your RV's freshwater intake valve.

While most public water systems in the United States are safe to drink, some rural RV parks may get water from their own wells. This water may contain things you don't want in your drinking water. You can add an inline water filter to your freshwater hose. It will remove large particles and minerals. If you are truly concerned about the water having bacteria, you can boil it.

 ESSENTIAL

If you travel to Mexico, always assume the public water system is unsafe and undrinkable. Drink only bottled water from a reputable source or carry your own with you. Keep your mouth closed when showering to avoid swallowing any water accidentally.

Mold and bacteria are prone to grow in warm, wet places and can contaminate the water in your onboard freshwater tanks. This tank and the plumbing that flows from it needs to be cleaned and sterilized monthly. You can buy chemicals for this purpose at any RV supply store. Follow the directions carefully to be sure all the chemicals are removed prior to filling it with fresh water for drinking.

Gray Water

The gray water tank collects waste water from your kitchen sink, shower, and bathroom sink. If you have a camping site with full hookups, you can drain your gray water directly into the campground sewer system. If you do not have full hookups, you will drain your gray water at the dump station at the camp or at some other location with a dump station. Always dump the gray water after the black water to help rinse out the discharge hose. Conserve water to decrease the possibility of having to dump your tank before you are ready to travel; it is much easier just to do it on the way out. Some campers choose to use the showers provided onsite to help reduce the amount of gray water.

You may be tempted to just let this waste water drain out onto the ground. Remember, though, that this water can be ecologically toxic as it contains soaps and detergents.

Black Water

Black water is the water and waste that is flushed by the RV toilet. It is dumped into the sewer system either at your site or at a dump station. If you have a sewer outlet at your site, don't keep the outlet open at all times but open it to drain when the tank is about three-quarters full. This will help to keep the waste liquefied and prevent clogs. Chemicals you place in the holding tank periodically also help break down waste and keep it from clumping. Cleaning out clogged black water tanks is a dirty, messy business and is best avoided if at all possible.

Water Heating

Most RVs have a propane-fueled water heater. There are also some that are dual propane-electric. These water heaters are either 6 or 10 gallons, depending on the size of the RV. Some will have an automatic ignition, while other must be lit manually. The heater is accessible from the outside through its ventilation grill.

Six to 10 gallons of water should be sufficient for at least a couple of showers if water is used judiciously. Most RV showers have a dial that reduces the flow of water. To save water, wet your body, turn off the flow of water and soap up, and then turn the water flow back to normal and rinse off. Leave your fifteen-minute showers for home with its 40-gallon water heater.

Baths and Toilets

RV toilets are different from residential toilets. Most RV toilets are plastic, not porcelain. Either a pedal on the base of the toilet or a lever on the back of the seat flushes the toilet. When the toilet is flushed, a trap in the bottom of the bowl opens while water enters the bowl from holes under the rim. After flushing the trap closes, leaving a small amount of water in the bowl.

Because the toilet waste is going into a holding tank, keeping the waste as liquid as possible will help it to drain. Toilet paper can quickly clog up a black water tank. Watch that children do not throw large amounts of toilet paper (or anything else) down the toilet or you may find yourself with a very smelly mess.

 ESSENTIAL

Save your comfy triple-ply toilet paper for home. Single-ply paper that will disintegrate quickly in water will be better for your RV plumbing. Put a single sheet of paper in a jar with about 4 ounces of water and shake. If it disintegrates quickly, it is suitable for use in an RV septic system.

There are many different shapes and sizes of bathtubs and showers found in RVs, depending on the size of the rig and the floor plan. Generally, you will find that bathtubs are barely two-thirds the size of the tub you have at home, and they are more suited for a shower than a long soak. The shower hose is attached by a fitting behind the spout. There is a diverted knob that directs water either into the tub or up the shower hose. The showerhead also has a valve that can shut down the flow of water and help conserve hot water.

Kitchen Appliances

Modern RV kitchens (usually called galleys) are remarkably well equipped and efficient to make the most of limited space. You will have at the least a refrigerator, range with three or four burners, and a kitchen sink. The larger and more expensive RVs may also have a microwave, coffee maker, convection oven, and side-by-side refrigerator/freezer with icemaker.

The oven and range are fueled by propane. Some have a pilot light, but more often they will have to be lit manually. Galley ovens are small; a 24-pound turkey is probably out of the question, but they will usually meet your needs. Many people never use their ovens, preferring to grill outdoors.

RV refrigerators are different from the one you find in your home. They are dual mode, switching from electric to propane power. While on the road, the refrigerator will run on electric power supplied by the batteries. When you arrive at the campground, you then switch the refrigerator to propane mode by lighting a pilot light or by flipping a switch.

RV refrigerators have a much smaller capacity; you will need to shop and pack carefully.

Beds and Bedrooms

Naturally, since an RV is your home on wheels, you will have a bed to sleep on. How that bed is configured is another story. Depending on the size of the RV and its floor plan, you may have a queen bed, bunk beds, a sofa that folds out to a bed, and a dinette that converts to a bed. Medium to large RVs can sleep several family members in comfort.

A popular floor plan in some travel trailers is the bunkhouse plan with three or four bunks for more sleeping spots in less space. The upper bunks often have a weight limit of 100 pounds, making them suitable for younger children only. Sleeping bags make great bedding for these bunks, as they are often in corners and using standard sheets is very difficult.

Other than the queen bed, which will use standard sheets, sleeping bags are often more suitable for all the sleeping spaces. Sleeping bags can be rolled up and stored when not in use.

Storage

Storage is usually limited in RVs. Class A and bus conversions will have the most storage, as these rigs will feature "basement" storage under the floor of the RV that will often stretch from one side of the rig to the other. They can often hold as much as two bicycles.

RVs should be packed carefully to maintain even loads that do not shift around. Cabinets with doors and drawers are preferable to open cabinets.

Some RVs have storage space under the bed. The mattress is on a board that sits on a box attached to the floor. The board with the mattress is lifted up to reveal a large storage space. If you have a luxury RV, you may even have a built-in safe suitable for storage of your valuables.

No matter how much or how little storage space you have, you will need to remember that everything you carry adds to the weight. The weight needs to be kept under the GVRW or you will have a very unsafe vehicle.

Entertainment

It sometimes seems that RV travel is not so much getting away from it all as much as it is taking it with us. Most mid- to larger-size RVs come equipped with state-of-the-art entertainment centers. You will find one or more televisions with VCR (or DVD) players. Many are equipped with built-in stereo systems, and most will have an antenna for television reception. It is not uncommon to find satellite dishes on many high-end motorhomes and travel trailers. Most new RVs have a cable television outlet and many campgrounds have cable. RV manufacturers also know that many people now travel with their computers. Many RVs have a place for your computer to access the Internet.

If your RV did not come equipped with built-in entertainment, you can always carry it along. If you have the space, you may be able to permanently attach a television in your RV.

Safety Features

Modern RVs are generally safe if not overloaded and if basic safety precautions are taken. When buying a new or used RV, there are some items you can add that will ensure a safe trip. Accidents will happen, but if you are prepared serious injury can be avoided.

Fire

Basic common-sense precautions will prevent most fires in RVs.

Make sure all cigarettes are extinguished thoroughly, and do not smoke in bed (or anywhere you might fall asleep). Better yet, only smoke outside the RV (but be sure to extinguish carefully in areas with high risk of forest fire). Best of all, quit smoking!

If you use candles in your RV, keep them on a sturdy surface where they will not be knocked over and away from flammable items. If you are using them just for the scent, try potpourri instead; it is much safer.

Keep flammable items away from heaters and open flames on the galley range. Never user gas space heaters in an RV (they are not recommended for the home, either).

Don't overload electrical circuits. If cords on appliances become worn or frayed, have the cords replaced. If a cord is warm or hot to the touch, unplug it until you get home and have it checked by an appliance serviceperson.

Keep the vents and ducts of all propane-powered **appliances free of dust and debris** that could burn.

Use outdoor grills well away from the RV and its awnings.

Have at least two (or more in a very large RV) fire extinguishers rated 5-BC. They should be easily accessible in case of fire, mounting on the wall at or near eye level is best. If you only have one extinguisher, it should be in the galley.

New RVs are equipped with at least one smoke detector. If you have an older RV or would like to install a second smoke detector, they can be easily added. Smoke detectors are inexpensive and are battery-powered. Make it a habit to change the batteries in your RV smoke detectors twice a year, spring and fall.

Have a family fire drill annually (or more often if you have small children). Make sure everyone knows how to get out of the RV if flames are blocking the way. Most RVs have an escape window in addition to the doorway in case of fire.

When camping in wilderness or forest areas in high fire season, listen for any warnings for wildfires in your area (anywhere within about 50 miles of your location). If there is a wildfire, experts suggest you pack up and move to a town or city where the danger of fire is lower. Use major roads to travel in these circumstances. Wildfires are unpredictable and can change direction at the drop of a hat. If fire is very close, just get out, even if means leaving some belongings behind. They can be replaced, but your loved ones cannot.

Pay attention to and follow burn rules. If you are camping in a wilderness area that has an outdoor burn restriction, follow the rules. If you start a forest fire, even accidentally, you could be liable for large fines, or worse, for criminal charges. Even an improperly extinguished cigarette can start a fire in very parched woodland areas.

Carbon Monoxide

Because so many RV systems depend on propane, you should have a carbon monoxide detector on board. Most new RVs are already equipped with these, but you can add one just as easily as a smoke detector. Another safety device you might want to consider is a gas "sniffer" that will detect propane gas leaks. Similar to carbon monoxide and smoke detectors, they are battery-powered and easily installed. Change all the batteries at the same time.

Personal and Property Safety

RV parks are generally safe, but always lock your doors and windows and either keep cash on your person or consider installing a safe that cannot be removed from the rig. Don't leave valuables in clear sight, and close the curtains when you are gone.

You may want to consider installing an automotive alarm system on your RV. These often deter potential thieves who will look for a rig without an alarm.

If you must stay overnight in a rest stop or parking lot, try to find one that is not totally deserted. Park in a well-lit location near other RVs or big rig trucks. If you feel uncomfortable or see some suspicious activity, leave. Motorized RVs are wonderful in these situations as you can leave an unsafe parking area without having to go outside.

 ALERT

A CB radio can be valuable in getting help in many situations. Many law enforcement agencies monitor CB channels and may be able to come to your assistance. Cell phones are tied to your service area and emergency calls (911) may be difficult to track and get to the closest authorities.

CHAPTER 9

Buying and Selling Your RV

BUYING AN RV is much like buying a second home. With such a major purchase, doing your homework is crucial. RV shows and exhibitions are great places to comparison-shop. You will usually find every type and brand of RV represented, all under one roof. If you have already decided on the RV and brand you want, shows can also be a great place to deal, especially if you find the perfect RV on the show floor. On their lots, most dealers will have a good selection of sizes and styles with the most popular floor plans, accessories, and interior colors.

Financing Your RV

Unless you are independently wealthy or selling your home and belongings, borrowing money to buy an RV is a reality for most of us. RV loans are available through banks, credit unions, and finance companies, as well as through RV dealers. Shop around for financing, and you may find a bargain. RV manufacturers, like car makers, introduce a new line of RVs every year. They may offer special financing or rebates to get last year's models off the lot. If you can live without that latest greatest widget that only comes on the new model, you may find you can save yourself a lot of money down the road.

If you have the available cash in the bank to pay for your rig outright, you may still want to consider financing. Interest rates for RVs, like home mortgages, have been at their lowest amounts for the last few years. While this may not last forever, it may be wise to take advantage of these low rates. Paying cash means that money is gone forever, taking any present or future earning power with it. You may find that you can negotiate lower interest rates by having a nice little nest egg in the bank.

Here are some things to watch for when considering dealer financing:

1. Compare the overall costs of dealer financing to other sources. Your RV dealer may boast a lower interest rate, but he may also have some hidden fees that actually make the loan cost more in the end.

2. Read the loan documents carefully for any clause that could cost you money. Some loans carry prepayment penalties that may end up being very costly.

3. Avoid costly loan "add-ons" that the loan salesperson may try to pressure you into buying. These additions may include an extended warranty or loan insurance that is overpriced to you but a significant moneymaker for the salesperson.

 FACT

Finding a lender to finance a used RV is usually more difficult than for a new RV. You may also find that interest rates are higher to match the higher risk. If you need to finance even a used RV, your best bet may be buying a trade-in from a dealer that also sells new RVs and has a finance department.

You may be able to walk into your RV dealer with financing in hand. Many lenders offer preapproved loans for buyers who are good solid risks. With a preapproved loan (it will be contingent on the appraised value of the RV you decide on), you can avoid the painful loan sales process with the dealer.

If you are having problems getting a loan, you may want to try increasing the amount of your down payment. Risking more of your own money will often persuade a reluctant lender to risk their money.

Warranties

When you buy a new RV, you will get a warranty—in fact, you will get several. Included with your purchase will be a bag or an envelope that contains the warranties and manuals that cover the construction and systems on your RV. If you purchase a motorhome, you will probably have a separate warranty for the chassis and drive train. While it may look like a daunting task, you should look though all of this material right away. Your RV manufacturer almost never manufactures the systems and appliances you find in your RV; most come from companies that produce specific RV parts. Dometic may make the refrigerator and the toilet may be from Thetford. The RV manufacturer usually provides and warranties the construction and installation of these separate parts, but each system or appliance will have its own warranty, terms of use, and restrictions. Reading thorough the material after you buy the rig and before you take a major trip may help avoid unpleasant surprises along the way. You may find that you have a system that breaks down far from home but also comes with a warranty restriction that requires a specific piece of paperwork that is sitting at home. Not reading the information could be costly in both money and time.

RV dealers are required to provide a written copy of all warranties before the sale is completed; do not depend on verbal promises from the dealer, as they are not binding. If the dealer will not put promises in writing, you might want to think twice about the purchase you are about to make.

Be sure to make note of the warranty terms, how long the item is covered, and how and where it gets fixed. If the warranty states that you have to ship the covered unit to a service center rather than take it to the dealer, look around. Your dealer should be able to handle all warranty work in-house. Ask other RV owners for their recommendations on service. You may have found the perfect RV, but if the dealer cannot follow up with great service, you may just be buying a headache.

 ALERT

As with most warranties, improper use of the product may void the warranty agreement. Improper use may include not carrying out maintenance recommended in the user manual. Keep documentation of maintenance in the event you have to make a warranty claim some day.

Warranties on used RVs through private sales are usually not available, unless you are buying a repossessed unit with remaining time on the factory warranty. Some dealers may offer a type of extended warranty on used RVs. Read the fine print closely, as it may not be worth the money it costs.

Don't forget to get it in writing if any towing or assistance with accommodations is available should your motorhome break down when you are traveling. Towing charges can be very expensive and the nightly charges even for Motel 6 can add up if your RV ends up in the shop for any length of time.

Authorized Dealers

When you dream of buying an RV, you are really dreaming about open roads and carefree traveling. For most people, those dreams do not include breakdowns, tow trucks, and service stations. Unfortunately, dreams are sometimes shattered, and RVs will need service and repair. On a more positive note, most new RVs are well built and most RV systems are very reliable, but it is still inevitable that at some point you will have a problem or need a repair. If that repair is to be done under warranty, it will need to be taken to an authorized service provider.

If you find the perfect RV but find that the dealers are only in a few locations, you may want to start looking again. While it may be the perfect RV, it will do you little good if you have to take it several hundred miles to have warranty work done. Remember to check for dealers in your immediate area and also for dealers in the areas you plan on visiting in the future. Not all RV service is of the same quality and reliability. Some RV owners suggest shopping for an RV by first going to the service department, and then heading over to the sales department to find the RV you want.

 FACT

If you don't know any RV owners to ask for recommendations on RV dealers or RV service, you might want to go online and get some information from some very friendly RV owners. Log on to *www.rv.net* and you will find some very busy forums that cover almost every aspect of RV ownership.

Another option for buying an RV is ordering one online from a "virtual" dealer. These dealers offer a wide selection of well-known RV brands you can specialty order. The prices are often much lower than you might find during special sales at local dealers. If you are considering buying an RV online, be sure to find out if the warranty will be honored by your local dealer and by dealers nationwide. Some RV dealers may not appreciate having to perform warranty work on RVs they did not sell. Before you buy online, get confirmation in writing that your warranty will be honored nationwide.

Care and Maintenance

Whether you buy new or used, an RV is a major purchase, and most buyers will want to protect that purchase to ensure many years of enjoyable travel. Some simple maintenance will keep your RV travel ready for many years.

If you are planning on selling your RV in the future and want to ensure that you get the best price possible, care and upkeep are important. Keep records of any and all maintenance and repairs performed on the rig during its lifetime. Most buyers will appreciate a maintenance history and will often pay a premium price for a used RV that has been well maintained.

Your RV owner's manual should contain a suggested maintenance schedule for the engine if you own a motorhome. Following this schedule will keep your RV in good running condition and keep it at peak fuel efficiency; it will also help ensure that your warranty is not compromised if you need major repairs.

 ALERT

Should your RV turn out to be a lemon, you will need thorough and accurate records of all maintenance and attempts to correct problems. If you do not have good records, you may not be able to file for relief under any "lemon law" in force in your state.

Routine maintenance should include the following:

• Clean the interior and appliances following the manufacturer's instructions for special cleaning products. Keep dirt out with a mat at the bottom of the outside steps.

• Clean the refrigerator and freezer with nonabrasive cleaners to prevent scratches and damage to the coils.

• RV toilets and baths should never be cleaned with the harsh chemicals used with porcelain residential toilets. Bleach can damage rubber seals and gaskets, leading to leaks and expensive repairs.

• Clean the exterior of the RV frequently to remove road dust and grime. There are products available for the type of exterior finish your rig has, either aluminum or fiberglass. It is a good time to examine the RV for any leaks at joints or on the roof and repair them as needed to prevent interior damage.

• Check all hitches, pins, chains, etc., for wear and tear, including cracks in the metal. Tighten any bolts that have become loose. Lubricate equipment if it is recommended by the manufacturer.

• Follow the manufacturer's instructions for storage if you will not be using the rig for an extended period. Block areas where mice and other critters can get into the rig and nest. If you are storing a rig in areas where freezing temperatures are expected, special antifreeze additives will be needed for water lines to prevent freezing and water line breaks.

Insurance

Like your automobile, your RV needs to be insured. If it is a motorized RV, most states require that you have insurance coverage. However, the company that insures your car is not necessarily the best company to insure your RV. Your auto insurance company may be able to provide you with coverage, but you will need to discuss the coverage with them. Most automobile insurance policies exclude coverage for the vehicle if you are living in the vehicle. Be sure to discuss this with your agent and have the policy modified to have that language excluded or modified to fit your needs. If your agent is unable or unwilling to issue a policy that will provide the coverage you need, it is time to look at other insurers that specialize in RV coverage.

When you are shopping for insurance coverage, be sure to pay attention to the scope of coverage. Some insurers may offer adequate insurance for the rig itself, but there may be minimal coverage for the contents of the RV. Take a minute to look at all the cargo you will be taking, and you will quickly realize that if you suffered a complete loss of your RV and its contents, the replacement costs would be substantial. Even if you need to pay extra for increased coverage for contents, it may be well worth the cost. You may also want to check your homeowner's policy. Under it, you may have some limited coverage for your possessions while in your RV. If you find the language of the policy confusing (as most legal documents are), check with your insurance company or agent.

 ALERT

One of the most important documents you need to carry in your rig is your proof of insurance. In most states, the laws mandate that you show proof of insurance (along with a valid driver's license and registration) at any traffic stop. Avoid a costly fine by keeping the proof of insurance and other documents in reach of the driver.

If you use your RV for business (and there are a number of people who do), your standard RV insurance policy may not cover those items you use for business. You will most likely need to purchase a rider to cover items used in business or purchase a completely separate policy for business-related items.

Make sure you have adequate coverage for all contingencies. Are you covered for liability if a visitor missteps and falls when leaving your rig after a card game? It can happen just as easily in your RV as it can in your home and you should be prepared.

Some RV insurance policies offer standard or optional roadside assistance and towing. This coverage can be worth its weight in gold when your rig has broken down in the middle of nowhere or even if you run out of gas. Generally, you will call an 800 number and the insurer will then contact a local towing company they have contracted with for service. Many auto insurers offer roadside assistance coverage, but you may have to pay extra for towing an RV instead of a car. Be sure to quiz your insurer if you are getting coverage from the same place as your automobile.

Should you break down and need to be towed without this coverage, you should be prepared for a hefty bill from the towing company. They will have to send a tow truck capable of towing such a large vehicle, and they don't come cheap.

Service Agreements and Extended Warranties

RVs are expensive. When you spend money on high-dollar items like cars and RVs, there is always the worry of the cost of repairs down the road. These fears of future bills prompt many people to consider purchasing extended warranties and repair service agreements. Extended warranties are very common and are offered on almost every large purchase you make.

Do you need an extended warranty? As with most other RV topics, there are two schools of thought on this subject. You will find a group of RV owners who swear that extended warranties and service agreements are a very necessary expense and will make your life more secure. Other RV owners will tell you that they are a waste of money—just another way for RV dealers to take money out of your wallet. Whom do you believe? The Service Contract Industry Council admits that 80 percent of extended warranties never have a claim filed against them. Newer RVs are generally well built and breakdowns are not generally an everyday occurrence. New RVs are also covered by a manufacturer's warranty (the length of which will depend on the manufacturer). In addition, most RV owners are usually very adept do-it-yourselfers who often find it easier to fix the small problems that crop up and to take care of routine maintenance.

When you buy a new RV, it is a given that the salesperson will offer you an extended or service warranty. These are very profitable add-on products that dealerships make a lot of money from. Your salesperson, working on commission, wants the final sales price to be as high as possible—and the more you spend, the bigger his or her commission check.

Some RV dealers use high-pressure tactics in promoting these products. Don't let a salesperson pressure you. Stand firm and only purchase this option if you really feel it is in your best interest to do so.

Before you buy these warranties or service contracts, read them over very carefully and ask questions if there is wording you don't understand. Don't take the dealer's word on what will and will not be covered. Look carefully at the restrictions and at the deductibles. It may be cheaper to just do it yourself and not pay the deductible. The contract should also specify where you can get service. If you are restricted to only a few options for service in the immediate area, this agreement will not do you much good on a cross-country trip.

You should also take a good look at your manufacturer's warranty. If you have a warranty that covers the rig bumper to bumper (or tongue to bumper) for seven years and you plan on trading up in three years, an extended warranty makes no sense, unless it is transferable (a rarity).

 ALERT

If you are considering purchasing an extended warranty or service agreement, investigate the company that offers this coverage. There have been many of these companies that have turned out to be fly-by-night operators who have gone out of business and left their customers high and dry.

If you do decide that an extended warranty or service contract is worth the cost, be sure to always carry the paperwork in the RV. If you cannot show proof of coverage, you may have to shell out a large amount of money that you did not plan on. You may be able to get reimbursed after the fact, but if you are already traveling on a budget it could end up changing your vacation plans.

There is one instance when an extended warranty may be a very wise choice. If you purchase a used RV from a dealer that sells new and used RVs, you may be offered an extended warranty during the sales process. Most used RVs are sold "as is" with no warranty available. If one is offered, look it over carefully and decide, based on the condition of the rig, its age, and the cost of warranty if it is a good deal. When you buy used, you also buy the previous owner's preventive maintenance (or lack of same). If the rig has been well taken care of, an extended warranty may be a waste of money.

 ALERT

Most extended warranties and service contracts contain language that will void liability for payment if the RV has not been used as recommended (overloaded, for example) or if recommended maintenance has not been done. Keep your receipts for proof when and if you need to make a claim.

If Life Gives You a Lemon . . .

The majority of RVs are well built and reliable. Most will give years of enjoyment to their owners with only routine and expected repairs.

Unfortunately, there are some RVs (both motorhomes and trailers) that cause nothing but nightmares for their owners. It is not hard to find a fellow traveler with the story of at least one example of a "lemon" to look out for. Problems can occur with any product we purchase, but when you shell out $100,000 for a motorhome that spends more time in the service bay than it does on the road, it can be a very frustrating experience.

It can be very difficult to pick out the lemons from the rest of the crop, as the rigs that turn out to be major headaches start their life looking just as new and shiny as any other quality RV. Lemons are not limited to any one manufacturer; you will find reports of them in all classes of RVs, from the least expensive trailer up to the most expensive luxury bus conversion.

If you buy a new RV and within a short period it has spent a good part of its young life in the repair shop, you may start to suspect that you have purchased a defective rig—a lemon. There are stories of RVs that spent more than 400 days in a period of two years in the shop for repairs. With some persistence, these RV owners were able to recoup the full purchase price of their RV plus any costs they incurred for repairs, lodging, and the costs of legal help if needed.

If you are not a good record keeper, it is important that you learn to be one when you buy an RV. Not only will you need to keep good records of your warranty information, but it is also very important to keep records of all service and repairs done to the rig. If you should have to make a claim under the "lemon law," this documentation will become your number-one piece of evidence to prove that the RV is defective. Make copies of all service transactions and keep the originals in a safe place.

 ALERT

Along with documentation of service records and maintenance, keep records of all phone calls and correspondence you have with your RV dealer or manufacturer. Get names and numbers, and record the exact time and date with a synopsis of the conversation. If the person you are talking to agrees, you can record the conversation.

As a consumer, what legal protection do you have when buying an RV? The Magnuson-Moss Warranty Act is a federal law that provides protection when you buy any product that costs $25 or more and comes with a written warranty. Its purpose is to ensure that repairs and/or replacement for defective products is performed within a reasonable period. If a product is covered by a written warranty, and any part of the product (or the product itself) is defective and cannot be fixed after a reasonable opportunity, the warrantor must permit the buyer either a refund or replacement or provide the buyer with monetary damages as compensation for the warrantor's failure to perform. Most states also have laws that offer the consumer protection from monetary loss due to defective products. Some states such as California have enacted more stringent warranty provisions than the federal act.

In some cases, you may have to hire a lawyer to help you. If you do and you are found to have a defective RV, the judgment should include coverage of the legal fees.

I hope you will not have any problems with your RV, and even if you do have problems, it is possible that your dealer and the manufacturer will do their best to make things right. They realize that RV owners are a very sharing group, and if they are unhappy with their rig or with the service they receive, they will gladly share that information with other potential customers.

Resolving Disputes

If you have a dispute with the manufacturer of your RV or with the dealer who sells it to you, you may be prohibited from initiating legal action. Even if you are harmed by the negligence of the builder or service provider, a clause in your sales agreement may limit your options. Many sales agreements include a clause that states that the buyer is limited to damages as awarded by an independent arbitrator and that the buyer of the product cannot initiate legal proceedings.

If you have signed a sales contract with a clause like this, most lawyers will not take on such a case once they have read the contract. The only indications for legal involvement would be in cases where the terms of the agreement were deemed to be misleading.

The moral of the story: Read all sales contracts carefully! If there are terms you feel are unjust or harmful, have them stricken. If the dealer or manufacturer will not change the agreement, you have two choices: leave and find another RV or accept the terms.

 FACT

If you are purchasing a very large and very expensive RV, it may be worth your while to have a lawyer review the contract. A lawyer can wade through the legal jargon and point out clauses that may be harmful to you.

Depreciation and Selling Your RV

Eventually, you will be ready to sell your RV. You might be unable to travel due to illness, or you might want to move to a newer RV with more (or even less) room. As your circumstances change so, too, will your RV. If you have done your homework, you will be prepared for the sticker shock of depreciation. RVs accumulate a lot of wear and tear traveling from place to place, just as your automobile does. Motorized RVs depreciate at a faster rate than towed RVs

It is usually better financially to sell your old RV before you buy a new one. Most RV dealers will offer you a trade-in on your old rig, but you may find you get a much better price by selling it yourself.

To get the best price for your old rig, you will need to know what the resale value is. You get the current market value from the *Kelly Blue Book*. Honestly appraise the condition of the rig, accounting for wear and tear and any additional options.

Once you have decided on the sales price, clean up the RV and do some basic maintenance—make it look well taken care of for any prospective buyers. Use some tips from real estate agents to make your RV appealing to potential buyers:

- Clean up the RV thoroughly, inside and out, including the windows. Have the carpets cleaned.
- Remove all personal belongings from the closets, cabinets, and drawers. All those empty spaces give the appearance of spaciousness and abundant storage.
- Clean out the refrigerator and add a deodorizer to remove that musty refrigerator smell.
- Clean out the holding tanks (especially the black water) and add chemicals to the toilet to prevent or remove any unpleasant odors.
- Perform any cosmetic repairs needed, tighten bolts or hinges, and apply oil to prevent any squeaks.
- Make copies of maintenance records that show how well the rig has been maintained.
- Make sure you have enough fuel, water, and juice in the batteries to give everything a test drive.

Where to Sell

There are many ways to let prospective buyers know that you have an RV for sale. Try putting an ad in your local paper, the classified section of magazines like *Motorhome* or *Trailer Life,* or in a national publication like *RV Trader.* Be sure to list the price to discourage calls from unqualified buyers.

RV consignment dealers are another option. They will advertise and show your RV in exchange for a commission when the rig is sold. You should have an agreement that specifies the commission and terms of the sale. Be sure that the dealer is reputable and that there are no hidden clauses that may end up costing you money you didn't plan on spending.

Be sure to keep the RV insured until it is sold. Accidents can happen anywhere and you don't want to lose your investment by trying to pinch pennies when trying to sell it.

CHAPTER 10

What to Avoid

YOU WILL NEED TO KEEP YOUR EYES OPEN when you are buying and operating an RV. You may run into a lot of people out there who will try to take your hard-earned dollars and give you little in return. Your own expectations for the adventure of RV travel, which might sometimes be a little more romantic than realistic, may also cause problems if you are not careful. To be a savvy RV owner, you need to know what to expect and what to try to avoid.

Buyer Beware!

As with any major purchase you make, you should do your homework carefully when buying an RV or RV accessory. Know what you want, know what fits your budget, and, most especially, know when to walk away. If the deal sounds too good or the claims are too hard to believe, then pay attention to that little voice inside and stand back. You will probably find the deal was not as good as it seems and that the claims are exaggerated, if not completely false.

You can buy a number of different after-market products for your RV. The largest outfitters of RV and camping products have catalogs that will tell you about the latest products designed to make your RV experience better, easier, safer, or more fun (or all of the above). Walking through the large camping stores, you're sure to see dozens of items that you feel you just have to have. Just make sure that any products you consider purchasing truly will make your life better, and that they won't just make your RV more cluttered and your wallet emptier.

Once you have found the RV that fits your needs and your budget, your shopping may only be half done. You will also have to deal with all the sales pitches for add-ons and after-market products that you will get. These will come not only from the RV dealer but also from the companies whose mailing lists you will land on because of your purchase.

You will get offers that claim they can save you money on insurance, or that promise ways to obtain discounts on items and services for your RV. Other products claim to help you save gas and get better mileage. While some good products are available, many are just ways to take money out of your pocket. Of course, some RV products are worth considering:

Gas detectors: While most RVs (especially new) come equipped with smoke and carbon monoxide detectors, you might want to consider adding a propane detector also.

Water pressure regulators and water filtration systems: These units will help prevent leaks and damage to your RV plumbing system from some municipal water systems.

Campground Memberships: Pros and Cons

When you buy an RV, your name and address will show up on many mailing lists for RV-related products. One group that is sure to send you offers through the mail sells campground memberships.

When buying a campground membership, the purchaser in effect "buys" a vacation campground site for a specific portion of a year or a certain number of weeks per year, along with several other "buyers" who share the campsite on a rotating basis. This is a similar concept to that of regular vacation timeshares, except that, rather than hotel rooms or condos, you are buying a space for your RV.

These memberships will involve a one-time purchase fee, plus a yearly membership or maintenance fee. As a member, you will still pay an overnight fee when you camp, but this will generally be about $8 to $9 per night for a full-service RV park. Compare this to the average overnight cost of most private RV parks, which is about $30 to $40 per night (you may be charged additional fees for more than two visitors).

If you buy a membership in a park that is affiliated with a reciprocal-use club, you will also be able to obtain a membership in that club. These memberships allow you to stay in any of their participating member RV parks (with some restrictions) for a minimal overnight fee.

Typical restrictions include length of stay limits (with an average of two weeks' stay in one park), and the restriction of no stays in a park within a 150-mile radius of your home park (the park you bought the membership in). Many people buy a membership in a park that is not in an area that they plan on visiting or traveling to.

QUESTION?

What if I have purchased a campground membership but have second thoughts and want to get out of the deal?
These types of sales are regulated by state governments and will contain a clause that allows a period of time for you to back out of the deal (usually three days). Read the contract or check with your attorney general's office.

Examine any membership offers carefully, and request a financial report from the park you are considering buying a membership at. If the salesperson refuses or hesitates to supply this information, run—don't walk—to the nearest exit. The membership is no good if the park goes out of business.

Read the membership agreement carefully, and get out the magnifying glass for the fine print. Are all activities and facilities included or are there extra fees? Extra fees could quickly boost your overnight rate to close to nonmembership parks.

You should request a trial period before buying a membership. Most membership parks will offer you a two- or three-night stay in exchange for listening to their sales pitch. This is a great way to see if this park is for you. Be prepared, though; these sales pitches are often very high pressure, and they are often presented on your first day there before you have had a good chance to look the place over. Typically, you will be presented with a special deal, which is only good if you sign up immediately.

Try to resist the pressure. If you are in an area that has several such membership parks, try out more than one. If you find one you like, go back to them and try to negotiate the "great deal" they originally offered. Most salespeople are willing to negotiate, especially if it is off-season and sales are on the slow side.

 ALERT

Many people get the advantages of a campground membership at a much better price by buying the membership secondhand. Many of these memberships are transferable and people sell for various reasons when RV travel is no longer possible for them. You'll find memberships for sale in the classified sections of most RV publications.

These memberships are not for everyone. You may find there are no campgrounds in the areas you want to travel to or you may not use the membership often enough to make it worthwhile. Take your time and avoid snap decisions.

Overscheduling

Many travelers, especially those with limited time for travel, may be tempted to pack too much in with too little time. Set a schedule and stick with as much as you can. Trying to pack too many activities into too little time while traveling can cause frayed nerves, temper tantrums, and little enjoyment of the RV lifestyle.

You should plan on driving only four to five hours each day, and take the time to make sufficient rest stops during your hours of driving. Stop early and find a place to enjoy the evening. Be sure to figure in the time it takes to set up camp and break down camp in the morning. There is nothing more frustrating than trying to back into an RV space in the dark.

Take enough time to travel. Many Americans have been forgetting about the two-week vacation and are now taking short vacations that consist of long weekends. This limits the amount of time they have and can cause more stress in the end.

A survey of several top executives around the country found that most felt their job performance was greatly improved after an extended vacation of two to three weeks. With more time to travel, you will not feel compelled to try to cram too much into too little time.

Curb Your Need for Speed

. . . along with all the other driving practices that you should avoid. For someone who is addicted to speed, driving an RV may be a little frustrating, but it is a good opportunity to learn to slow down, relax, and enjoy the drive.

Driving an RV, while not much more difficult than a large car, does require quite a lot more concentration by the driver. Passengers should not do anything to cause unnecessary distractions, such as becoming overly upset about little things like making a wrong turn, getting nervous in heavy traffic, or making the driver feel that he or she should get to their destination as quickly as possible.

Driving at Night

According to the National Safety Council, the number of traffic deaths is three times greater at night than during the day. Avoid driving at night if at all possible, and plan your trip accordingly. If you need to get there that quickly, perhaps you should just consider flying rather than driving.

Driving While Medicated

Taking medication while operating your RV can clearly affect your alertness and ability to concentrate. Prescription and over-the-counter medications both have the capability to cause impairment. If you are taking any medication and plan to drive your RV, it's important to read the drug label before getting behind the wheel to confirm that drowsiness is not a side effect. Alcohol can enhance the effects of these medications.

 FACT

Carry all medications (even over-the-counter medications) in their original packaging in order to retain the warning labels. Many medications interact with each other, and not knowing what they are may prove deadly.

Fast-Talking Salespeople

Watch out for fast-talking salespeople who try to bully you into making a snap decision on anything from the RV to the add-ons and accessories that you may or may not need. According to one RV owner, "Buyers of new RVs are among the least informed of any consumer class or group in the United States. It is a phenomenon rarely found in any other sector of consumer products. This is amazing considering the average cost of a RV purchase."

No matter how friendly the salesperson is, always remember that his or her job and goal is to sell; this person is not there to be a friend but to make a living. If that means being somewhat deceptive, that is often a compromise that he or she is willing to make.

The objective of the dealer and the salesperson is:

- Not to allow the buyer to leave the lot without buying
- To hold or maximize the "gross profit" on the sale
- To pay the least that they can for the trade-in (if one exists)

Many RV buyers lack important knowledge about the basics when they decide to buy an RV. Go to any RV show and talk with the salespeople. Often what they are trying to sell is the lifestyle, hoping that once you are hooked on the dream, you will quickly follow with a purchase.

It is amazing, considering the cost of an RV, how many are purchased as impulse purchases, just look at the "sold" signs at RV shows. Many buyers are pressured with assurances that they are getting special deals at the show and that if they wait, they lose out.

Buyer's regret is growing, it seems. The RVDA (Recreational Vehicle Dealers Association) is reporting greater numbers of lawsuits involving RV dealers and their sales practices.

 FACT

If you develop buyer's regret immediately after purchasing an RV, you do have some recourse. Most states mandate a grace period or cooling-off period after a major sale. During this time, the buyer can cancel the sales contract without penalty. Your RV dealer should supply this information at the time of sale.

Don't Skimp on Safety

When you begin driving an RV, you may need to relearn how to drive defensively. If you have been driving smaller vehicles for many years, your defensive driving skills may easily have slipped. Your current driving habits may work fine for a maneuverable automobile, but driving a vehicle the size of an RV requires better skills and habits.

RVs have many blind spots for their drivers. To prevent serious accidents, you will need to learn to use your mirrors and signals properly. Don't think that you can see everything on the road with your mirrors, and always be aware of what is going on around you. Large trucks, those vehicles that are even bigger than your RV, also have even larger blind spots, so their drivers may not see you. Always be ready to respond defensively to any dangerous situation that suddenly arises.

This really should go without saying, but it needs to be said anyway: Always wear your seat belt. As the driver, you also need to make sure all passengers in your RV wear seat belts whenever the vehicle is in motion. If there is an accident or sudden stop, any passengers who are not buckled in may be thrown around inside the vehicle and seriously injured.

Tire maintenance is another important safety consideration. To help avoid tire problems, you should maintain proper tire pressure, inspect tires regularly, avoid excess loading, and drive at a safe speed. Before each trip, check to make sure that your tires are properly inflated and have the correct tread depth.

QUESTION?

How can I learn to drive an RV safely?
There are numerous RV driving schools across the country to help drivers gain the skills and confidence needed to maneuver their homes on wheels safely across the country's roadways. Do a search on the term "RV driving schools" on the Internet and you will be sure to find one in your area of the country.

CHAPTER 11

Plan Your Trip

SOME PEOPLE PREFER TO TRAVEL to wherever the wind blows them. They like stopping at places on a whim, and, when they have seen enough, just packing up and moving on to the next stop. Other travelers would rather make plans. Before they begin a trip, they already know how far they will drive each day, where they will stop, and what they will see when they get there. Even if you are in the carefree former group, you probably find that at least some planning helps prevent stress and anxiety. If you are traveling with children, you will find that some planning is an absolute necessity.

A Short Shakedown Trip

Most dealers and manufacturers recommend that, before heading across the continent, you take your new (or new to you) RV on a shorter trip first. You may find a few problems with your new RV, and you will be closer to help if you do.

Taming the Systems

Like most travelers who are new to RV travel, you probably want to jump immediately into the driver's seat and hit the road. While that is understandable, your first trip should be a destination that is only an hour or two from your home. It may not seem like a lot of fun to take your new toy only a few miles down the road instead of on the cross-country trip you have been planning for years. However, if you save the cross-country trip for a little while, you will be much more prepared when you take it. Your long trip will be much more likely to be enjoyable and trouble-free.

As experienced RV travelers can tell you, no matter how well you think you have prepared for a trip, you will always forget something important. Think of your first excursion as a "test" trip, where you will be able to check out how well everything is working and how comfortable you are on the road.

 ALERT

If you have problems with any systems or construction of your RV, be sure to retain all documentation of the complaint you have and the repairs that were or were not done. If your problems continue, this documentation may help you in getting items replaced or in filling a "lemon law" claim.

A good RV dealer will offer you instructions on how to operate all of the systems that are available on your new RV. Depending on your level of experience with RVs, these instructions could be very brief or a little lengthier; if you are an experienced RV owner, you will probably just need a refresher specific to your new rig. Before you leave the lot, make sure that you know:

- How to hook up and unhook your trailer or fifth-wheel from its tow vehicle.
- How to stabilize and level your RV.
- Where the utility hookups (water, shore power, and sewer) are.
- How to turn on and turn off the propane tanks for cooking and heat.
- How to light the stove and water heater (if it is manually lit).

- How to work the refrigerator (most work on electric or gas mode with the flip of a switch, but some may still have to be "lit").

If you find it to be helpful, take notes as the dealer explains all of this to you. Be sure that you get all of the user's manuals (and the warranty cards) that go with these systems.

Your first RV trip to an RV park close to home will give you the chance to try out all systems to discover any problems that need to be corrected before you head cross-country. Most new RVs are very well built and problems should be minimal, but you should have them dealt with promptly.

Driving the Beast

A short first trip will help you get a feel for driving your new RV, with considerably less pressure than you would have on a longer trip. If you are an inexperienced driver, you also may find it helpful to have an experienced copilot along for support.

A drive of an hour or two should give you a feel for the brakes, steering, and cornering.

 ESSENTIAL

For the complete novice, RV driving schools are available in many areas of the country. The course will generally last two to three days and cover the basics of RV driving and driving conditions with an experienced instructor by your side. The certificate you earn may also qualify you for an insurance discount (you will need to check with your insurance company).

Try to plan your first trip to get some experience on demanding roads if possible. It may be difficult to find any steep grades in Iowa, but you should be able to find some routes that will give your driving skills a workout.

Basic RV Driving Skills

In some ways, learning to drive an RV can be like going back to those nervous early days of driver's ed. Here are some things to keep in mind when starting to drive an RV for the first time, or when driving an RV of a type and size that is unfamiliar to you.

Driving in traffic can be a white-knuckle experience for an inexperienced RV driver. Plan your first trip to avoid the heaviest traffic times and areas. This is not the time to get stuck in rush-hour traffic.

Plan your trip to take you on a highway with on and off ramps. This will give you experience in accelerating to highway speeds and decelerating to exit. You will find that an RV weighing four to five times as much as most cars will not be as responsive on acceleration or braking. Try changing lanes when traffic is light.

Do try some in-town driving, to get a feel for turning corners on narrow streets and stopping suddenly. This is a great way to get oriented to the size of your rig.

Practice backing up and parking your RV into a camping space–size area before you get to your destination. Mall parking lots are great places to practice, especially early on a weekday. Motorhomes can be fairly easy to park, at least compared to travel trailers and fifth-wheels. Drive-through camping spaces are great, especially for novices, but can be difficult to find in many areas. Learn to back into a parking space and you will find that you will have a much greater variety of campgrounds to choose from.

Where to Go

Planning your trip can be half the fun. It is exciting to think about the places and sights you want to see. Perhaps you have been dreaming about a trip to Alaska for years. You see yourself in the wilderness, drinking in all the fresh air and sights and sounds. Dreams are wonderful, but time, money, and equipment challenges often step in to spoil them.

If you have unlimited time to travel, the world (or at least the continent) is at your feet. But if you are like most, your travel time is limited by your job and all the other commitments you have. You can still have some wonderful and memorable travels with limited time.

Planning a trip cross-country in a week or two is foolish. Even if you could cover that many miles in the time allotted, it would be both stressful and dangerous.

To avoid falling asleep at the wheel, you should plan on driving no more than 200 to 250 miles in a day. If you have more than one qualified driver, you may be able to cover more miles per day. Be sure that each driver gets adequate rest periods.

During the summer months, you will find a wider variety of places to go. You will also find more people on the roads and in the campgrounds. Summer is the traditional time when families with school-age children can travel.

 ALERT

Prepare for higher fuel prices during the summer months as more motorists hit the road in search of rest and relaxation. Gasoline prices generally rise just before the Memorial Day weekend, staying high until after Labor Day travelers have returned home.

Many RV parks in northern areas are open on a seasonal basis from April to September/October. While there may be less traffic on the road, there also may be fewer places to stay.

During the winter, you may find RV campsites in short supply in the southern states because of the influx of "snowbirds" from the cold weather states.

What to See

There are great places to see and visit all through the United States, Canada, and Mexico. Fortunately, most of them are in areas where there are plenty of places for RV travelers to stay. (See the Appendix for a guide to some of the many parks and campgrounds that welcome RVs throughout the United States and southern Canada.)

According to the Recreational Vehicle Industry Association, there are great destinations for RV travelers to visit nationwide. You may find a wonderful destination an easy day's drive from your home. The following destinations have a wide variety of activities and sights for all the members of your family.

Cooperstown/Otsego County, New York

In Cooperstown, you will find the home of the National Baseball Hall of Fame, National Soccer Hall of Fame, and Corvette-Americana Hall of Fame—plenty to keep the sports fans and car buffs busy and entertained. Nearby Otsego Lake boasts swimming, fishing, and boating. For those interested in educational opportunities, Fenimore House and Farmers' Museum give a glimpse into the early days of a young United States. There are approximately 1,200 campsites close by to accommodate almost any kind of RV.

Nashville/Brown County, Indiana

With over 300 arts and crafts shops, Nashville is a great place to browse and shop. Nashville also boasts 700 campsites within four miles. For those who enjoy outdoor recreation, Hoosier National Forest, Brown County State Park, and Monroe Lake beckon. Music fans of all persuasions will enjoy the Little Nashville Opry.

San Antonio, Texas

San Antonio is the favorite Texas destination for travelers looking for a place where history and fun come together. You can remember the Alamo, enjoy the thrill rides and entertainment of Sea World and Fiesta Texas theme parks, and pick up a bit of south of the border culture. Generally mild winter temperatures make it a great destination for snowbirds trying to flee the cold.

Myrtle Beach, South Carolina

The Myrtle Beach area boasts more than 7,000 campsites along with miles of white sand beaches for family fun. It is also a golfers' haven with seventy championship golf courses and mild weather for year-round enjoyment.

Sandusky, Ohio

Home of Cedar Point Amusement Park, known for having more roller coasters than any other park, Sandusky is a great destination for the late spring and summer months. As it sits right on Lake Erie, there are many opportunities for beach fun.

Wind Cave National Park/ Badlands National Park, South Dakota

This is a great destination for travelers who want to mix the great outdoors with some great sightseeing. This area boasts Mount Rushmore, Jewel Cave National Monument, Crazy Horse Monument, and Wall Drug Store, along with some great opportunities for cave exploring. There are a wide variety of campgrounds available for all.

Gatlinburg/Pigeon Forge, Tennessee

From shopping to country music to water sports, the Gatlinburg area is a great destination for the whole family. The area boasts more than 300 shops featuring arts and crafts produced by local artisans. Dollywood is a celebration of the music, history, and culture of the Tennessee hills, and local lakes provide opportunities for water sports of all kinds.

North Carolina's Outer Banks

Visitors to this area can see where the Wright brothers achieved their dream of man in flight. There are also several fine museums and exhibits that celebrate early settlement and history. For the outdoors enthusiast, the mild weather and beaches are a bonus.

Cheyenne, Wyoming: Frontier Days Celebration

Frontier Days is a nine-day celebration of the Old West. One of the finest rodeos in the country is held annually in the summer. After the rodeo, enjoy the lakes and nearby mountains.

Pennsylvania Dutch Country/ Lancaster County, Pennsylvania

This area is known for its Amish and Mennonite communities with their unique lifestyles that hearken back to a simpler time. You'll be able to enjoy shopping for unique items and enjoy some of the best food in the country. For dessert, visit Hershey, Pennsylvania, the chocolate capital of the world. Get off the main roads and enjoy some unique museums and farmers' markets.

Alaska

Visiting Alaska is a once-in-a-lifetime dream for most of those who enjoy RV travel. Because of the distances involved, this trip is best planned for travelers who can devote more than three weeks to a trip. Enjoy rugged landscapes, Native American culture, Denali National Park, panning for gold, big-game hunting, salmon fishing, and much more.

 ESSENTIAL

Most travelers forget the adventures that are available in their own backyards. Contact your state (or nearby state) department of tourism for information on attractions. Many states have publications that highlight different attractions and seasonal activities. These publications can be a great resource for travel planning.

Making Reservations

It is the foolhardy traveler who fails to make reservations and instead depends on luck to find a place to stay after a long day of driving. Popular RV resorts in favorite tourist destinations fill up quickly, and reservations often need to be made many months ahead for stays during busy times.

Most RV parks require a deposit on reservations. While a credit card is usually the easiest way to guarantee a space, some campground owners may hold a spot with a check (don't forget to get it in the mail). Your credit card should not be charged until you actually check in, or only one night should be charged in case you have to cancel your trip at the last moment.

When you make reservations, ask about the campground's late arrival policy. No matter how well you plan, you may run into delays on the road or mechanical problems. If you are late, you will need to know how to get to your camping space with as little disturbance to other campers as possible.

 **ALERT**

If you own a large RV with multiple slideouts, you should make sure that the campground you are considering has RV sites that are wide enough to accommodate your rig comfortably. Get it in writing if possible, but at least get the name of the person you spoke with just in case.

Some public campgrounds do not take reservations for camping but work on a first-come, first-served basis. If they do make reservations, they may only have a limited number of sites for larger RVs, or, in many cases, they will not be able to accommodate them at all. Public campgrounds often do not have full hookups (or even any hookups). These are all things to consider and ask about when you call for reservations.

Cancellation Policies

Many RV parks have cancellation policies that are similar to many hotel/motel chains. Generally, if you cancel by a certain time or date before you are to arrive, there will not be a penalty for cancellation. Some will cancel your reservations if you do not show by a certain time but will still charge you for the first night.

Another common cancellation policy is to allow you to cancel up to the date of arrival but still charge a small "service" fee. Other RV parks do not charge any type of fee; these are the campgrounds that are always in high demand. They don't worry about cancellations, because they know they will always be able to fill the space.

Ask about cancellation policies when you make the reservations and get this in writing or at least get a name. If you do end up canceling a reservation, be sure to follow and check your credit card statement to be sure you were not charged for anything other than what you agreed to when making the reservation.

You may also want to check on cancellation policies if the campground does not measure up in quality or amenities. Most RVers have at least one horror story of the "campground from hell," where the advertised amenities don't exist. When you make reservations, ask if there are any contingencies for refunds if the accommodations are substandard or unavailable. Money-back guarantees are basically unheard of, but you can always give it a try. Frequently, a threat to call RV clubs like "Good Sam" with your complaints may persuade a campground owner to refund at least a portion of the fee. If the campground is truly at fault and negligent in fixing problems, ask for a refund. If you get a refund, great; if not, nothing is lost for asking.

Know Your Roads

One of the most valuable set of tools you will carry in your RV are the maps that help you get from place to place in safety and comfort. A good map contains most of the information you will need to make a good trip into a great trip.

Maps are available in most large grocery and department stores like Wal-Mart and Target. You'll find maps at gas stations, convenience stores, and bookstores. There are even some stores that just sell maps. You can get maps almost anywhere, and they are relatively inexpensive or even free.

Some of the best maps are provided by state tourism departments. They are usually the most up-to-date with accurate information about roads and road improvements or long-term road construction projects. These maps will generally also include listings of state and local parks, hospitals, rest stops, campgrounds, and fees. Most maps include elevations (useful when traveling in mountainous regions) and often will indicate roads with steep grades. Read the map carefully and learn what the different markings and symbols on the map indicate. You might want to avoid that unimproved country road in Colorado; it may involve going up a mountain with hairpin curves.

 ESSENTIAL

If you are a member of the American Automobile Association, one of your membership privileges includes Triptik maps. AAA will compile your trip information into a booklet the size of a folded map that maps out your route using the most up-to-date road information available with exit numbers and services clearly marked. You can specify whether you want the shortest or the most scenic routes.

If you don't have a current map of a state you are visiting, make the tourist information center your first stop after you cross the border. Besides maps, you will also find information on points of interest and events that you may never have heard of. Looking through the racks of brochures, you may find directions to a fascinating smaller museum, or to a renowned local festival that just happens to be taking place the weekend you are there.

If the tourist information center is staffed, ask for current information on road construction and closures and for any tips on avoiding areas that may be difficult to traverse in RVs. You will find that most people staffing these centers are friendly and helpful and understand that tourism and travelers are very important to the economic health of their state. Replace your travel maps at least yearly and keep them within reach of the copilot.

If you are staying in one place for awhile and are interested in learning more about local history, call on the local county clerk's office or historical society. They will often have maps that will help you discover some gems of local history.

Where in the World Are You?

One of the handiest tools for RV travelers was actually developed by the military for use in the battlefield. Its application for RV travel is much more peaceful, especially as it may help prevent fights about asking for directions.

The Global Positioning System (GPS) is a worldwide radio wave navigation system formed by twenty-four satellites and ground stations. These form manmade reference points that that can calculate your position down to a matter of a few feet. The advanced forms of GPS the military now uses can calculate positions down to a few inches (very helpful when trying to pinpoint a target). The GPS receivers are very small with miniaturized circuits; as with most technology, the prices have been coming down over the last few years. The receivers work in conjunction with commercial software that you install in your hardware (a laptop PC or PDA). You can also buy hand-held units that can be easily used in many situations. These receivers must have a clear view of the sky without obstacles in order to work properly. Generally, you enter the information about your trip with start and ending points with any side trips or stops you would like to make. The software will calculate the best route for your trip along with estimated times and mileage information. Most of these systems have a voice prompt that will warn you when an exit is coming. You will be able to see your progress on the map. Many software programs also have information about campgrounds, restaurants, rest stops, and gas stations built in.

 ESSENTIAL

GPS systems, like many technology products (such as computers and cell phones), have become very affordable over the past few years. Many mid- to high-end motorhomes now come equipped with GPS systems as either part of the standard package or as a very useful option.

How Far Today?

One of the most frequent causes of accidents is drivers who become overtired and fall asleep behind the wheel. A sleepy driver is the most common cause of single-vehicle accidents involving RVs. It is the nature of traveling that you want to get there as quickly as possible so the fun can begin. Pushing yourself to go one more mile can be a dangerous move. It is always advisable to have more than one person who is able to drive the rig. If two drivers spell each other, they may be able put in more miles before stopping. Just make sure that the resting driver is really resting.

If you are traveling with children or pets, plan to stop at least every two hours to let them stretch their legs and run around a bit. While a fifteen- to twenty-minute break every two hours may mean fewer miles in a day, it will make those miles much more pleasant.

Don't depend on being able to drive 65 miles per hour at all times. If your travels take you on many interstate highways, you may achieve that, but you may also encounter long stretches of construction or large accidents that will slow you down. If you are traveling on secondary roads, you will have to figure in slower speeds for any towns you will have to travel through. You are almost certain to encounter road construction at least once on your travels, especially during the summer months in more northern areas. You may be taking advantage of milder weather for travel and so are the various state highway departments. Winding roads and steep grades will also slow you down, as will unexpected stops for mechanical problems or illness.

 ALERT

> If luck is on your side and you end up covering that 300 miles in less than six hours, don't be tempted to keep driving and take your chances at finding a place to stop for the night. You may find yourself coping with rest stops that are full and campgrounds with no vacancy signs. Just stop where you planned and enjoy the extra time to unwind from the drive.

Taking all these things into consideration, you should not plan on traveling more that 250 to 300 miles a day. Using these numbers as your goal for a day's driving; you can then plan for your stop for the night.

CHAPTER 12

Packing for the Trip

WHETHER YOU ARE GOING for a quick weekend trip or are leaving for a three-month cross-country trek, you will need to plan and pack for the trip. While many people outfit their rigs with necessities for the road, your destination will affect the optional items you will have to pack. Planning ahead will make your trip much more enjoyable.

Less Is Better

Every discussion of RV travel will begin and end with the weight limitations of your RV. The amount of stuff you can take with you on a trip will depend on the weight limitations of your RV, but with some creativity you will be able to take along what you need (though maybe not everything you want).

Approach the packing of your RV in a logical manner. Think about the things you need and want to do while on your trip. Remember that your RV is there to provide the basic items you need for a safe and enjoyable trip. If you pack based on your basic needs, you will find life much easier.

What are your basic needs while traveling? You will need:

- Shelter
- Food

- Water
- Sleep
- Cleanliness
- Clothing

You do not need to take along or duplicate the entire contents of your kitchen or your closets. Always remember that you are on vacation and probably will be doing a lot of cooking. Think about what you'll be doing and what you will be seeing. What kind of clothing will you need? If you will be doing a lot of sightseeing, you'll need comfortable clothing and comfortable walking shoes.

Plan your meals and then do your shopping. Remember that you have limited space for food in both cabinets and in your small RV refrigerator. You will not often find that you are far from a place to buy food. Plan on shopping for food along the road and be flexible with your meal plans to take advantage of regional foods or specialties you find along the way. Look for food products that can be reconstituted with water when needed. Dried beans and peas weigh much less than their canned or frozen equivalents.

If you will be staying at an RV park with full hookups, carry only a small amount of water while you are traveling. Water is very heavy; a full freshwater tank may put you very near to your weight limits. Plan on using public restrooms while traveling to minimize the use of water (remember that the waste water goes along with you in the black and gray water tanks).

 FACT

If you want or need to take a computer along on your travels, you would be wise to invest in a portable laptop, rather than a desktop model. A laptop can save 30 to 40 pounds or more in weight, plus it is much easier to use and store while on the road.

Plan for Changes in the Weather

Be sure to plan for the weather as you pack for your trip. There are some areas of the country with fairly dependable weather, but others can have extremes that you will need to plan for.

With the Internet, there is really no excuse for not knowing what to expect about the places you will be visiting on your travels. If you are going to Florida's Disney World in November, a quick visit to the Orlando weather Web site gives you historical weather data to help in planning your trip. The average temperature on November 1 in Orlando runs from a high of 71 degrees to a low of 61. Knowing this will help you plan your clothing needs. As you will be in Florida at the end of the hurricane season, it is always wise to take along rain gear or an umbrella, but you will not need winter clothing footwear. Layering is always in style.

 ESSENTIAL

Comedian George Carlin has a hilarious comedy routine called "A Place for My Stuff" about our human foible of wanting to carry everything we own with us everywhere we go. It will make you think about the stuff you really need to take on your travels. Warning: As with most of his routines, Carlin does use some language that is not suitable for children or the faint of heart.

Always plan for rain; it can occur anywhere—even in the desert. If you plan menus exclusively for outdoor cooking you may find yourself standing out in the rain with your food getting soggy on the grill. Bring along a rain slicker with a hood; it is not easy to hook up your RV while holding an umbrella.

One of the handiest things you might want to think about adding to your RV is one of those folding wooden clothes dryers. You can find them at Wal-Mart in the same department where they sell irons and ironing boards. These are great for setting up in the bathroom tub for drying small items or bathing suits.

Limited Space

There are many strategies the RV traveler can use to live comfortably in the limited space of an RV.

Cook Outside

Carry a portable grill or use the outdoor grill to cook as many meals in the great outdoors as possible. Food always seems to taste better when cooked over a charcoal file. Pick up a cookbook of recipes for the grill to keep your meals varied and interesting. Hamburgers and hot dogs every meal would be pretty boring, to say the least.

Contain Clutter

A place for everything and everything in its place. Clutter in a confined space can quickly become overwhelming. Visit your local discount store and look at the bins and boxes and storage options they sell. Here's one way to contain clutter: save hotel-size containers of shampoo, soap, and lotion for use when traveling. Most discount, grocery, and drug stores carry travel-size packages of most of these grooming items. If you run out, you can replace them easily.

 ESSENTIAL

Camping and RV stores are a treasure trove of smaller travel-size items, but they can be expensive. Before you buy anything at these stores, check with your local discount store for similar items at a better price.

Necessary Items

There are items that are necessary for safe and comfortable travel. These checklists provide a guideline for those things you may want to bring along. Adapt them for your needs.

Kitchen (Galley)

❑ Lightweight pots and pans (aluminum is good) with nonstick surfaces for easy cleanup
❑ Mixing bowls that can be used in a microwave
❑ Set of measuring cups and spoons
❑ Pot holders and kitchen towels
❑ Lightweight, unbreakable dishware (including drinkware) that can be used in the microwave
❑ Heavyweight zippered plastic bags in various sizes
❑ Lightweight utensils
❑ Plastic wrap
❑ Aluminum foil (heavyweight foil is generally wider)
❑ Plastic containers with lids for food storage
❑ Paper towels

Bathroom

❑ Toothbrush, toothpaste, and dental floss
❑ Shampoo and hair care products (repackaged in travel-size containers if possible)
❑ Hand and bath soap
❑ Towels and washcloth
❑ Toilet paper

Cleaning Supplies

❑ Small spray bottle of all-purpose cleaner
❑ Cleaning cloths
❑ Small sponges

ESSENTIAL

If you have a computer, type up a master checklist as a Word document and save it. Print out a copy and check off items as they are loaded into the RV. If you find there are other essentials for the trip that are not on your checklist, write them in and update the document when you get home. It may take a few trips to get the list finalized for your needs.

Remember Your Medications and Health Records

No matter how long or short your trip is or the state of your health, it is essential that you have accurate health records.

Keep these health records in a safe place. You may decide, as many RV travelers have, that is it is worthwhile to add a fireproof safe to your vehicle. The safe does not have to be large, and you should put it in an inconspicuous spot. It makes for a great place to keep valuable documents and records.

If you are going to be traveling for an extended period, be sure you take enough medications with you for the duration of your trip. If you are not able to get a supply that will last because of an insurance company policy or for financial reasons, ask your doctor for a new prescription that you will be able to fill while on the road. No matter how well you plan, your return home could be delayed by a mechanical breakdown or weather and you may need to get a refill on your medications before you get home. If you fill your prescription at a national chain, you should have no problems obtaining refills while on the road.

Among the documents you carry with you, be sure to have the name and phone number of your personal physician. If you are in need of medical care and are unable to give a history of your health problems, a call to your physician for that information may be necessary.

Before you leave home, check with your physician and fill out the paperwork that will allow him or her to give a doctor or hospital information on your medical history if needed. Privacy laws have limited the amount of information that health care providers can provide without written permission from the patient. You should also carry documents that give any health care provider rendering emergency care on your behalf permission to release information to your doctor at home. While one hopes that these laws would not impede any care being provided, it is best to be prepared.

 QUESTION?

Will Medicare cover any health-related emergencies while I am traveling in Canada?
Medicare does not cover health care outside the United States. You will need to purchase traveler's health coverage for emergency care while in Canada. Older travelers can check with AARP for information on policies.

If you have prepared a living will or any sort of advanced directives, carry a copy of those with you also. These legal papers document your wishes for health care if you become incapacitated and are unable to direct your own care. No matter what your age or present state of health is, everyone should have these documents prepared. While laws may differ from state to state on the legal basis of these documents, they will make your wishes known to health care providers.

If your health insurance is provided by an HMO, or health maintenance organization, you may be limited to coverage only for emergency conditions while you are away from home. Your health care card should have a toll-free number you can call for information and guidance should you become ill while traveling.

Vital Information

There are many other vital pieces of information and documents you will need to carry with you on your travels. For the organized traveler, this should be an easy assignment, but for the rest it may take a bit more time.

 ESSENTIAL

Before you leave on a trip, especially an extended one, check that everything is up-to-date, including your driver's license and insurance. If they would expire during your trip (or if your trip is extended by illness or a breakdown), take steps to get everything current before you leave.

If you purchased your RV new, you should have received a pouch or folder with all the important papers and documents about your RV, including proof of ownership and warranties. Also included in this information should be the owner's manuals and instructions for operating the various appliances and systems in your RV. You should have studied all these documents and books shortly after you took delivery of your RV to familiarize yourself with its operation.

Keep these documents in one place. Visit your local discount or office store to find a container. There are several mobile filing systems that would work great for this purpose. Try to find one that is waterproof and fireproof. Label the sections with the type of document contained for easy retrieval. The basic documents you should carry include the following:

- Warranty information
- Insurance information, including proof of insurance
- Owner's manuals
- Emergency contact information

- Credit cards and ATM card
- Proof of citizenship

Crossing Borders

There are many wonderful places to visit in the United States, but you may also want to explore the neighboring countries of Canada and Mexico. All three countries are connected by road and RV travel is relatively easy. Always remember that you are entering a foreign country and will need some special paperwork.

Entering Canada

Canada and the United States have enjoyed a relatively warm relationship over the years. The cultures and language are similar (even in French-speaking Quebec, most people speak and understand English). Canada is very safe and welcoming to visitors.

Residents of the United States and Canada are still able to cross borders relatively easily, though security measures have been increased as concerns about terrorism have grown. If you carry the correct paperwork, your border crossing should be relatively free of hassles.

Visas are not required for U.S. citizens entering Canada who are coming from the United States. You will, however, need:

1. Proof of U.S. citizenship. This could be a U.S. passport or a certified copy of your birth certificate issued by the city, county, or state where you were born. (For information on how to obtain a U.S. passport, check with a local passport agent, which may be located at a nearby post office.) If you are a naturalized U.S. citizen and you do not have a passport, you should travel with your naturalization certificate. An important note to remember: A driver's license or Social Security card is *not* valid proof of citizenship.

2. Photo identification, such as a current, valid driver's license.

Here are some other rules to be aware of:

All U.S. citizens who are entering Canada from a third country must show a valid passport.

Alien permanent residents of the United States must present their Alien Registration Card (commonly called a "green card").

If you are a dual U.S./Canadian citizen, you should present yourself as a Canadian citizen when you are entering Canada. However, U.S. citizens should use their U.S. passports when entering or leaving the United States.

Because of the international concern over child abduction, single parents, grandparents, or guardians who are traveling with children will often need proof of custody, or else a notarized letter from the other parent authorizing travel. (This requirement is in addition to the proof of citizenship explained above.)

Any person who is under the age of eighteen and traveling without his or her parent or guardian should carry a letter from the parents or guardians authorizing the trip.

Mexico

Each year, between 15 and 16 million U.S. citizens visit Mexico. Most visitors enjoy their stay, though some will encounter minor difficulties and occasionally even serious inconveniences.

You shouldn't expect travel conditions in Mexico to be just the same as you will find them in the United States. Fortunately, the Department of State and its embassy and consulates in Mexico offer various services to assist U.S. citizens who run into problems while in the country.

The State Department offers the following tips to those planning on traveling to Mexico.

Before You Go

As you travel, keep aware of local news coverage. If you plan a stay in one place for longer than a few weeks, or, if you are in an area where communications are poor or some natural disaster or civil unrest has occurred, you are encouraged to register with the nearest U.S. embassy or consulate. Registration takes only a few moments, and it may be invaluable in case of an emergency.

Other useful precautions include:

- Leaving a detailed itinerary and the numbers of your passport or other citizenship documents with a friend or relative back in the United States.
- Bringing either a U.S. passport or a certified copy of a birth certificate and photo identification.
- Carrying your photo identification and the name of a person to contact with you in the event of serious illness or other emergency.
- Photocopying your list of traveler's checks and keeping them with you in a separate location from the originals and leaving copies with someone at home.
- Leaving things like unnecessary credit cards and expensive jewelry at home.
- Bringing traveler's checks, not cash.
- Using a money belt or concealed pouch for passport, cash, and other valuables.
- Not bringing firearms or ammunition into Mexico without written permission from the Mexican government.

 QUESTION?

Can I use my cell phone while out of the United States?
Check with the customer service department of your cell phone carrier. There are different service plans that may or may not provide service in Canada or Mexico. Be aware such service can be expensive if you do not travel out of the country regularly.

CHAPTER 13

Food for the Road

HERE'S ONE BIG REASON RV TRAVEL is less expensive than other forms of travel: all the money you can save by not eating in restaurants. At a time when the price of a typical fast-food meal can run more than $5 per person, the money you would need for eating out for every meal quickly adds up. And don't forget the high cost to your health and waistline of all those burgers and fries. Many people also find it difficult to follow special diets when faced with restaurant menus for each meal. Cooking in an RV can be a challenge, but if you plan well, it can be a fun activity as well.

Plan Ahead

If you want to have a great trip with great food, you'll need to plan ahead. An RV galley usually has much less space than your kitchen at home, and you'll need to use every bit of it as well as you can. You also always to need to consider the weight of what you're bringing along in an RV, and all of your food and kitchen items will need to be packed and loaded properly.

When you're planning your meals, keep your travel plans in mind. If you will be going through more populated areas, you will be able to plan meals that require a regular stop at a supermarket for more fresh ingredients. If you are setting up camp in a remote area that is miles away from the nearest convenience store, you will have to stock everything you need before you arrive. You'll also to make sure that you only bring foods that will keep fresh for the time you're there.

Even if you are unable to buy fresh foods very often on your trip, you can still make a number of delicious meals without too much fuss if you plan ahead. Keep things as simple as you can; you don't want to spend all your time behind the stove or cleaning dishes and pots—you could have stayed home and done that. Think of creating the meals that you enjoy that use the minimum number of ingredients and utensils, as you will have limited counter space and storage areas. Don't bring along all the electronic appliances you have in your home kitchen; they take up space, add weight, and require power. An RV trip is a good time to reacquaint yourself with how your manual can opener works, or to dig out that hand-operated beater from the back of your kitchen drawer.

 FACT

If you have time to stop at roadside produce stands, do it. You will usually find just-picked freshness combined with low prices. These small farmstands are selling directly to the public (you) and cutting out the intermediary. Don't be tempted by the low prices to buy too much; you'll have no place to store it.

In a midsize trailer or motorhome, the typical RV galley has a refrigerator-freezer combination, two to three burners, an oven, a microwave, and a double sink. These amenities will not be the full-size versions you find in your home kitchen; they have been downsized and designed to work in the confines of your RV galley. Your cooking will have to adapt to the space you have.

RV refrigerators are smaller than and not nearly as efficient as your home unit, though they have improved over the past few years. Usually they are dual power, meaning they can switch over from electricity to gas cooling units as needed. You will find that food will spoil faster in your RV refrigerator. If you are traveling with children, pack powdered milk for use after the liquid milk runs out or spoils; this is a particularly good idea if you will be traveling somewhere where buying a quart of milk might require a 10-mile drive.

You'll find that RV ovens are small and have a limited cooking capacity. Preparing a large Thanksgiving turkey is probably out of the question. Beyond the oven limitations, storing the leftovers from a large meal is also a challenge. You can more easily make a traditional Thanksgiving dinner in your RV by cooking one of the turkey breasts most grocery stores carry (this will also eliminate the traditional fights that the kids have over who gets the drumsticks). Add side dishes of instant mashed potatoes and vegetables, and you'll have a tasty meal much like the one you'd have back home.

Other points to remember:

- Try to limit leftovers that can be difficult to store.
- Keep a variety of different sizes of heavy-duty (freezer weight), zippered plastic bags on hand for food storage.
- Transfer foods from glass to plastic containers before putting them in your RV. Glass breaks too easily in a moving RV.
- Stock your galley with items that can serve more than one purpose, or will be used on a regular basis.

Plan for storage of countertop appliances while you on the road. If you can't store it safely, don't bring it. Blenders and food processors are wonderful add-ons to well-stocked home kitchens, but in an RV galley, they take up valuable counter space and can become dangerous projectiles in a moving vehicle. Another consideration is the weight of the items you are adding to the galley. If you add a blender, you may have to eliminate another item that will prove much more useful in your travels.

Stocking Your Galley

RV travel requires some careful planning of supplies and provisions to ensure that you are able to prepare easy and nutritious meals that will appeal to all the members of your family. Even with the largest RVs, you will face storage and weight limitations that will determine how much you can carry in your rig. Unless you are planning a trip to a wilderness area with limited grocery shopping options, you should be prepared to restock along the way.

When you are stocking your RV kitchen, you also need to consider that it is not going to being staying in one place. No matter how smooth the drive is, you will still occasionally experience bumpy roads and sudden stops. Those occurrences can cause a big mess if you are not prepared.

 ESSENTIAL

Check your grocery or discount store for rolls of nonslip shelf lining. This thin, foam-like material can be cut to fit your cabinets and drawers. It will help keep things in place while you are traveling and will keep damage to belongings to a minimum in most situations.

Do not pack glass items if at all possible. Glass is much heavier than plastic and is breakable. Leave your good dishes at home; no one is going to expect meals served on china and crystal.

To avoid having to pack and unpack your RV at the beginning and end of every trip, purchase a set of dishes that stays in your RV. You can find very nice and serviceable sets of unbreakable plastic in most large department stores. Keep the number of dishes you carry to a minimum to save space and weight. Any dishes that can serve double duty are a much smarter purchase.

For holding various kitchen items neatly and efficiently, small plastic baskets are a good choice. Also handy are those wire dividers you can purchase at home stores like Home Depot or Lowe's. You can use them to divide cabinets into smaller units for greater efficiency.

 ESSENTIAL

Before you put anything into your RV kitchen, look at it with a critical eye to be sure it is really needed. If only one person drinks coffee, do you really need a 12-cup coffee maker taking up a lot of counter space? You can find very good single-serving coffee makers.

Some basic items are useful or necessary for just about everyone who travels in an RV. The following list will give you the most common basics.

- Seasonings and spices (including salt and pepper)
- Sugar and artificial sweeteners
- Baking soda (useful for putting out small fires, for upset stomachs, and as a substitute for toothpaste)
- Food staples such as rice, beans, and pasta
- Powdered milk
- Basic pots and pans (easy to clean)
- Basic cutlery (stainless steel)
- Basic cooking utensils
- Kitchen linens
- Paper towels
- Trash bags
- Dishwashing liquid

Simple Menus

Most veteran RV owners find that planning menus for the trip before you leave the house helps make traveling much easier and more enjoyable. If you plan your meals before you leave, you will know what you need to shop for at home, what you will need to buy along the way, and what additional cooking utensils you will need to take with you for the trip.

You may find it easier to make some meals beforehand, especially if you have a day or two with long drives before you reach your destination. What could be easier than just heating up a homemade dinner after a long day's drive? Trying cooking a large roast with all the fixings a day or two before you plan on leaving. You can enjoy a wonderful meal, make a stew with the leftovers, and then freeze the stew in a plastic container. On a later day, put the frozen meal into the RV galley refrigerator before you hit the road in the morning, and it should be thawed by the time you stop for the evening. Pop it into the microwave for a few minutes and you will have another home-cooked meal in a few minutes.

 ESSENTIAL

You can save time and cleanup on mornings you are traveling or trying to get an early start on sightseeing by precooking your bacon before you leave home. Cook it until it's almost done and it will just require a quick turn in the microwave to heat and eat. You will need to plan on eating this within a day or two after you leave home.

Plan your menus for the trip around your activities. If you are going on a wilderness trip where you will be out exploring the wilds during the day, you should plan on having a fairly large, satisfying breakfast with a light carry-along lunch and a larger evening meal. If your plans involve early sightseeing, you may want to plan to have a large breakfast and then buy a light snack at your destination if carrying food is impractical.

Plan on eating at least a couple of meals in restaurants, especially if you are visiting cities that boast unique regional foods. What would a trip to San Antonio, Texas, be without some authentic Tex-Mex cooking, or a trip to New Orleans without some Cajun jambalaya?

Try to plan your menus to take advantage of local produce that may be in season. If you are traveling in any of the southern states, you will find a wide variety of fresh fruits and vegetables available almost year-round, much of it imported from Mexico.

When you have planned your meals for the trip, you can do your initial shopping before you leave home. You can also add any utensils or pots and pans that you may need, but don't normally keep in your RV. When shopping and stocking for your planned meals, pack only what you will need. This is not the place for left-overs. If you have leftovers and don't use them within a day or two, they will usually end up in the trash. With the limited space in RV refrigerators, a lot of leftovers can limit the variety of foods you can carry and make for boring meals.

Be sure to plan several meals that can be cooked outside on either the grill at your campsite or on a portable grill you carry with you. Getting out in the fresh air makes food taste better, and cooking is usually less of a chore and more of an adventure when you use an outdoor grill. If you are traveling in areas where the weather is extremely hot, cooking outside will help keep your rig cooler.

Prepackaged Meals

Many people, especially empty nesters, find that cooking large meals once or twice a week and freezing leftovers into single-meal packages make life simpler. They find they can have a variety of nutritious meals with minimal fuss. You can use this same strategy for preparing meals for your travels.

You can of course visit your local supermarket and find many frozen and packaged meals. While these are certainly convenient and handy, they can also be expensive and wasteful. Check the number of servings on the package; if it serves more than the number of people you are traveling with, or if one or two of those with you are small children, you may find you are confronted with a lot of leftover food at the end of the day. With the limited food storage available on board, you have few choices on what to do with the leftovers.

Prepackaged frozen dinners that you find in the grocery store can be very high in fat and sodium. If you have a family member on a special diet, these meals may not be a wise choice. Learn to read labels, especially the nutrition labels for information on the food you are buying. If you have a family member who has allergies, check the list of ingredients for dangerous foods.

 ESSENTIAL

A handy gadget you might want to consider buying is a home vacuum packaging system like the Foodsaver. You can use it to package foods in vacuum-sealed bags that are easy to store, keep food fresh, and won't break like glass jars and containers can. The bags can also be used as cooking containers in the microwave or in a pot of boiling water for meals like stews.

There are many ways to prepare before you leave that can cut down on the time spent in your RV kitchen on the road. The cook is on vacation, too, and does not want to be stuck in the galley the whole time. One of the easiest ways to prepare is to pull out your family's favorite recipes and adapt them for the road. It is generally best to stick to trusted foods and recipes, especially when you have young children. Children don't always adapt well to change, and travel can sometime be unsettling for them. Familiar foods can help ease the transition and make mealtime much more pleasant.

Precook meats such as chicken and beef. Cut them into bite-size pieces and freeze the amount needed in heavy-duty freezer bags. You can pull out a bag from the freezer and thaw it to use in a quick meal. Use the beef as a basis for stew or chili. The thawed chicken along with flour tortillas can quickly become quesadillas on the grill or in a pan on the stovetop. Add a salad (the prepackaged salads are a great value) and you have a fast, tasty, and satisfying meal.

Another way to save time and energy in the galley is to premix dry ingredients. You can prepare the dry ingredients for brownies, corn bread, muffins, etc., and pack them in resealable plastic bags. When you are ready to make them, just mix in the wet ingredients and bake.

When buying fruits and vegetables for the road, precut fruits and vegetable are wonderful for RV travel. You can find packages of carrots, celery, broccoli, and cauliflower already washed, trimmed, and ready to eat. Buy the smaller packages to maximize space and variety in your RV refrigerator. You can stock up on these products on the road.

The packaged salad mixes seemed to be made for RV travel. You can find a wide variety of salad mixes, including some that come with dressing, croutons, etc. One bag generally feeds four to six and adds the fiber and nutrients we all need in our diets.

Food Storage

For most RV owners, limited storage is the major downside to RV travel. Lack of actual storage (cabinets and drawers) is obvious, but weight restrictions also factor into the limited amount of provisions you can carry in most RVs.

Many RV owners suggest a trip to your local discount or grocery store to stock up on small to medium-size plastic containers for food storage. Square or rectangular shapes are best for limited storage space. Stackable containers will stay in place during travel more readily than containers with curved tops.

One brand you may want to look at for your RV is Gladware, found in the plastics section of your grocery store. These containers are lightweight and see-through (which helps eliminate mystery food) and very inexpensive. They can go from the refrigerator or freezer to the microwave and are dishwasher safe on the top rack (for those lucky RV owners with dishwashers).

If they become damaged, they are inexpensive enough to toss in the trash.

 ESSENTIAL

Tupperware is a well-known brand of plastic ware that boasts a wide variety of containers. You may even be able to find a friendly Tupperware consultant who can look at your RV galley and suggest storage solutions. Tupperware is more expensive than many other brands of storage containers, but it does have an excellent warranty that provides replacement parts with few questions asked.

Cooking on the Road

There may be times when you are traveling that it will be hot enough to fry eggs on the pavement, but that is not the kind of road cooking we are talking about here.

When traveling from point A to point B, you will need to eat. If you are traveling in a motorhome, it will be very tempting for the passenger to fix a meal in the galley while the vehicle is in motion. Once it is done, you can make a quick stop to eat and then get back on the road. Or taking it to the extreme, the food can be prepared by the passenger and the driver can eat while driving. While this is possible in a motorhome, it is not advisable. Moving around in a moving RV can be very dangerous. If a sudden stop is necessary, unrestrained passengers can become missiles, harming themselves and possibly other passengers at the same time. If you must get up and be out of your seat belt, make sure it is for only a very short time.

If your travels include a long road trip to get to your destination, plan on stopping for all meals. If you plan ahead for light, easy-to-prepare meals, you will still have the time to put in many miles toward your destination. Be sure to pack sandwich fixings for quick meals on the road. Keep a jar of peanut butter in the cupboard along with some jelly in the refrigerator; add some bread and you have a quick, satisfying meal. If peanut butter is not your favorite, most cold meats pack easily and keep well in an RV refrigerator.

 FACT

The adventurous traveler in you may want to check out the book *Manifold Destiny: The One! The Only! Guide to Cooking on Your Car Engine.* The book contains recipes that use the heat your engine generates to cook dishes that are wrapped in foil and cradled on top of your engine manifold. Those who have tried it swear they get great-tasting hot meals at the end of a long drive.

During meal stops, you should take the opportunity to get outside your motorhome or tow vehicle and walk around to stretch your legs. If you have circulatory problems, it is especially important to change your position on a regular basis. This helps prevent any pooling of blood in the lower extremities that could lead to dangerous blood clots.

Special Occasion Meals

There will be times during your travels when you will want to plan meals for special occasions. While you may not be able to cook an elaborate Thanksgiving dinner with all the fixings in your RV galley, you can prepare a wonderful and memorable meal for your family.

You may want to check with the proprietor or manager of the RV park you are staying at. Some have small "party" rooms with kitchen facilities you can use while staying there for a small fee or cleaning deposit. Some families have their own RV family gathering or reunion with several families and generations meeting for these special occasions and this type of party room is great for that type of gathering. You will still need to plan carefully to prevent too many leftovers, and you will generally need to supply dishes and table coverings. These are the times when disposables are especially wonderful.

 ALERT

RV campgrounds in southern states that cater to the long-term snowbird escaping from winter weather often provide special parties for events like Thanksgiving and Christmas. For a fee that is usually reasonable, you get Thanksgiving dinner and entertainment with no dishes to wash and no leftovers to store. What a deal!

Plan to Shop

If you are going to be traveling for more than a few days, you will need to stop to shop for provisions. You will also need to pay for those provisions. Be sure to carry enough cash or checks to pay for restocking your pantry or you may find yourself going hungry. Some large grocery stores do accept credit cards for purchases. Many smaller stores may not take credit cards and may not accept out-of-state checks (this will vary from place to place).

While prices may not be the most important thing you look at when shopping for food supplies for your travels, there are some things that you can do to save money. Prices on most items will generally be lower in large chain stores than in smaller independent grocery stores. You may also find lower prices in larger urban areas with many stores and more competition for shoppers. One exception is fruits and vegetables in season. Look for roadside farm stands selling fresh-from-the-field goods. Prices are often much better than in supermarkets, as is the quality.

You should also shop carefully for the freshest meats and produce you can find. Your RV refrigerator is not as efficient as the one at home, and fresher foods will last longer in it.

 ESSENTIAL

> If you are traveling with a group or with friends, you may want to take advantage of cost savings of larger quantity buys. While not everyone will need the same things, there may be items such as rice and beans that can be purchased very economically in large quantities and divided for all-around savings.

Unfortunately, you may find the overall cost of some items is higher because you are not buying them in bulk while you are on the road. With the limited storage an RV affords, getting a bargain on that twelve-pack of paper towel rolls from the shopper's club (or even buying a value-priced jumbo bottle of ketchup) is not a realistic option.

Paper or Plastic

Considering how difficult it can be to bring along and wash regular dishes on an RV, it can be very tempting to use only disposable dishes when you are traveling. You go on a vacation to get away from the rigors and chores of everyday life and enjoy a bit of rest and relaxation. For many that means no dishes, especially when you do not have an automatic dishwasher on board.

While it may be tempting to bring along nothing but disposables, that is not always practical. Paper products are generally lightweight but they are bulky, taking up a lot of room in the limited storage area of an RV. You also may want to consider the environmental impact of your choice of products, and whether they will be easily recycled.

The best advice from many experienced campers is to bring along a combination of disposable and lightweight plastic tableware. The disposables are wonderful for those quick stops along the road for meals and rest as you are traveling. Make quick sandwiches that require no cooking for these types of meals. Use disposable dishes and your cleanup will be fast and easy to get you back on the road quickly.

 ALERT

> One exception for using nothing but paper dishes would be for those travelers who are renting an RV. Whatever you put in the RV will need to be removed when you turn it back in. It would be better to lose a few paper plates than several good dishes because you forgot them in the rental.

Once you get to your final destination, it is time to put away the paper and bring out the washable dishware and cutlery. Don't bring along your best china in the RV. It is best to use some type of heavy-duty plastic dishes and glassware. You can get some very sturdy and attractive plastic ware that will serve you well.

Do not plan on keeping a twelve-place setting of dishes in your RV. You don't have the room and don't need that many dishes. If your usual camping group consists of four, you only need pack four or five dishes. Your RV galley is very small and it is much easier to just wash everything up as soon as meals are over. You also don't want to take the chance of attracting more bugs or critters.

CHAPTER 14

Are We There Yet?

RV TRAVEL MAY SEEM TO BE ONLY FOR RETIREES and empty nesters, but many young families are finding that it is great for their families. It can be challenging, but going by RV is a great way to promote family togetherness away from the hectic activity of everyday life. You may also find that RV travel is great for getting your children into the great outdoors and away from the television set—whether at home or in a typical motel room.

Traveling with Children

If you are having nightmares remembering annual family vacations that consisted of nonstop driving, crammed in the backseat of the family Buick, you may be a little hesitant to try RV travel with your children. Forget those visions of travel past. RV travel is very family-friendly if you plan carefully and try not to overschedule.

In this age of stressed-out, overscheduled families, RV travel is the perfect way for family members to stay in touch with each other. Nothing encourages people to talk with one another and engage in shared activities like a trip in an RV. According to a Harris Interactive Survey, "Ninety-four percent of parents who own RVs overwhelmingly consider them the best way to travel with children."

RV travel can help foster a love for the outdoors in your children as well. RV owners surveyed by Robert Hitlin Associates cited teaching a respect for nature as an important benefit of family RV camping. Of those who camped as children, 95 percent said it had a positive effect on their adult lives, helping them develop an appreciation for the outdoors and insight into different people and places.

 FACT

With many of the newer tow vehicles and RVs, getting there is half the fun. More vehicles are coming equipped with state-of-the-art stereos, TVs, and DVD players. You can even get game systems as an option to keep the kids occupied.

Games and Activities for the Road

When the kids have tired of movies and music, you can keep them occupied by planning some games that can be played while traveling. Encourage these activities as they help foster creativity.

Travel journal: Older children might enjoy keeping a journal that documents their travels. This is a great activity while driving, and it gives you something that you may treasure long afterward.

License plate game: Print a list of all fifty states (and the Canadian provinces if you like) or bring a copy of a U.S. map, and let the kids put a check for each state when they see a car with that license plate. Promise a small reward for the child who spots the most states or provinces.

I spy: Pick out an object that everyone can see from where they are seated. Give everyone a clue by saying, "I spy something that is . . ." (tell the object's shape, color, or size). The other players ask questions about what you see, and you are only allowed to answer with "yes" or "no." The first player who guesses right becomes the new spy.

A to *Z* **game:** Find objects or animals beginning with *A* on signs around you. Have the players take turns, after *A*, go to *B*, and so on. An easy example for *A* would be "automobile." Try to get through the whole alphabet; if you want, you can skip letters that may take too long to find.

Hangman: With just a piece of paper and a pencil, you can play hangman. One person thinks of a word or phrase and then draws a series of dashes, one for each letter in the answer (leaving spaces between words). The other person guesses individual letters; when a guess is correct, the first person writes the letter above each dash where it is found. For each letter that is guessed that isn't in the word or phrase, another line in a gallows and stick figure is drawn. The first player is the winner if the "man" is hung before the second player can guess the word or phrase.

Board games: Look at local toy and discount stores for travel versions of favorite board games like Battleship, checkers, and bingo. Many of these miniaturized games have metal boards with magnetic pieces to keep them from falling off with each bump in the road.

 ALERT

If distracting children with games and activities does not alleviate whining, it might be a signal that it is time to stop for a while or even for the night. Children have much less tolerance for long stretches of driving. Often just letting them out to stretch and run will help.

Overcoming Boredom

Even the best travel planning cannot control the weather. If your travels have taken you to the beach for sun and sand, a week of wind and rain may lead to frayed nerves and arguments if you have children cooped up in an RV. Always have alternative activities planned. If weather could be a factor in derailing your travel plans, be sure to have backup plans.

If an outdoor attraction is on the agenda, have an alternative activity in an indoor or weather-sheltered venue. If rain sidelines a day at the beach, find a museum or indoor amusement park to visit instead.

Make sure you have a variety of books, movies, and games along to pass the time when the weather is bad. Board games are a great activity for RV travels, allowing family members to interact in a fun way without the stress of work and school.

 ESSENTIAL

A standard deck of cards is inexpensive and easily replaced. Card games are ideal for RV vacations as they don't add much weight and are compact. Get a good card playing book (*Hoyle's Rules of Games*, for example) for hours of fun.

Books and Movies

Books and movies are great for keeping kids entertained while traveling. Most motorhomes have an entertainment system that includes a videotape player or a DVD player. Many vans, trucks, and large SUVs have a TV included with a player as well.

If possible, it is desirable to have headphones to keep the noise level tolerable. Headphones will also lessen road and wind noise for those using them. Make sure the television is not distracting to the driver to help avoid mishaps.

Best Movies for Kids

There are many fine movies for children. The Disney animated movies are always favorites. Most children will enjoy watching them over and over again. It is well worth the money to buy the video or DVD of particular favorites.

Books

If your children enjoy reading, long road trips are the perfect place for a bookworm to get in some uninterrupted reading time. Encourage your child to put the book down at intervals to stretch and move around. Reading for long periods in a moving vehicle can lead to motion sickness or headaches, especially for readers who become very engrossed in the book and don't look up periodically.

If you do have a child who suffers from motion sickness, be sure to be attentive to indications that there may be a problem. Many children do not realize that they are sick until it is too late to stop.

 FACT

If you have a portable game system, you may be able to hook it up to the television. Purchase an inverter, which allows you to power the game system using the automobile power system rather than batteries. You will quickly recoup the money you spend on the inverter.

Things to See

The number of places you can go in an RV in North America is almost unlimited. There are some destinations that are more kid-friendly than others. Depending on your family's interest and budget, the world is your playground. Trying to list all the family-friendly destinations would take too much space. The destinations listed here will give you a taste of some of the best places to take your children.

Florida

Florida is one of the best places in the country for traveling with children. You'll find a lot to see and do in various spots all over the state, and many attractions are within easy driving distance from each other. Here are some of the most popular:

Amusement and Theme Parks

Orlando is home to two large theme parks: Disney World (which includes Epcot and Disney-MGM Studios), and Universal Studios and Islands of Adventures. Both parks can easily take more than a day to explore and are great for kids of all ages. The prices of the daily passes are expensive, but a three-day pass can be a better deal. With younger children, it is often wise to spread your visit over a few days to avoid child and parent burnout.

Take breaks from the parks to rest and refuel. If you stay at the Disney campground Fort Wilderness, you will be able to get a shuttle back and forth from the parks.

Kennedy Space Center

This is a great place for families with school-age children to spend the day. If you have ever dreamed of being an astronaut, this is the place for you. There are various tours of the facilities, interactive exhibits, and movies to fill an entire day with dreams and education.

Daytona Beach

For the family that loves not only the beach but motor sports, this is a great destination. *Florida Monthly* magazine calls the public beach in Daytona the finest in Florida. It is a great place for family fun. Be advised that it is also a top destination for college-age spring break revelers. That might be a time to choose another destination.

Daytona is also home to the Daytona Raceway, and one of the biggest sporting events in the country, the Daytona 500, in early February. RV parks and campgrounds fill up months prior to "Speedweek." There are numerous race-related activities for families during nonrace times that include tours and interactive exhibits at Daytona USA, an amusement park for racing enthusiasts.

Everglades National Park

Located in the southern part of Florida, Everglades National Park is the only subtropical preserve in North America. You'll encounter a wide variety of ecological communities, from sawgrass prairies to cypress swamps. The park is known for its rich bird life, particularly large wading birds, and it is the only place in the world where alligators and crocodiles live side by side. During the winter months, the park has ranger-led walks, talks, and bike hikes, along with special kids' programs.

California

California is another popular place for family camping, with lots to do from theme parks to some of the most interesting educational opportunities in the country.

Southern California

The Los Angeles area (Anaheim) is home to the original Disney theme park, Disneyland. The Magic Kingdom is a great place for young children and teenagers alike. Just up the road are Knott's Berry Farm, the original Universal Studios, and Six Flags Magic Mountain, which has some of the best roller coaster rides you will find anywhere. Down the road in San Diego is Sea World with its wonderful wildlife shows. You will also find some of the nicest beaches and great seafood. There are several very nice campgrounds in the area.

Monterey

Home of John Steinbeck and Cannery Row, Monterey boasts one of the finest aquariums in the world. Your children will be fascinated by displays of the wonders of the ocean, in many cases from an up-close and personal view. The aquarium will take a full day to enjoy completely. Just up the road in Santa Cruz is a boardwalk with carnival rides and games and some of the most entertaining sea lions you will ever see (or hear).

Sequoia and Kings Canyon National Parks

These parks share miles of boundary and are managed as one park. Sequoia was the second national park designated in this country. Home to the giant sequoias, and teeming with wildlife, these parks are spectacular. In summer, there are ranger-led field trips for the entire family that kids can enjoy. Be forewarned: there are bears, so you should be cautious in your adventures and watch that small children do not wander off.

 ESSENTIAL

There are many family and child-friendly places to visit that are just too numerous to list here. One of the best resources for information is the Web site *http://travelwithkids.about.com.* You will find information on kid-friendly places to visit along with other useful travel information.

Safety First

While it may be tempting to let the kids loose in the RV and stop the whining while traveling, this is very dangerous and against the law. Seat belt and child restraint laws are not just for drivers of cars; RVs are subject to the same laws.

When buying an RV in anticipation of a growing family, be sure to look at the number of seat belts. In newer motorhomes, every seat that can be used while the motorhome is in motion is required by law to have a seat belt. This includes seats at dinettes and couches (even those that turn into beds). Seating that is not anchored to the frame of motorhome is not designed to be used while traveling.

If you are buying used, older motorhomes may not have enough seating with seat belts for your family. Seat belts can often be installed after-market, though it may be expensive.

If you have a large family, there may not even be enough seating, and you may not be able to travel together safely. Keep this in mind when shopping for a motorhome, new or used.

If you have a larger than average family, a travel trailer pulled by a vehicle with adequate seating and restraints may be a better choice. The typical full-size van or large SUV with three rows of seating can comfortably carry seven to eight passengers with seat belts for all.

 FACT

Children under four years of age and less than 40 pounds should be in specially designed car seats while traveling. This is the law in the United States and in Canada. It is the driver's responsibility to ensure that all passengers under the age of sixteen are protected by safety restraints.

Medical Emergencies

If your child is injured or becomes ill while traveling it can be very scary, especially if you do not know where to go for help. Good maps will often show hospitals where emergency care can be obtained.

Carry a basic first-aid kit in your vehicle or motorhome and check it at least every six months to replace any items that are out-of-date.

Carry a list of poison control centers (you can print one right from the Internet). If you suspect a poison-related incident, call the center closest to your location (from a cell phone or pay phone) for directions on care or information on the nearest emergency care.

Prevent Injury

Take the same precautions in your RV as you would at home:

- Keep poisonous substances out of the reach of children, or in locked cabinets.
- Turn the handles of pots and pans away from the edge to prevent a young child from grabbing one and getting burned.

- Check the temperature of hot water coming from the taps to prevent scalding.
- Do not put young children in upper bunks without bars to keep them from rolling off the edge.
- Watch children closely around swimming pools to prevent drowning.
- Never leave young children alone outside in wilderness areas where wild animals may wander.

 FACT

Even young children can learn what to do in case of fire. Have a fire drill on a regular basis and make it fun. Give a reward for the fastest escape. Children who know what they need to do in emergencies are less likely to panic if one occurs.

CHAPTER 15

Plan for Emergencies

NO MATTER HOW WELL YOU PLAN FOR TRAVEL, emergencies can happen when you least expect them. That is why it is always prudent to plan ahead on how to deal with them. Proper preparation requires having up-to-date information and also on running safety drills when necessary. Being prepared can help eliminate some of the panic that can occur in crisis situations and also prevent the injuries and damage that may result.

RV Safety Features

When you are at home or in your car on the road, you will be dealing with many different situations or factors that can affect your safety. The same is true when you are traveling in your RV. Weather, fire, and traffic accidents are all hazards that can affect your safety while traveling. Most RVs, especially newer RVs, are well built and very safe, but accidents do happen and it is good to know that your RV is prepared for those times.

Propane Gas

Liquid propane gas (known as LP) is used in your RV to cook food, heat water, and also cool your refrigerator. While many people travel with the gas on to help keep food cooled, it is much safer to turn off the gas while the RV is in motion. LP gas is highly volatile; should the gas line be broken during an accident or other incident, a single spark could trigger a devastating explosion and fire. Most modern refrigerators will keep food cool for long periods if the door is not opened too frequently. Stay safe and turn off the gas while traveling.

Fire Extinguishers

All new RVs will have a fire extinguisher as a part of their standard equipment. According to the rules mandated by the National Fire Protection Agency (NFPA), RVs are required to have a 5-pound BC-rated fire extinguisher near each exit. Make sure you know how to use it! Here's a tip: A fire usually starts at the front of the rig and moves to the rear.

 ALERT

Besides knowing where the fire extinguishers are, learn how to use them. If a fire were to break out, that is not the time to start reading the directions.

You should carry four to five extinguishers in your RV (this will depend on the type of RV). This usually means purchasing additional extinguishers unless you have a very generous and safety-conscious RV dealer. Fire extinguishers should be placed in the following areas:

- The driver's compartment
- The kitchen
- The bedroom
- Under the coach in a storage compartment
- In your towed vehicle

If you travel with children, make sure that they know where the extinguishers are located; if they are old enough, they should know how to operate them. Make sure that children understand that extinguishers are not toys and are only to be used in case of fire.

Escape Routes

Safety regulations state that *Emergency Exits* must be a part of all RVs; one such escape route is designed to be opposite the door or entrance to the RV, while the other route of escape must be in the bedroom area. Basically, what this means is that the occupants of an RV must have two ways out of every separate room.

Besides the door, there are windows that function as escape routes in case of fire. They are large enough for most adults to crawl through and have latches that allow the window to fall out of the way while you escape.

 ALERT

Have fire drills on a regular basis, especially if you have young children who may need to have the information reinforced. Emphasize that they need to get outside and away from the RV—even a small fire can quickly grow out of control.

Emergency Kits

Every RV traveler should carry those items that are necessary in case of emergency. Depending on where your travels take you, these supplies may vary somewhat, but should include items that will enable you to survive without help for a few days, or to repair your RV in the event of a breakdown in a remote area.

The most important advance in obtaining help in the event of emergency is a technology we are quickly taking for granted. The humble cell phone can put you in touch with help at the push of a button. With the decreasing prices and expanding service areas available today, RV travelers should consider a cell phone a necessity rather than a luxury.

Be sure to keep your phone charged at all times, and invest in a car charger that will keep the phone charged while you are on the road. Invest also in an earphone accessory that allows for hands-free phone operation as you are going down the road.

Tools

You should carry tools with you for simple repairs that can get you to an RV service center. A basic set of tools should include:

❑ Bright spotlight
❑ Emergency red flashing light
❑ Car adapter or batteries for the lights
❑ Extra car fuses
❑ Tire pressure gauge
❑ Hammer
❑ Various screwdrivers
❑ Allen wrenches and a crescent wrench
❑ Pliers
❑ Can of tire sealer inflator
❑ Flashlight signal cone
❑ Booster/jumper cables
❑ 12-foot tow rope
❑ Battery terminal brush
❑ Emergency rain poncho
❑ Well-stocked first-aid kit
❑ Emergency blanket (fire resistant)
❑ Roll of PVC tape
❑ Emergency water bag
❑ Rain poncho
❑ Assorted cable ties
❑ Siphon pump
❑ SOS banner

You may also want to bring along some ready-to-eat meals, which have a long shelf life. These are similar to the MREs (Meals

Ready to Eat) that are a staple of the military in the field. They can supply adequate nutrition for a few days until help can be obtained if you are stranded in a remote area.

 ALERT

Clean water is the most important nutrient you will need if stranded or injured. Humans can live much longer without food. Use water sparingly whenever possible so that you can preserve it for drinking only if you become stranded and help is a long way off.

Tracking Bad Weather

If you watch the news at all, you know that although predicting the weather has improved over the last few years, it can still be an inexact science. Whenever storm systems crop up that could produce dangerous weather situations, it is difficult, if not impossible, to predict the exact area where they will occur. Most forecasters can only give a general area where the conditions are ripe for events such as tornadoes or hurricanes.

No matter how carefully you plan your trip, bad weather can seemingly pop up without warning. It is up to you to stay alert and informed to help prevent injury if bad weather occurs.

Keep Your Eye on the Sky

Be observant as you are driving. If the skies ahead are dark with ominous clouds looming in the middle of the day, you can be almost certain that you will be driving toward bad weather. How bad or dangerous a storm you are looking at is much harder to determine, unless you have accurate weather information.

One of the most valuable devices you can buy for your RV travels is a NOAA Weather Radio receiver. NOAA Weather Radio (NWR) is a nationwide network of radio stations that continuously broadcasts current weather information directly from a local National Weather Service office. The network broadcasts National Weather Service warnings, watches, forecasts, and other hazard information 24 hours a day. To receive NWR, you need to have a special radio receiver or scanner capable of picking up the signal. You can find these at electronics stores, at many RV and camping equipment stores, or through mail-order catalogs or the Internet.

 ALERT

> Many of the NOAA Weather radios come equipped with a feature that allows you to leave the radio in "standby" mode until an alert is issued by the National Weather Service. When that happens, an alarm sounds, followed by an audio message that gives the details of the alert.

NWR also broadcasts warning and postevent information for all types of hazards. These include natural disasters (such as earthquakes and volcano activity) and manmade crises (such as chemical releases or oil spills).

Be alert for reports of heavy rains and flooding. Do not drive into areas that are under any amount of water. Many dry areas in the Southwest States are subject to flooding during certain times of the year. If heavy rains occur while you are on the road, pull over when it is safe and wait out the rain.

Driving in high winds can also be dangerous in a high-profile vehicle like an RV. Slow down and stay alert. If winds and cross-winds start pushing your rig around, it is time to pull over and wait it out.

Snow and ice are also very difficult for RVs to traverse safely. Drive cautiously or just pull over and wait it out during more severe conditions.

Medical Emergencies

Medical emergencies can happen anywhere, especially if you have a chronic illness. If you plan on traveling and plan on enjoying your travels, try to stay healthy:

- Have a checkup at least yearly and more often if recommended by your physician.
- Follow your doctor's order concerning medications and recommendations for medications and diet.
- If you are overweight, ask your doctor for information on weight loss diets that are appropriate for your health status.
- Stop smoking.
- Educate yourself on the signs and symptoms of conditions that require immediate medical intervention, such as heart attack and stroke.
- Take a Red Cross first-aid class to help provide immediate aid on the spot for medical emergencies and accidents.
- Wear a medical alert bracelet to notify first responders of any special medical conditions or needs.

If you are planning on camping in a remote area, do not do it alone. Use the buddy system to ensure that help can be obtained if an emergency should arise.

Heart Attack and Stroke

Heart attack and stroke are major medical emergencies and among the leading causes of death among adults over the age of sixty-five. Learn to recognize the symptoms that you or your travel companion may exhibit if you are suffering from either of these conditions.

Heart Attack

Some or all of these symptoms may be observed:

- Pale, sweaty skin
- Cyanosis (blue discoloration) of the lips or nail beds
- Complaints of chest pain or heaviness—it may be either sharp or dull
- Pain on the inside of the left arm or left lower jaw
- Shortness of breath
- Pain that mimics indigestion but does not subside with antacids

If you observe someone with these symptoms, call for help (911 if available) and stay close to provide assistance. Help the person to a comfortable position as he or she wishes. Know CPR and be prepared to provide it if the condition progresses to a stopping of the heart.

 ALERT

Taking an aspirin at the first sign of a heart attack has been shown to decrease permanent damage to the heart by about 30 percent. Under no circumstances, should you give aspirin to someone suspected of having a stroke. Aspirin is a blood thinner and, in some cases of stroke, can cause more damage.

Stroke

Stoke is a condition in which brain damage is caused by either blockage of a blood vessel by a blood clot, or by bleeding into the brain caused by rupture of a blood vessel. If treatment is initiated early in the event, full or near full recovery can be expected. If treatment is delayed, paralysis or death may occur.

Some of the symptoms that may be seen include the following:

- Slurring of speech
- Inability to move one side of the body
- Double vision

- Difficulty swallowing
- Severe headache

Call for help immediately or get the victim to an emergency room as soon as possible.

First Aid

The independence of RV travel also means that you often have to fend for yourself in the case of injury or illness. Many experts recommend that at least one adult in the family take a basic first-aid course. This is especially important if you are camping in wilderness areas, where it may be a long distance to any type of health care facility.

You should also carry a basic first-aid kit in your RV on all trips, no matter how long. Add the first-aid kit to the list of things to check every year.

You can buy a well-equipped first-aid kit at stores like Wal-Mart. They come equipped with all the supplies you will need for providing basic first aid while on the road.

If You Are Lost

Despite your best efforts, it is still possible to get lost while traveling. There is nothing more frustrating at the end of a long day than to discover that you don't know where you are. Even the most up-to-date maps can be made obsolete by the whims of road construction and weather.

Try to limit your driving times to daytime hours if possible. If you do become lost, it is much easier to find help and directions during the day. Many smaller towns have few establishments that stay open late and you may not be able to get help with directions.

If you are a member of AAA or some other auto club, you can contact their roadside assistance for help with directions. You will need to be ready to tell them the address or location you are at, but they should be able to help you.

If you do need to stop to ask for directions, make sure you can do it in a safe manner. Most gas and service stations are a safe bet. Park in an area that is well lighted with easy access to the road, especially if the area does not seem especially secure or safe.

 ALERT

> If you are unable to find a place to ask for directions that appears safe, keep your eyes open for a police station or for a police car. Public safety officers are a great resource for directions.

If all else fails, consider stopping for the night if it especially late. Spending hours wandering around trying to find your way only leads to fatigue and frustration. Even a less than desirable campsite can provide you with a place to get some well-needed rest.

Staying in Touch

It is very important to stay in touch with family or friends while traveling. If you were to become sick or have an accident, access or information about your health history could be important. While you should carry this information with you while traveling, a second set at home is also important if those records are lost or destroyed.

Many travelers now carry cellular phones on their trek. These compact devices have become one of the most popular and efficient ways of staying in touch while on the road.

If you plan on traveling for long periods to destinations far from home, a nationwide plan is probably the most cost efficient for you.

Many people are canceling their land-based service as they find that cell phones meet all their needs, often at a lower cost. If you are frugal with your calls and try to call when you have free air time, it can be a real cost savings.

 FACT

> Online services like Yahoo! and Hotmail offer free e-mail accounts. Even if you don't have a computer, you can sign up online at your local library and use your account to pick up and send e-mail from online computers wherever you go.

If you plan to travel outside the United States, you can purchase additional cell-phone coverage for Canada or Mexico. Your financial situation and the amount of time you plan on spending outside the country should be taken into consideration when purchasing these additional services.

You can also stay in touch by e-mail. Many campsites have or are adding service to let their visitors log on. If you do not travel with a computer or cannot get access at your campsite, the public library is another option. Most have computers with Internet connections. While they may limit the time you can use them, you should have enough time to send a few e-mails.

Stop for Sleep

While official estimates place the number of sleep-related deaths at about 3 percent of all fatal crashes, some feel the numbers are grossly underreported. RV owners are not immune from this type of crash.

According to Florence Cardinal at About.com Sleep Disorders, "Drowsiness impairs a driver's reaction time, his judgment, and even his vision. Some drivers may fall asleep for very brief periods. Others will become so drowsy and fatigued they will actually fall sound asleep without realizing they have a problem. Drowsy driving is as dangerous as driving drunk, and not nearly as easily detected." The size and weight of RVs does give the RV occupants more protection in case of accident, but it also puts any other vehicles involved at a severe disadvantage. A compact or subcompact automobile hit by a motorhome is very likely be a death trap for the driver and occupants, while the RV occupants may walk away unharmed or with only minor injuries.

 QUESTION?

What causes sleep disorders?
Sleep disorders can have various causes, including some medications or obstructions from being overweight. These disorders can be diagnosed by your doctor or a specialist and are treatable.

A law passed in New Jersey takes aim at sleepy drivers by allowing them to be charged with reckless driving. The law allows prosecution of drivers who fall asleep at the wheel or who have an accident and have not slept in twenty-four hours. Other states following New Jersey's lead are considering similar laws.

Many people are chronically sleep deprived, either because of lifestyle choices or due to sleep disorders. If you find you are always feeling tired, even after sleeping for several hours, see your doctor. A checkup may reveal a sleep disorder that may be corrected with a medical procedure or a device designed to improve sleep.

The best way to prevent sleep-related problems while you are traveling is to set a reasonable schedule of driving and stopping. Pace your trip. If you want to visit a far-flung destination, set aside a reasonable length of time for travel. If you cannot set aside enough time to safely cover the distanced needed, save that destination for another time. There are no magic pills or tricks that will keep you awake behind the wheel. While you may get advice such as open a window for fresh air, drink a caffeinated beverage, or try blasting the radio, experts will tell you the only thing that will help a sleep-deprived driver is sleep.

Plan your trip with the goal of covering no more than 250 miles per day. Ideally 100 to 150 miles per day is best. If you must drive farther, plan on having at least two qualified drivers taking turns behind the wheel. If both drivers are exhausted, it is time to stop and sleep. You are bringing your bed with you, after all; it is the foolish traveler who falls asleep at the wheel with a bed just a few feet behind him.

 FACT

Sleepy drivers are the main reason that Wal-Mart parking lots have become so popular with RV owners. They are generally well lighted and are often patrolled by a security guard. If you explain that you are just going to catch a few winks to prevent falling asleep behind the wheel, you will probably be left alone for a few hours of sleep.

Crime Prevention

For the most part, RV travelers are an honest group of people. It is the other folks you come into contact along the road that you often have to worry about. Taking some simple precautions can help prevent the savvy RV owner from becoming a crime victim.

Leave Valuables at Home

RV windows and doors are not as secure as your locks at home. To provide an additional emergency exit, every RV has at least one window that can easily be pushed out from the inside and is big enough for an adult to crawl through. This unfortunately makes for somewhat easier access into the RV. Do not bring expensive jewelry or other belongings along unless it is absolutely necessary. Avoid large amounts of cash, use credit cards when possible, and bring along an ATM card for obtaining cash along the way. You will find ATM machines in most cities in the United States and Canada that work with your card. With advances in technology, out-of state checks are accepted more readily in most places.

 ALERT

If you can't leave home without a precious valuable, make sure to have a safe place to keep it. Some of the high-end RVs come with a built-in fireproof safe. If you add one of these after-market, make sure it is inconspicuous and out of the way.

Rest Stop Bandits

Out-of-the-way rest stops are favorite places for those with a criminal bent to prey on innocent travelers. If you must stop at one of these places to catch a few winks before you fall asleep behind the wheel, try to find one that is not totally deserted. Park your RV in an area that is well lighted, preferably near other RVs or big rigs. Lock your doors and windows. If you have a motorhome, don't venture outside if you don't have to. If someone knocks on the door saying they are law enforcement, demand to see proof before you open the door.

If you feel uncomfortable, leave just as soon as you can grab a few winks and try to move on to a location that instills a greater sense of security.

CHAPTER 16

Find the Right Campground

CONSIDERING THAT THERE ARE THOUSANDS of campgrounds dotting the countryside, finding the perfect place to stay should not be difficult. Unfortunately, not all campgrounds are created equally. There are ways for you to find the perfect place to set up your RV and enjoy your travels.

Campground Directories

There are several campground directories you can purchase with listings of campgrounds organized by state or region (or by province or region in Canadian directories). You should plan on carrying at least one (or more) of these directories in your rig at all times.

These directories should be an integral part of your resources for trip planning. Used along with a good, up-to-date map, they will make your trip planning easier. You can find these directories at most bookstores, usually in the travel section. You can also find them at large RV and camping stores (such as Camping World) and at many of the large truck stops found along most major interstate highways.

The best-known and most popular directories are the *Trailer Life Campground Directory* and the *Woodall's Campground Directories*. These directories, which could be mistaken for the yellow pages of a large metropolitan city, contain listings for private campgrounds indexed by state or province. Both update their directories every year with any changes in rates, dates of operation, and amenities. The *Trailer Life Directory* is also available on a CD-ROM for your computer. If you are concerned about weight, this might be a better option, especially if you are traveling with a laptop computer. The *Trailer Life Directory* in book form weighs five pounds, as compared to the CD, which will only add a few ounces at most.

Here are some available guides that you may want to look at purchasing as resources for your travels:

Woodall's Campground Directories
(full North America and regional directories available)
Phone: 1-877-680-6155
Web site: *www.woodalls.com*

Trailer Life Directory
Phone: 1-800-234-3450
Web site: *www.tldirectory.com*

Anderson's Campground and RV Park Directory
Phone: 1-866-RV-DIRECT (783-4732)
Web site: *www.andersonsdirectory.com*

Wheelers Guide
Phone: 1-800-323-8899
Web site: *www.wheelersguides.com*

The RVer's Friend (lists fuel locations and camping services)
Fax: 1-727-443-4921
Web site: *http://truckstops.com/rvers.asp*

KOA Kampground Directory
Phone: 1-406-248-7444
Web site: *www.koakampgrounds.com/orderadirectory*

American Automobile Association (members only)

Web site: *www.aaa.com*

Yogi Bear's Jellystone Park Campground Directory

Phone: 1-513-232-6800

Web site: *www.campjellystone.com*

 FACT

You may want to consider carrying more than one directory. You may find campgrounds listed in one and not another, especially those that only list chain-affiliated campgrounds such as KOA or Yogi Bear.

Using the Internet

The Internet has evolved into a goldmine of resources for the RV traveler. Every day, more and more campgrounds are adding an online presence to their informational and marketing efforts. Many either advertise on campground directory Web sites or are building their own Web sites.

Along with the Web site, many campgrounds are taking advantage of the strides technology has made and are offering online reservations and payment. For those who are still leery of the safety of giving your credit card number over the Internet, you might take comfort in knowing that it is much more secure these days. Studies have shown that your credit card number is more likely to be highjacked at a restaurant than from an online transaction. If you are still not sure, most Web sites will list a phone number for reservations.

Online directories are more likely to have updated information than printed directories; a printed directory may contain information that is a year or two old depending on their policies. Do check the Web site for information on the last date it was updated; if you have it bookmarked, refresh the information when you open up the site in order to have the latest updates.

 ALERT

> When making reservations online, make sure you are getting a campsite for your needs, and check for cancellation policies. How will you get a refund if you need to cancel due to illness or other emergency?

Internet directories should list the basic amenities and services available, the dates of operation, fees, and activities. Many also have photos.

These online directories are a good place to find information on RV campsites:

- Woodall's—*www.woodalls.com*
- RV Park.com—*www.rvpark.com*
- Go Camping America—*www.gocampingamerica.com*
- Campground.com—*www.campground.com*
- RV Central—*www.rvcentral.com*
- CampSource (Canada)—*www.campsource.com*
- Camp USA—*www.campusa.com*
- CampNet America—*www.campnetamerica.com*

Tourist Agencies

There are times when you will be ready to stop for the night, but you will not have reservations at an RV park in the vicinity. Illness or mechanical problems are among the situations that may throw the best planning off schedule. These can be the times when you end up finding either the campground from hell or an undiscovered gem.

Local and state tourist agencies are a goldmine of information on places to stay in the area. Even if you have reservations at a campsite, you may find a backup or an alternative for future trips.

Many fine campsites have small advertising budgets, especially those in areas with limited seasons. Some well-placed brochures will often garner more business, especially repeat business, if the brochure is followed up with a great camping experience.

Talk to the staff and volunteers in the tourist stops if they are staffed. They can often be a great source of information on camping areas. Ask if there are any downsides to a camp you are considering. The brochure you pick up will not show the train tracks that sit right next to the campground, ferrying miles-long freight trains every night, but a volunteer who lives in the area may be able to give you a warning about this type of situation.

State tourist agencies are also a great source for up-to-date maps. You may have to pay a small fee for these maps, but they are generally well worth the cost. Look also for information on local attractions that may not get national attention. If you enjoy crafts or quilting, cars, or county fairs, you will find information at the local tourist agency kiosk.

 ESSENTIAL

You can often find discount coupons for out-of-the-way campgrounds or services in the free papers you see at rest stops on major highways. These are an inexpensive advertising venue for owners of tourist- and traveler-related businesses.

Ask Your Friends and Family

The best recommendations for places to stay often come from friends and family. RV owners are a naturally helpful group of people. If you are considering visiting a new city or area of the country, ask another RVer and you will get some great suggestions on places to stay.

Be advised that Uncle Joe's idea of the perfect place to stay may not be what you imagined for yourself. You may get suggestions on places to stay prefaced with the words "wonderful" or "perfect," and then find yourself wondering if the person making the suggestion was even staying at the same campground.

 QUESTION?

What if I find that a park has been deceptive in advertising?
If you find a park in a campground directory making a false claim for services or facilities, you can notify the publisher of the directory. These publications need to keep the trust of their users so that they will be willing to buy an updated future edition.

Another great place to get honest information on the pros and cons of RV parks is the Internet. One of the best places to get unbiased reviews of RV parks and campgrounds is on the Web site *www.rvparkreviews.com*. This site does not allow RV parks to advertise because that could affect the reviews, and it does not allow campground owners to post reviews. There are more than 5,000 reviews on the Web site, covering the entire country.

The site is organized by state and then by city (the city nearest the park if it is in a rural area). This could be a great place to get a recommendation for parks in an area you are unfamiliar with or in an area you have visited but were unhappy with the place you stayed.

As with any recommendation, these reviews are based on the needs and perceptions of the person writing the review. Their needs and expectations may be very different, but overall, most are honest and straightforward in their comments. Consider the following comments on the same park in the Phoenix, Arizona, area.

> "   *This is a very interesting park, considering it
> is next to Picacho Peak (a national monument)
> and approximately halfway between Tucson and
> Phoenix, and only a short distance to Casa
> Grande and the old Casa Grande ruins. We stay*"
> *there every chance we get.*

> "   *Why the low rating? Because of noise from
> I-10. We were given a site that backed up to the
> freeway and we did not sleep a wink as semi-
> trucks and traffic zoomed by all night long. Our
> RV literally shook and vibrated from the racket.
> We left the next morning. If you stay here, be sure"
> to ask for a site in the back. We won't return.*

Are Children Welcome?

While the general public may equate RV travel with retired couples
or empty nesters, more families with children are now enjoying the
RV lifestyle. Some RV parks have embraced the concept of welcoming families with children while others have not.

Some RV parks are quite open about not wanting or allowing
children. Advertising or directory listings will give clues to the focus
of the park, whether it is oriented toward adults or toward families
of all sizes and ages.

Look at directory listings for fees. If the listing says "per
family," you have a great clue that children are welcome. Look
also at the recreational activities listed. If the park has a game
room, kiddy pool, or playground listed, you can be sure children
are welcome.

Many RV parks charge an additional per-day fee for more than
two visitors per site. Some travelers feel this is unfriendly to families with children. This is a very gray area, however. In some cases,
this is a way that RV parks encourage older RV couples and discourage families with children. It may also be a way of generating

income for parks that have lower rates to entice visitors and then add on an additional fee.

You will have to decide if the park, based on its location and amenities, is worth the additional fee. If you wait to make reservations for a busy travel time, you may also have no choice in the matter if you want to travel at all.

 FACT

Additional fees for additional visitors may be justified if utilities are not metered. More people will use more water, produce more waste, and use more electricity. This is a reasonable excuse for these fees.

Playground Safety

If you are traveling with children, especially young children, safety issues are a big concern. Young children need nearly constant supervision. While you may have taken every precaution at home to safeguard your children, you have no influence over the conditions at the RV park.

Questions to Ask

If you are making reservations at an unfamiliar park, feel free to ask questions about their safety standards.

- What are the posted speed limits within the park and are they enforced?
- Is there a swimming pool? If there is a pool, is it enclosed with a high fence and locked gate? Is the pool supervised by a trained lifeguard?
- Is there a playground? Does it meet safety standards? Is it enclosed with a fence?

- What about wild animals? Are there precautions in place to keep wild animals away from campers?
- How close is the nearest medical facility? (This could be important if you have a child with a medical condition such as asthma.)

Children's Programs

The National Park Service is responsible for running and maintaining all national parks. Part of their mandate is to provide programs for all ages that help to preserve these precious natural resources for generations to come.

The park service has a program called Junior Rangers for kids ages five through twelve. Each park with a Junior Ranger program has an educational program that is set up specifically for that park, whether it is a national historic monument or a national park.

These are excellent programs that teach kids about the history of the park and the region, the flora and fauna of the area, and the geography. All this knowledge will help children appreciate and want to protect the great outdoors.

Besides educational programs, many parks have organized activities for children. Look for crafts lessons, swimming lessons, and movie screenings aimed at kids. Most park operators find that offering these programs is a great way to entice families to spend time at their parks.

 QUESTION?

Whom do I notify if a campground is unsafe?
Contact the campground owner initially for safety issues. If you do not get satisfaction from the owner, you can notify the associations they are associated with. If they are a Good Sam Park, then let Good Sam know your concerns. They may inspect the park and reduce their rating if safety problems are not corrected.

Making Reservations

There are many ways to make reservations for the parks you plan on visiting. Most campground directories list both phone numbers and mailing addresses. Generally, you will phone (perhaps they have a toll-free number) and find out about availability on the dates you are planning on traveling. This is a great time to get information on the park's amenities and ask any questions you have about the listings.

If the park accepts credit cards, you may be able to give your number over the phone. If they do not, you will need to mail payment. Payment usually needs to arrive within a specific time to guarantee the reservation. You should ask for confirmation that the payment has arrived.

You will also need to decide if you are going to make reservations for the entire stay or for just one night to see if it meets your expectations. If you are making reservations at a new campground, you may be hesitant to commit to a long stay. You will need to decide if you can risk not finding another park if it is a busy time of year.

Many RV parks now have a presence on the Internet. While some are just informational, some also have the ability to make reservations and take payment online. For RV owners who have embraced this technology, it is a very convenient option. It is also cost efficient for both the park owner and the traveler.

 ALERT

If you make reservations on the Internet, be sure to print out a hard copy of the confirmation. Many shopping carts on Web sites generate an e-mail confirmation that you can print out and save on your computer. This confirmation will help prevent problems when you arrive.

Educational Opportunities

There are numerous educational opportunities available for RV travelers who want to combine travel and learning. Older travelers especially seek out and participate in the various learning opportunities available around the country

You can even learn more about RVs and their operation. RV Life on Wheels (✑ www.rvlifeonwheels.com) runs weeklong conferences to teach both new and longtime RV owners how to operate their RVs in a safe and efficient manner.

National Parks

The National Park System is worth mentioning again for the numerous educational opportunities they provide. Docents lead nature and history programs for all ages.

Senior Summer School

This program offers various educational programs on college campuses across the country and in Canada. They are on the Internet at ✑ www.seniorsummerschool.com.

Create Your Own Educational Program

Bring along a small telescope if you can, along with a star chart. Far away from bright city lights, the night skies are much more visible. Collect unusual rocks, take pictures of wildlife and vegetation you don't see at home, and learn about a different part of the country. You can purchase bird identification books at most bookstores (the Audubon Society books are among the best) and take up bird watching as a new hobby.

CHAPTER 17

The Family Pet

IF ONE OF YOUR FAMILY MEMBERS is of the four-legged kind, you will probably want to take him along on your RV adventure. Most pets are wonderful traveling companions—just as long you provide them with the things they need to stay safe and comfortable. Traveling with pets can be challenging and requires planning, but many people would never think of leaving their family pets at home, missing all the fun.

Are Pets Allowed?

If you are planning on taking your family pet along on your next RV trip, you will need to find out if that option is feasible. As you plan your trip, think about whether having your pet along will fit with what you want to do. Be fair to your pet; don't just bring him along to save the cost of boarding. Perhaps he would be better off being boarded.

As you plan your trip and start looking at RV campgrounds, be sure to check the listing for their policy on pets. Depending on the campground directory you are using, you may get very detailed information or may just see "Pets Not Allowed" or "Pet Restrictions."

"Pets Not Allowed" is a very straightforward statement. If you want to bring your pet along on your travels, you will need to find another place to stay. Don't plan on trying to sneak a pet into a campground that does not permit them. Pets are very difficult to hide. If you are found out, you will probably be asked to leave (as that is the RV park owner's prerogative), usually without a refund (as is the park owner's right). Trying to beat the system can be expensive.

 ALERT

Some RV resorts and campgrounds are able to provide "pet-sitting" services (for an additional fee) for the pets of registered guests. Ask when you make reservations if they have this type of service available, or if they have names of local pet sitters who could come to the campground to sit on those days when you will be away from the RV for extended periods.

If your RV campground directory listing says "Pet Restrictions," you may also find a definition of the restrictions in the listing or you may have to contact the campground directly to have those restrictions defined. Some of the more common restrictions (or combination of restrictions) you may come across include:

- Only dogs allowed
- Only cats or dogs allowed
- Only one pet per RV allowed
- Only dogs under a certain weight are allowed (20 pounds is a common limit)
- Pets allowed but cannot be left alone in RVs if the owner is not in the park
- All pets must be on a leash (this includes cats)

In addition, wild or exotic pets are almost never allowed in RV campgrounds. Your pot-bellied pig may be a great pet, but she will not be a welcome guest in most RV parks. Depending on the city, country, state, or provincial restrictions, exotic pets may not be allowed in the areas you are visiting. Find someone to watch your pet ferret; don't insist on bringing him along.

 ALERT

> If your travel plans include spending some time at attractions such as big amusement parks, find out if they have pet parks or boarding for park guests with pets. Your pet would probably enjoy some human contact while you are enjoying the park, rather then being left locked up all day in the RV.

You may also need to pay an extra charge for the privilege of having your pet with you or you may have to leave a hefty "damage" deposit. An extra charge may make sense for those traveling with dogs to account for the cleanup chores some rude visitors may leave, but if the pet you travel with is a cat that never leaves the trailer you might want to protest this charge. If a deposit is required, make sure it is refundable and who decides on damage.

Be Kind to Your Neighbors

If you do bring your pet along on your RV travels, be a responsible pet owner. Your campground neighbors are not going to appreciate your dog's wandering over to their space and "doing its business" any more than your next-door neighbor at home would. If you are staying at a campground or RV park that allows pets, you will also have to follow the rules governing those pets if you want to stay. Most park operators take complaints seriously. If your neighbor complains about your dog barking, you will generally be the one asked either to leave or to move to another space.

Many parks have designated areas for "toileting" your dog. You may or may not have to clean up waste, but generally it is required.

Doggy waste can be very toxic to grass (think about those patches of brown grass in your own backyard), and if there is a lake nearby for swimming it may also be unsanitary.

If the park rules state you need to clean up after your own pets, do it! Chances are there will not be "potty police" stationed in lookouts around the camp trying to catch offenders. Just think, though, how you would feel if you were out walking in the evening and you saw that offending brown mound on the ground.

When you take your dog out for a walk, carry along some bags for collecting and containing their waste. One or two (doubled) grocery bags do a great job of collecting the waste. Once you have collected the waste, tie off the bag and then dispose of it in an outdoor receptacle (many parks do provide waste receptacles near dog runs) and continue your walk. You may want to carry two sets of bags, as some dogs may go more than once during a walk.

 ALERT

Be very careful when chaining up your dog. Tying a chain around a tree trunk could cause significant damage to the tree and, if the dog is tied up for a length of time, damage to the grass around the tree. You may want to bring along a heavy steel stake for the chain. When using a chain, make sure you have one that is heavy enough to restrain your dog.

It will also be your responsibility to keep your dog on a leash or chained at all times. RV park owners do not want guests' pets running wild around their parks, nor do other guests. Not all travelers are animal lovers. If your dog should jump up on an older visitor using a cane or walker and knock her over, you could be liable for damages.

Best Bets for Travel

Is there a perfect pet for travel? Ask any group of RV owners that question and you are going to get a different answer from them all. The most popular pet by far for travelers are dogs.

There are some who do travel with cats, but generally they are not quite the travelers that dogs are. Cats are very much creatures of habit, and most don't like to be taken out of their environment. There are stories of families who have moved cross-country and had a cat disappear and show up at their old home years later.

Remember that you will need to account for the weight of your pet when adding provisions and luggage to your RV. If you plan on traveling with your 200-pound mastiff, that is 200 pounds of luggage, water, or provisions that you will not be able to carry with you. The other consideration is space. The bigger the dog, the more space he takes up. If your dog is used to sleeping with you in your king-size bed at home, how will you manage in an RV-size bed? If you are pulling a fifth-wheel trailer with a crew cab truck and two children, where will the dog sit? These are all things you need to consider.

 FACT

Animals can get homesick, just like young children. You might bring along a favorite toy, pet bed, or blanket. Older dogs especially don't always cope well with changes and something familiar can ease the anxiety.

What do you do with the dog that does not like to ride in a car? How will you get him to travel long miles in an RV? If you plan on having a traveling dog, it is best to start her traveling when she is very young. The noise and confined spaces of cars and RVs tend to frighten many dogs, and they need to be acclimatized on short trips that get progressively longer.

Some breeds of dogs are naturally very anxious and high-strung. When traveling they tend to pace and pant. They never seem to get used to traveling. You may want to talk with your vet about a sedative or tranquilizer to use when traveling. These medications will help ease the dog's anxiety and let him sleep while traveling.

If you have an RV and are considering getting a pet to travel with you, you might want to consider a smaller dog of a breed that tends to be fairly calm and comfortable when meeting new people. Obedience school is highly recommended to teach your new pet proper manners.

If you don't want to have to worry about house training and accidents, stay away from very young dogs. A dog older than six months is much easier to train. Puppies are willing but often do not have the needed control. Puppies are also notorious for chewing on things. Once they have their adult teeth, this behavior usually stops.

ESSENTIAL

Some dogs, especially young ones, suffer from motion sickness when traveling. Your vet can give you a supply of medication that will prevent motion sickness. Give it to the dog at least thirty minutes before you get on the road. Be sure to cover the car seat or floor with an old towel—just in case.

Keeping Shots Up-to-Date

If you will be traveling with your family pet, it is very important that he be healthy and have up-to-date shots. Your dog should have a health checkup annually and have any shots updated at that time. This is probably the most important thing in keeping your pet healthy and safe.

Ask your vet about special precautions for certain parts of the country you may be visiting. Lyme disease is spread by deer ticks found in certain areas. Lyme disease can be deadly for pets. Fortunately, there is a vaccination that can prevent your pet from contracting this disease.

If you are camping in a wilderness area, where rabies could be prevalent among the wild animal population, be sure that your pet is up-to-date on her rabies vaccination and that she is wearing an up-to-date tag. If you become separated from your pet, or if she is attacked by a rabid animal, that tag could mean the difference between life and death.

If you have a dog, be sure to have the vet check his teeth and clean them if it is time. Not only will it keep that doggy breath a little fresher, but it will help to preserve teeth by preventing gum disease. Healthy teeth will help your dog eat better and improve his overall health.

 FACT

Be a responsible pet owner and have your dog or cat spayed or neutered. There are too many unwanted animals running loose or being euthanized in shelters every year. No one really wants to deal with a pet in heat while traveling, especially as it may bring unwanted wild animals to your campsite.

Healthy Travel Tips

Here some other things to consider to ensure a happy, healthy RV trip for your pet.

Never leave your pet alone in your RV during warm weather. Even with an open window, the temperature in the car can rise to over 120 degrees in just a few minutes. If you have a motorhome or other RV with a generator, you can run the air conditioner when necessary.

Ask your vet or other RV owners for the names of veterinarians in the area you will be traveling to. If your pet is ill or injured, it can be reassuring to have a place to get treatment that you can trust.

Bring along first-aid items for your pet. Include hydrogen peroxide, cotton swabs, any medication the pet is taking, and tweezers (for removing ticks).

Your dog may pant more due to travel anxiety and will need more water because of this. Be sure you always keep an abundance of fresh water available for your pet.

Make frequent stops for bathroom breaks. If your pet is drinking more water, he will need them. He will also enjoy the chance to get out of the vehicle and move around (on a leash, of course).

Dogs especially do not react well to a change in diet. If your dog is used to a certain brand of food, be sure that you can get it where you are going, or take enough along for the trip.

Be sure your dog or cat is up-to-date on their flea or tick medication. You may have treated the area around your home, but that may not be the case at your campground.

Never leave your pet outside on a leash by itself. If you are in a wilderness area, there may be wild animals that would love a light lunch featuring your pet.

 **ALERT**

If you are planning to travel into or out of Canada, you must have proper documentation of shots for your pet. To enter Canada, you must have a certificate from a licensed veterinarian that clearly identifies the animal and certifies that the dog or cat has been vaccinated against rabies.

Pet Health Insurance

While health insurance for you and your family is common and necessary, health insurance for pets is a fairly recent phenomenon. Compared to health insurance provided by your employer, it is fairly expensive. Many insurance policies only provide basic accident and illness coverage. Coverage for vaccinations and other preventive services may not be available or may only be available for an additional payment. Is pet insurance necessary? That is a decision that pet owners who are considering it will need to answer for themselves.

Signs of Illness

Your pet may get sick while you are traveling. A sick pet will not be a happy traveler and may disrupt your travel plans. Not all conditions require veterinary care, but some other conditions may require intervention. If your pet's symptoms persist or worsen, you may want to have a professional treat them.

The American Veterinary Medical Association, therefore, suggests that you consult your veterinarian if your pet shows any of the following signs:

- Abnormal discharges from the nose, eyes, or other body openings
- Loss of appetite, marked weight losses or gains, or excessive water consumption
- Difficult, abnormal, or uncontrolled waste elimination
- Abnormal behavior, sudden viciousness, or lethargy
- Abnormal lumps, limping, or difficulty getting up or lying down
- Excessive head shaking, scratching, and licking or biting any part of the body
- Dandruff, loss of hair, open sores, and a ragged or dull coat
- Foul breath or excessive tarter deposits on teeth

Remember the Leash

Keep at least one extra leash in your RV and one in your tow vehicle. No matter how well behaved your pet is, she needs to be on a leash whenever she is outside the RV. The only exception to this is if you bring along some type of outdoor enclosure. If there is room on your site, you may be able to have an enclosed yard or run. Never leave animals alone or unattended; they may figure out an escape route and break free.

There are some great products available for pets that are ideal for the RV traveler. You can find portable pet runs and kitty condos that keep the animal safe and sound while allowing them some freedom from the leash.

 ESSENTIAL

A great product for the traveler with a cat or small-to-medium dog is a pet enclosure call the Puppywalk from Midnight Pass, Inc. It stakes into the ground, is made with "chew-proof" netting, and is expandable with additional units. It folds up for travel and comes with its own carrying bag.

Keep your animal restrained at any time when the RV door is opened to prevent him from darting out the door and into danger. In most RV parks, you are in very close proximity to other campers, which makes them dangerous places for small animals.

Keep your animals restrained while traveling in the motorhome or tow vehicle. Just as seat belts save human lives, a pet restraint can help to save your animal's life.

There are a wide variety of restraints available. The type of restraint you choose to use will depend on the size of your pet and her travel needs. Many small dogs and cats travel quite well in kennels or carriers. Most like the feeling of security they find in an enclosed space. If your pet does travel in a carrier, remember to restrain the carrier while the vehicle is in motion. Your pet may be protected within its confines, but the carrier can become a missile if a sudden stop is made. Check your local pet store for restraint systems that work with the vehicle's seat-belt system.

You can also use a seat-belt restraint system specifically designed for pets. These restraints are actually harness systems that fit around the animal's body and attach to the seat-belt mechanism. The safest of these fit around the front legs and chest, especially for larger dogs. These restraints give the animal some freedom of movement when traveling (they should be able to stand up and lie down with it properly adjusted), but in case of an accident or sudden stop, they will keep the animal from flying around in the vehicle.

 ALERT

> If you must travel with your dog in the bed of a pickup truck, make sure it is restrained. While your dog may not try to jump out, he could go flying if you stop suddenly. You can use a restraint system that attaches to the bed, and this will keep your dog safer.

Finding Fido

Losing a pet can be heartbreaking. If your pet wanders away from home, most owners know where to find them, or know who to call for help finding them. If your pet disappears many miles away from home, the problem of finding her is compounded by the unfamiliar setting.

The best way to avoid losing your pet when traveling is to leave him at home in a kennel or with a dog sitter. The next best way is to keep him restrained at all times when outside the RV. If your pet fights a leash or has bad manners on a leash, it may be wise to think about obedience classes. These are invaluable for dogs under the age of two to three years old. Older dogs are hard to break of bad habits.

The most common reason pets get lost is because they become disoriented by all the new sights and sounds they encounter when traveling. Dogs and cats that have been used to open spaces and freedom will often find the small scale of an RV restrictive.

Most pets are creatures of habit; a change in their daily schedule can induce unwanted behavior. Try to keep them on a similar schedule to the one they follow at home. Allow them to eat and exercise on their normal schedule. Make sure you pack their favorite blanket and toys. Something familiar from home will help maintain a feeling of security.

Your pet should wear a collar with identification tags at all times. Check the collar regularly to make sure it is still strong and will not break with excess strain. It should be loose enough not to impede breathing but tight enough to stay on the dog and not slip off easily. Make sure the information is current and correct.

 ESSENTIAL

Most large pet store chains provide identification tag–making services that will produce an ID tag on the spot. Information that should be included is the pet's name, address, and a phone number to call if found. You may want to include your cell phone number; a home number is not much use when traveling.

Another popular method of identification for your pet is the implantable microchip ID. These microchips contain information about a pet that will help authorities to locate owners in case of loss. They can also include medical information on illnesses or medications that could mean the difference between life and death for your pet. The microchips are implanted under the skin by a veterinarian after being programmed with the information supplied by the owner. The procedure is relatively simple and almost painless for the pet. These microchips are very small and once inserted will not bother the animal.

Most animal control shelters have the technology in place to read these chips. How aggressively they attempt to contact owners depends on the individual shelter. They may have very limited resources available for tracking down the owners of lost pets.

 FACT

Check with your veterinarian for information on the microchip ID systems. If your vet does not provide this service, he or she may be able to direct you to another veterinarian in your area who can inject one. These microchips are relatively inexpensive, generally running less than $100.

If you have to leave the area before your pet is located, prepare to be responsible for transportation fees if and when she is found. You will be responsible for traveling to the shelter to get her and may have to pay some type of finder's fee to have the pet released.

Do not leave your pet tied up outside the RV without supervision, especially in wilderness areas. Many wild animals will find your pet a tempting meal, and even the strongest collar will prove no barrier. If you are camping in areas with large populations of wolves, coyotes, or bears, watch your animal closely and never let it run loose.

CHAPTER 18

Budget Travel

ONE OF THE GREAT ATTRACTIONS OF RV TRAVEL for
most people is its usual low cost compared to the price of expensive flights and costly hotels. There are many ways for the savvy RV
traveler to save even more money and still have a wonderful and
memorable trip. It just takes a little planning and creativity.

The Wal-Mart Parking Lot

Mention Wal-Mart on any of the online RV boards, and you will
inevitably spark a lively discussion. One of the busiest of these
forums is Open Roads on RV.net. Log in anytime, and someone
will have a comment pro or con about Wal-Mart. You will find
advice on which Wal-Marts allow overnight stays and advice on
those that don't.

Most of this discussion arises because for years Wal-Mart has
been a favorite place to stop overnight or to catch some needed
sleep before hitting the road. Wal-Mart has been an ideal place for
boondocking. RVers found secure, level places to park, with a place
to restock supplies. Although they did not encourage RVers to use
their parking lots for overnight stays, Wal-Mart generally did not discourage it either. This is understandable. Why take the chance of
offending some of your best customers?

There is a potential for RV owners to abuse the privilege, however. There are stories of RVers who pulled into parking lots and stayed for days or weeks. Rather than paying the nightly fees at an RV park, they made the parking lot their headquarters.

 QUESTION?

What does the term *boondocking* mean?
Boondocking is one of the terms RVers use to mean they are camping without any hookups. Other terms with the same meaning are "dry camping" and "primitive camping."

This type of abuse has prompted some stores, and many communities, to ban overnight stays in these areas. Before you pull in and park, check with the store manager to see if it is okay. If it is late and the store is closed, you might want to chance it, but be prepared for a knock on the door in the middle of the night. If it is a security guard or the local police asking you to move on, don't put up a fuss; you don't have a leg to stand on.

Other places that can provide a place to set up camp for a few hours (or longer in some cases) for free include:

- Truck stops
- City parks and beaches
- Friends' and relatives' driveways
- Unoccupied office buildings
- Malls

None of these places is a given. You may feel uneasy in terms of safety, or you may have a security guard knocking on your door asking you to leave. If you do not feel the place you have stopped is safe, leave as soon as you can. If you are sleepy and feel that driving any farther is dangerous, you should stop, but be sure to check that doors and windows are closed and locked.

Club Discounts

There are many clubs or groups you can join and, as a perk of membership, receive discounts on camping. There are other discounts available if you are over a certain age (senior citizen discounts) or if you are active duty or retired military. Not all offer the same level of discount and not all campgrounds offer discounts, but if you are a frequent traveler, you may want to consider one or more of these programs for saving money during your travels. Compare the cost of membership to the potential savings to determine if they are right for you. Here are a few groups to consider:

- Good Sam Club
- AAA
- KOA
- FCMA

If you or your spouse is a member of AARP, you should take full advantage of the discounts that members enjoy. A discount on the National Parks Pass is just one example.

Length-of-Stay Discounts

If you are a full-time RVer or are considering hitting the road full-time after retirement or when the kids are gone, extended stays in places may well be a part of your plans.

RV parks in the southern states and along the Mexican border are full of RV travelers who arrive in early November and stay until the last snow has melted from the ground in their northern homes.

Many of these "snowbirds" spend six months or more away from their homes enjoying the milder weather in these southern resorts. Not all of these travelers are rich or with the means to afford a second home, most are just savvy bargain hunters who have been able negotiate a deal.

Most RV park owners in the country face the ordeals of a seasonal business. Other than southern California, most areas face extremes of weather. Arizona is sunny and mild in the winter, but it turns into an oven from May through September.

 ESSENTIAL

> The Internet is a great resource when trying to save money on your travel costs. New Web sites are being added every day. Look for the Web sites of individual campsites. You may find "Internet-only specials."

Most RV owners love the snowbirds who travel south and stay put for four to six months at a time. It makes life easier and budgeting more predictable to have all those RV spaces filled rather than having to depend on the whims of overnight campers.

To encourage those long-term stays, many RV parks will offer discounts for campers who stay for a month or more. You will often have to ask for the discount and it may not be advertised, but they are generally readily available.

Many RV park owners will also give good deals to "regulars." Many people go back to the same place year in and year out. If the surroundings are pleasant, convenient, and fit your needs, staying put for a long time can make sense, both for the traveler and for the park owner. In those cases, most RV park owners are more than willing to give discounts to these regulars, who may also become close friends.

Off-Season Rates

Arizona is teeming with snowbirds in the winter, but when they migrate home, many RV park owners find they have lots of open RV sites. Many RV owners either close up or sit back for the season or offer discounts for those willing to deal with the heat.

Most popular tourist destination campgrounds have certain rates for in-season and other rates for off-season. If you can travel during times that are not considered peak, you will save money and your travels will be much more enjoyable. Avoid Disney World during the week between Christmas and New Year's and during spring break. Travel to these popular areas instead in October and January for the smallest crowds and best prices.

It is also much easier to get reservations during these nonpeak periods. Parks in the vicinity of Disney World in Florida and Disneyland in California are often booked a year in advance for peak travel times.

Campground directories may or may not show off-season rates. They generally list a range of overnight rates. Some of the difference may be based on the type of campsite (full hookups vs. partial or no hookups). But some of the range in rates may be based on peak times. Weekend rates may be higher than weekly rates and there may be minimums for weekends.

 FACT

> Some RV parks and campgrounds are listed in multiple directories. Compare the listings for these parks in the different directories. You may find a wide variance in rates between the directories. You can often use these variances to negotiate the lowest price available.

RV parks off the beaten track are also more likely to offer discounts for off-season. Parks that enjoy a full house during peak travel seasons and are located near busy highways can often compensate for the slow season due to location. Off-season slowdowns can be made up with those travelers who just happen to be driving by and need a place to stay for the night. RV parks and campgrounds off the beaten track do not enjoy this advantage. If they are not visible from the interstate, they often miss those one-night stays that can help pay the bills. Carry a campground directory and look for parks that are off the highway (but still convenient). If you pull in and see many empty spaces, don't be shy about asking for a discount, especially if you are only staying for a night or two. A place that might be insufferable for a month may be tolerable for overnight at the right price.

Work It Off

If your RV travels are limited due to income, there are ways to increase your income while traveling. This is not a pitch for some fly-by-night pyramid scheme but a discussion of some real-life ways that travelers can supplement their incomes or work off their travel expenses while enjoying their RVs.

RVs for Business Travel

If you have an RV and also travel a lot for business, you may have found the perfect combination that mixes business and pleasure. Check with your company to see if using your RV for business travel meets with their business travel guidelines. Most companies offer a per-mile stipend for use of a personal vehicle. While an RV will have higher costs for fuel and maintenance, these stipends are often generous enough to nearly cover the costs. Most companies provide guidelines or have contracts with hotels for guaranteed rates for business travel. These rates will always be much higher than the overnight rate at even the most expensive RV resort. You may be able to negotiate a higher per-mile stipend by demonstrating the savings of your RV over stays in hotels and costs of rental cars and restaurant meals. Using an RV for business travel for the small business owner is also a great way to travel in comfort, knowing you have familiar surroundings and your own bed to return to after a day's work.

If you are using your RV for business travel, you will need to keep detailed records for tax purposes. Record starting and ending mileage and keep all receipts, including those for gas purchases and food or restaurant meals. It is preferable to have an accountant prepare your taxes to be sure you take full advantage of tax laws. Unless you use your RV exclusively for business (and can prove it to the IRS), you will not be able to take a home office deduction for your RV itself or write off depreciation on the rig.

Support Your Hobby

If you are a serious artist or crafter who wants to sell your wares, an RV is the perfect way to travel to the various shows and markets that dot the country. Visit any craft show or flea market and you will find the vendor parking full of RVs, many towing trailers as well.

As with any enterprise, keeping accurate records is a must for tax purposes. You will also need to check into local and state regulations concerning resale licenses and sales tax. Be sure to do your homework before you embark on any type of business that involves selling to the public. Some states and localities are easier to sell in than others.

There are directories (national and regional) available that list flea markets and craft fairs with dates and requirements for vendors. Many are operated by event companies. Check with them for fees and requirements.

If you are a crafter who plans on working from your RV, make sure you have a craft that is compatible with an RV lifestyle. Woodwork and metalwork in an RV would be difficult. Jewelry making and other decorative crafts can be produced in an RV. The best crafts are those that do not require a lot of heavy equipment or supplies; remember the weight and storage limitations.

Finding Jobs on the Road

Many full-time RVers find work along the road of their travels to support their lifestyle. While many are able to find temporary employment in their field, others find seasonal employment at parks, campgrounds, and tourist areas. Most of these jobs are lower paid or minimum wage, but they are often enough to help the traveler meet expenses and enjoy the road. Many of these employers are more than pleased to hire temporary seasonal help from the ranks of RV travelers. They often find that these employees are more reliable and dependable than the usual temporary employees. Many seasonal employees have come back to the same jobs year after year.

 FACT

> An excellent resource for finding temporary employment while you are traveling is the *Workamper News*. A one-year subscription will run about $25. Call ☎1-800-446-5627 or log on to ✐*www.workamper.com* for information.

Many RV parks hire guests in exchange for a place to park their RV. You will often find that the person who is checking you in at arrival is also a guest at the park. Many park owners find that it is a mutually advantageous arrangement. Most RV parks are never completely full and giving up a space in exchange for work is usually mutually beneficial.

Volunteer Opportunities

Another way to get free or reduced-rate camping is by volunteering. Most national, state, and regional parks have programs for volunteers that can help you to save money as you travel.

In exchange for assignments that vary from providing basic maintenance to providing educational opportunities for other campers, volunteers have the opportunity to stay in some of the most beautiful surroundings for free.

AARP and the Good Sam Club are good sources for locating volunteer opportunities. If you are a member of either organization, look in their publications for information on volunteer positions.

The national parks have a program for volunteer positions in the more than 360 national parks they manage. This program recruits volunteers called VIPs or Volunteers in Parks. You will need to fill out an application, and a physical examination may be required for some physically demanding areas or jobs. The application process lets you highlight your interests and abilities for placement in a position best suited for you.

Most volunteers find these jobs to be both enjoyable and rewarding, if not monetarily then in the pride they bring. Many have been volunteering for years and are a very valuable resource in keeping the parks as a valuable resource for all of us.

Do You Need Cable TV?

If you are traveling on a budget, you will have to make some decisions about the luxuries you can or cannot live without. When you look through campground directories, be sure to take note of what is and is not included in the fees. Look at the park itself and decide if those extras are really necessary.

Cable TV

Is an additional fee for a cable TV hookup really necessary? Did you travel a thousand miles to sit and watch TV? If you did, you could have saved money and stayed at home. Most RVs have a TV antenna and you should be able to pick up at least one or two local channels. If you are out enjoying nature or the attractions all day, you may only want to catch the news and weather before you fall asleep at night.

If you have kids, this is a great way to encourage activities that don't involve TV watching. If you are worried about what to do with them if the weather is bad, bring along card and board games or books to read. What a great way to promote family togetherness!

Air Conditioning

Your destination and time of year will help you decide if the extra fee for running the air conditioning is worth the cost. If you are staying in a campground without shade in the middle of summer, you would probably need to have the air conditioner on, at least part of the time. If you must stay in a place where running the air conditioner is an extra charge, you may find sometimes it is billed as a flat daily fee or you may have to pay a metered charge based on the overall power used. If you are staying in Arizona in July you will need air, so look for a park that charges a flat fee rather than one based on usage, or you may end up with a bill you cannot pay.

Campground Activities

Many campgrounds that cater to families have found that videogame arcades are a great source of income. The quarters dropped into the slots can add up to a tidy little sum. If you are a parent watching the pennies, you may have a battle on your hands. The best way to avoid problems is to set the ground rules before the trip begins. If trips to the game arcade are not allowed, let your kids know it. You might want to set a spending limit—say a dollar (or some amount you are comfortable with) a day—and when it is gone, it is gone. Let your child decide whether to spend it all at once or save it for later, or to use that money for something entirely different. This can be a great learning experience in budgeting for your children.

 ALERT

While you may plan on depending on fresh air and breezes for cooling to save money on electricity costs, you may find it is neither safe nor practical. Fresh air means open windows and curtains. If you are staying in a park that is not secure or in an area that is less than desirable, you may not want to leave windows open. The cost of electricity may be worth the extra security it brings.

CHAPTER 19

Luxury Travel

SOME PEOPLE TRAVEL IN AN RV to save money. For others, an RV is an ideal way to travel in luxury while still being free to come and go as you please. They also are happy to avoid the hassles that often occur when traveling using airlines and hotels. With the many features and fine appointments that are available in the most upscale motorhomes, you can definitely travel in style as you embark on your RV adventures.

Spa on Wheels

The larger, more expensive RVs are also more luxurious. Even the lower-end Class A motorhomes are running in the $100,000 range, and the prices only go up from there. Some of the bus conversions that are available can cost five times the average cost of a home these days.

These luxury RVs come equipped with the latest, highest-quality amenities and appointments. In some rigs, you will find furniture uphol-stered in fine leather and Italian marble on the bathroom countertops.

Top-of-the-line RVs like these are often built on a bus chassis and equipped with a diesel engine. While expensive, they are well built and designed for many thousands of miles of RV travel. These are the type of RV that your favorite music star uses to tour the country in. In fact, you may need the income of Britney Spears if you want to buy one.

If you have the money, these luxury RVs are well worth the price. For the driver, they are a joy to drive rather than a nightmare, as some RVs can be. They are stable and not affected by most bad weather situations. Wet roads and wind won't send them into dangerous territory.

Because these vehicles are wide-body to start, with they are very roomy. Many of these RVs come with at least two and sometimes three slideouts, making them even more spacious. With the addition of an optional washer-dryer combination, they are truly self-contained.

 FACT

Luxury bus conversions will always be powered by a diesel engine. When buying one of these RVs, be sure that you are also getting a quality diesel engine. Look for names like Cummins or Detroit Diesel for long-lasting, trouble-free travel. The engine is not the place to skimp on quality.

Other options and amenities you may find on these luxury RVs include:

- Wine coolers
- Fireplaces
- Second bathrooms
- Security alarm systems
- Fireproof built-in safes for valuables
- Intercom systems
- Washer and dryer
- Dishwasher
- Side-by-side refrigerator-freezer combination with icemaker
- Satellite tracking systems
- Home theater entertainment systems with surround sound
- Controlled security entry

- Remote-control awnings
- Cedar-lined closets
- Built-in power inverter
- Towing service

You should remember, though, that more options equals more things that can break and require repair.

Resort Vacations

There are many RV campgrounds that should correctly be classified as luxury resorts. These privately owned campgrounds often rival exclusive resorts in the amenities they offer. They are often found in the more expensive resort areas and offer a luxury RV experience to travelers who prefer not to stay in hotels, but demand high-quality, luxurious surroundings.

These resorts are not cheap, with overnight fees rivaling many upper-end hotel chain prices. They will cost less than the nightly charges at an equivalent luxury resort, and provide many of the same benefits. You also have the comfort of your own bed and belongings and food of your own liking.

You will find that these RV resorts cater to the large Class A and bus-conversion RVs by providing pull-through concrete berths for ease of entry and setup. These sites will have full hookups, many including 50-amp services, in addition to the standard water and sewer. You will often have cable TV hookups and telephone service. You may also find attractions such as:

- Golf course with full pro shop
- Massage services
- Child-care facilities
- Self-improvement classes
- Dance classes
- Exercise facilities
- Meeting and conference facilities

- Game rooms
- Shopping
- Pet sitting
- Pool and sauna
- Transportation and discounted tickets to local attractions
- Entertainment

 ALERT

When you make reservations at one of these resorts, watch out for hidden costs. The up-front fee may only cover the basic costs of the RV site. There may be additional, (and costly) fees for the extras.

Package Vacations

Guided RV tours and package vacations are other higher-cost options for the RV traveler who is willing to pay a bit more for a vacation. There are numerous companies that offer guided tours to exotic locations or special events for a price. You will travel in a caravan with a group (the number of units will depend on the company and destination) led by an experienced guide. These are wonderful opportunities for travelers who want to be adventurous while avoiding many of the dangers of the lone RV traveler.

These package vacations can also be ideal for those who want to maximize the attractions they can see in a limited time and leave the planning to someone else. Well-established tour companies will know the best places to stay, the best sights to see, and the places to avoid.

There are many companies that offer these types of tours. Some specialize in tours to Alaska, and others in travel to Mexico and Central America. There is even one company that offers major league baseball tours. This tour was offered for the first time in 2003, as a group of dedicated fans traveled in a caravan for three months and took in thirty major league baseball games. Have you dreamed of following the Lewis and Clark trail or sitting in the bleachers watching the Rose Bowl Parade? You can find a company that offers just about any tour that you might imagine.

Talk with friends to find the best company for your needs. If someone has had a bad experience with one of these companies, you may want to ask for references before booking a tour. Be sure to ask about cancellation polices and contingency plans for bad weather, emergency situations, and other events that could affect your trip. Get the details in writing of what is included.

 FACT

There are some companies that include all activities planned in the overall cost of the trip and some that offer these as options that you pay for separately. This is a good option; you may not be interested in participating in every activity offered and may want more flexibility.

For the inexperienced RV traveler in particular, guided RV tours are wonderful. This is a great way to gain experience in the actual day-to-day operation of your rig with an expert nearby to help with problems.

If you are planning a trip to Mexico or Central America and you are worried that the language difference can cause problems, these tours are an excellent choice. Experienced guides can help communicate with the local people, and they can prevent you from traveling to places that are less desirable, or even dangerous. If you have a problem or accident, the guide can help you avoid being ripped off because of the language difference. Your rusty high school Spanish class will be of little use to you if you have a major breakdown with your rig.

Always check on cancellation policies. Illness, emergencies, and natural disasters cannot be planned. A well-established company with a good track record may cost more but give better values in the long run.

 FACT

There are some tour companies that can supply you with a rental RV for the duration of the tour (at additional cost, of course). If you are not an RV owner but are considering buying one, this could be a great way to try out the lifestyle.

Theme Park Camping

Visiting one of the many theme parks around the country is a great way to spend a family vacation. Using your RV as home base lets you have a place to wind down in familiar surroundings and avoid expensive restaurants. Theme parks are very expensive, although they do offer a lot of entertainment for the whole family.

Disney World

Disney World in Orlando, Florida, leads the list in theme parks for families, especially for RV families. Disney World has some of the best hotels in the Orlando area and Disney's Fort Wilderness Resort & Campground is their offering for RV travelers. They boast 784 private back-in lots that are equipped with hookups for essentials like water, electricity, and sewer. You'll have a level, paved driveway pad, parking for one vehicle, a picnic table, and a charcoal grill.

Fort Wilderness is one of the more expensive campgrounds. Its prices range from around $40 per day in the off-season to over $80 per day during the most popular times of the year. It also books up quickly for certain periods; the most popular vacation times, such as the week between Christmas and New Year's, are often booked a year in advance.

The resort features two swimming pools, nightly campfires, and many daily activities. This is a great choice for families with children. Disney does vacations the right way—though you will pay top dollar for it.

There is free transportation to and from the various Disney parks available from this RV camp. Especially appealing for families with young children is the opportunity to visit the theme park at your leisure. If a young one is getting tired and cranky, just hop on the shuttle back to your RV for a nap or just to wind down after the excitement of the rides. You can return to the park later in the day for more fun. Just be sure that you get your hand stamped for re-entry.

Remember that there are many other attractions in the Orlando area besides the Disney World attractions. Universal Studios and its Islands of Adventure are entertaining and popular family theme parks you may want to visit. If you plan on including these attractions in your visit, make sure there is transportation available when choosing a place to stay. If you stay at Disney's Fort Wilderness, you will be on your own for transportation to other attractions in the Orlando area.

The Disney theme park in California is much older and in an area that is more built up and urban. It does not have its own RV resort, but there are many very nice RV campgrounds in the vicinity. Southern California is another very popular tourist area that offers many amenities to the traveler. Once again, check for transportation to the various local attractions.

Travel to these popular tourist destinations requires advanced planning. If you are able to travel off-peak, you will find a better selection of places to stay with better rates. If you are traveling at peak times, you will pay premium rates.

Join a Travel Club

There are many travel clubs available for RV travelers, some with the budget-minded traveler in mind, and others that cater to the more upscale and luxury-minded traveler. There are also clubs for owners of specific types of RVs. The most important part of belonging to these clubs for many is the experience of getting together with like-minded people, making friends to possibly travel with and socialize with on the road.

Another advantage to joining one of these clubs is that very often RV owners are able to get discounts and group rates on items like insurance and service that are not available to the lone traveler.

The best-known of these RV travel clubs is the Good Sam Club. It began in 1966 when a group of RV owners put Good Samaritan bumper stickers on their rigs so that fellow members of the club would know they could get help on the road. From those humble beginnings, it has grown to more than one million RV families. Some of the benefits include:

- One year subscription to *Highways* magazine
- Discounts at over 1,600 RV parks and campgrounds in the United States and Canada
- Discounts on RV parts & accessories at hundreds of RV service centers
- Discounts on long-distance telephone services
- Discounts on eye exams, contact lenses, and eyewear
- Local chapters
- RV trip routing
- Mail forwarding
- Preferred member rates on RV and auto insurance
- Good Sam RV Emergency Road Service (at additional cost)

Local chapters are plentiful and many hold gatherings or rallies called Samborees that offer programs that include live entertainment, craft shows and classes, contests, games, seminars, tours, and food. Usually held over a weekend, these offer a great opportunity to get together with other RV owners. Many clubs offer seminars that can help the do-it-yourselfer brush up on the latest and greatest tools and methods of RV repair. Additionally, at these gatherings, you will meet people with many different brands of RVs. It is a great place to get a recommendation from the owner's mouth on the pros and cons of that new RV you are considering. As one Good Sam member said after nine years of attending Samborees, "It is a friendly 'neighborhood' where you can share the RV experience and compare notes with folks just like yourself. You can meet many friendly people at campgrounds, and that's fine, but you just can't seem to beat the Samboree or rally experience."

 QUESTION?

How much do these memberships cost?
Membership prices vary from a current cost of $19 for Good Sam (if you join a local chapter, there will be an additional fee) to $35 or more for membership in clubs of owners of specific brands.

Getting What You Pay For

As always, it pays to remember the advice, "Buyers beware." If you have not inspected a campground, you will have to depend on the RV park owner to give accurate information in the advertising brochure or on the Internet site. Look out for misleading information or for those keywords that let you know that this place might not be as great as they advertise. Some examples:

"Coming Soon"—If you are making reservations in January for a trip in August, the phase "pool coming soon" does not necessarily mean the pool is under construction and will be ready for your visit. "Coming soon" could mean next week, or it could mean sometime in the next couple of years.

"Wide Sites"—Your idea of a wide RV site and the owner's idea could be literally yards apart. Look for specifics, especially if you have an RV with slideouts. If you need a site that is 35 feet wide for your rig, look for specific numbers in the listing or ask for details.

"Accommodates Slideouts"—Will the slideout that expands your bedroom put you within inches of your neighbors' living room (and loud TV)? Not all slideouts are equal. Get specifics on exact widths of the sites rather than depending on the park's estimates.

"Children's Area"—Is there a safe and fun area for your children or grandchildren to play in, or does the owner's definition of a children's play area consist of a swing set and sandbox (that stray cats may use too)?

If you book a place sight unseen, insist on looking around before you pull in and set up. If the actual park does not meet your expectations, let the owners or manager know your displeasure. An honest owner will offer a refund or rate reduction. If no refund or discount is forthcoming, you have a couple of choices. You can leave and find another place (and spend more money) or you can stay and voice your complaints. It is sometimes helpful to let the owners know that you will be letting all your RV friends and acquaintances know how disappointed you are.

 ALERT

While it may sound cynical, many people depend on creative advertising to get business in. Learn to read advertising with a critical eye. Remember, you often get exactly what you pay for. You may find you spend a lot of money trying to save a few bucks and end up with a disappointing travel experience.

CHAPTER 20

Roughing It

CAN YOU REALLY ROUGH IT IN AN RV? While dedicated tent campers might disagree, it can be done. Many RV owners travel to remote wilderness areas and live in close harmony with nature. From the smallest truck camper and foldup trailer to the largest motorhome, RVs are self-contained vehicles capable of providing shelter in all sorts of remote locations.

Wilderness Campgrounds

The vast North American wilderness areas provide many camping opportunities for those travelers who might have doors and wilderness. Many of these campgrounds are run by the federal or state governments. Canada also has vast areas of untouched wilderness that are wonderful for camping. Many of these campgrounds are free or very low priced. The National Forest Service and Bureau of Land Management administer most of these campsites. For long stays, you may need to obtain a permit. These campgrounds do not have hookups; there is no electricity or water and no sewer. Your RV needs to be self-contained. Before you decide to stay in one of these wilderness campgrounds, be sure that you are prepared. Fully charge batteries and top off your provisions at the local supermarket. Make sure you have all tanks full of gas and water, and check your propane. You may also need to carry extra water, especially if you're in a very dry, hot desert area. When adding these extra provisions, be sure that you keep within your weight limitations.

You will need to conserve your water and power while camping in the wilderness. If you enjoy long showers, then wilderness camping may not be for you. It is better to spend a day without a shower than to run out of water to drink.

RV batteries will run down very quickly. Be sure to monitor the battery power levels regularly and keep the batteries in good condition. You also might think about replacing the incandescent bulbs used in RV fixtures with fluorescent bulbs. This can save a lot of power. Check your local RV store for information on adding solar power. This can be a good way to keep your batteries charged when you are in areas that have a lot of sunlight. Keep your generator in good working condition; if you don't have one, consider buying a portable model. You should also realize that you will not be able to use your air conditioner. Plan your trip accordingly.

Isolation

Wilderness camping can be very isolating, and it can also be dangerous. If you experienced an accident or illness, would you have any way of getting help? To avoid mishaps, it is always wise to camp with at least one other couple.

If you are camping in an area that is prone to fire during dry summer months, be sure that you have a clear exit in case you have to evacuate quickly. Wildfires can spread just as fast as their name implies. Narrow, overgrown mountain roads are a road map for disaster if you do not move quickly at the first sign of fire.

Make your first wilderness camping trip a short one. You may not enjoy living without modern conveniences. Many wilderness campgrounds are far enough away from civilization that you will not pick up TV or radio signals without a satellite dish. Even with a battery-powered radio, you may be limited for entertainment. Can you put up with all that clean air, clear sky, and solitude? If your idea of a fun vacation is a whirlwind of activity and sightseeing, you may find the wilderness dull.

If your idea of the perfect vacation is listening to the grass grow and sitting in a lawn chair with a good book for hours on end, however, this could be the perfect vacation spot for you. If you are afraid your children will self-destruct without television and videogames, you may be in for a surprise. Children will adapt to new things and will probably enjoy being able to get outside and enjoy nature.

If you are prepared for the inevitable bug collections that they will want to cart home, you will find that wilderness camping is a great way to get to know your kids again. It is amazing how much you can find to talk about without the distractions of modern living drowning out their voices. Many families will tell you that often the only time they ever get together for a meal is when they are camping and away from all those distractions.

 **ALERT**

Invest in a set of good walkie-talkies that are compatible with those owned by other RV families you are traveling with. These are invaluable tools for communicating in the middle of the night when needed or if the group splits up.

Is My Rig Too Big?

Many RVs are just too big for wilderness areas. Narrow, winding roads with low overhanging trees are nearly impossible to traverse in the big rigs. If you are planning on camping in an area that can only be accessed on dirt roads, how will your rig behave in the rain? It won't be much fun trying to get a tow truck out to the middle of nowhere to pull you out, but it will definitely be expensive. Areas that are prone to snowfall (and some mountain areas get freak snowstorms in August) are also not the best places to take some of these larger RVs. It is definitely not for the inexperienced or the faint-of-heart.

Many national park campgrounds have limits on the length of RV that is allowed to use their facilities. Remember, the longer the RV, the heavier, and the more people it can accommodate. Many of the national parks are located in pristine wilderness areas. To accommodate the larger RVs, vegetation may have to be cleared for space, and the demands on resources such as water may impact vegetation and wildlife. Before you make plans to visit any of the national or state parks, find out what they do and do not allow in terms of RVs and additional vehicles at the properties.

 ALERT

If your goal in traveling to a national park is to get away from civilization and back to nature, you might want to think again. Some of the more popular parks are very crowded during peak travel times, and you may encounter more people on your wilderness trek than you do on a normal day back home.

You can find information on the national parks, including information on reservations, regulations, restrictions, activities, and services on the Internet at ✑*www.nps.gov.* The National Park Foundation chartered by Congress in 1967 to raise private support for national parks, sells guide books priced at about $20. The sale of these books and other merchandise helps to support the national parks. This support includes improvements to the facilities and establishment of educational opportunities in the parks.

Preparing for Cold Weather

Traveling in cold weather can be exciting, but it can also be perilous if you are not prepared. RV owners who live in northern areas generally do one of two things with their RV during the winter:

They store it or they travel south with the well-known migration of other RV snowbirds.

Winter camping in places like Wisconsin is difficult at the least. Most RV parks in these areas are seasonal, closing for the winter (their owners often travel south for the winter themselves). What this means is camping without hookups, depending on batteries or a generator for electricity, and carrying all the water you need.

Your RV may not be equipped for extremely cold temperatures. If you are in the market for a new RV and plan on doing any winter (cold weather) camping at all, you may want to consider buying a motorhome that has been equipped with a winter package. Most manufacturers offer this package as an option.

To be prepared for winter weather, your RV will need upgraded insulation, improved heating options, and insulated water pipes. If you have one of the larger RVs, you probably have at least two air-conditioning units. If you plan on winter camping trips, you will want two furnaces on your big rig.

 **ALERT**

According to Jim Kerr in *Canadian Driver*, your battery may need to be charged for thirty minutes just to get warm enough to accept a charge in very cold temperatures. If you are camping in this type of weather, you might want to consider using an electric battery blanket to keep your battery charged.

If your motorhome is powered by diesel fuel, you may find that your rig does not start as well in cold weather. Diesel fuel thickens when it is cold. If it is especially cold, the fuel may not flow well from the tank to the engine. If you are using your diesel rig in winter, it should be equipped with heaters in the manifold to help keep the fuel at the proper consistency. You may also consider using the winter mix of diesel fuel. Most truck-stop gas stations that cater to long-distance truckers carry this winter mix (check your owner's manual for information, as the winter mix may not be approved for your engine).

 ALERT

> The owner's manual for your motorhome has a wealth of information on the care and use of the diesel engine. Look under "cold-weather operation" for information on fuel and fuel additives that will keep the diesel fuel at the needed consistency for proper operation.

Additional Cold-Weather Tips

Here are some other things you should do when setting off on a cold-weather RV excursion:

- Keep roof vents clear. Birds love to nest in these, but if blocked they can cause a dangerous buildup of carbon monoxide.
- Add antifreeze (available at your RV supply dealer) to the holding tanks in order to prevent their contents from freezing.
- Add insulation to draperies and keep them closed to retain heat.
- Check for wear and replace weather-stripping around doors and windows if necessary.
- Camp in areas that are sheltered from the wind but allow for thermal heating from the sun.

Protecting the Environment

If you love camping in the wild, you also know how fragile some of this country's wilderness areas can be. Every summer it seems there are sensational news stories about wildfires; many are set accidentally by campers. Fires are not the only environmental damage that a careless camper can cause. The air, the water, and native animals can all be harmed by campers in RVs. The wise camper will follow the Scout example and "pack it in, pack it out," meaning that whatever you carry into the wilderness you carry out to dispose of in the proper way.

Remove Trash

Many wilderness camp areas do not have trash pickup; if they do, it may be limited. So try to reduce the amount of trash you produce. If you use disposable plates, buy the cheap thin, flimsy ones and use them with a set of reusable paper-plate holders. This type of paper plate produces less waste than the sturdier and more expensive type.

If you do use paper plates, you can burn them in your campfire (if fires are permitted). Just remember that some food wastes (like bones) do not burn and should be removed to trash bags even after being incinerated.

 ALERT

One ingenious traveler who camps in the wilderness on a regular basis with his pet dog suggests letting the dog help with the cleanup. If your dog is accustomed to eating table scraps, let it lick the paper plates before you burn or otherwise dispose of them.

Bring an ample supply of heavy-duty trash bags along when wilderness camping. Heavy-duty bags will be less likely to tear and will do a better job of containing smells. Trash should be locked up and kept away from the sleeping areas if you do not want a midnight visit from a bear.

As you are leaving, police the area and make sure that all trash is picked up. There are many things humans use regularly that can be toxic to animals.

Cooking

If you cook outdoors, be sure to follow established safety rules. In areas with a very high fire danger, any type of outdoor fire may be prohibited or limited. If you break the rules, you could face a very hefty fine if caught. You could face criminal prosecution, and even jail time, for starting an illegal fire, particularly if your actions cause harm to persons or property.

If fires are allowed, use established fire rings that are well contained. Do not start a fire when it is very windy, as a single spark has often been known to start a deadly fire. Put the fire out completely when done (don't leave a fire burning when you go to bed), and then bag up the ashes and take them out with the rest of the trash. Keep fires away from rivers and streams to prevent potentially toxic ashes from contaminating the water.

Face-to-Face with Wildlife

One of the most exciting things about camping in the many natural wilderness areas around the country is the possibility of seeing wild animals in their natural environment. Imagine sitting outside as the sun comes up, the only sounds you hear are the birds chirping as you watch deer grazing in the distance. This is the way you want to commune with nature; unfortunately, you may also meet nature in a face-to-face encounter with a bear.

Most wild animals are afraid of humans, but hunger can help overcome those fears. If you hear about drought and fire danger on the news, you may find that the wild creatures are bolder than normal. Some simple precautions can help keep your RV from being attractive to animals.

Food Storage

Store all food carefully; do not leave food in coolers outside your rig. Bears have a wonderful sense of smell and will find those coolers during middle-of-the-night food raids. Limit food waste and dispose of it in bear-proof containers that are kept well away from your rig. You can also bury food waste, although be sure it is well away from water sources and from your rig.

Mating Season

Be especially careful when wild animals may be mating and giving birth. Generally most wild animals are afraid of humans, but this fear may be much less after giving birth. As with most new mothers, bears are very protective of their young and will attack if they feel threatened.

 ALERT

> If you do find yourself face-to-face with a bear or large cat, wave your arms and yell loudly. You may scare a potential attacker off. If it is not prohibited, carry bear spray (similar to pepper spray) and keep it in hand. According to National Park Service rangers, it is very effective at close range.

Pets

If you bring along a pet, do not leave it outside alone or on hikes where you may encounter a hungry bear. A bear may be afraid of you, but your poodle, on the other hand, may look like a great snack.

The following tips are from the National Park Services program to teach children about camping in bear country, but they are commonsense tips for everyone:

Be a Noisy Hiker . . .
Sing, talk, wear a bell.
Give Bears Space . . .
Watch and photograph from a distance.
Respect a Bear's Meal . . .
Stay away from dead animals.

Keep a Clean Camp . . .
Cook and store food away from your camp.
Leave Your Dog at Home . . .
Bears and pets don't mix.

FACT

Don't be afraid to admit that the wilderness is not right for you. If you find yourself yearning for a vacation with more action and less nature, wilderness camping may not be your thing. Move to a campsite with more modern conveniences and enjoy your stay.

Natural Disasters

No matter where your travels lead you in the United States, Canada, or Mexico, you will always need to be prepared for natural disasters. There is not an area of North America that is exempt from some type of natural disaster. The key to safe and enjoyable travel is being prepared for any natural disaster that might occur.

If you are traveling with children, make sure they understand the emergency plan your family has devised. Children as young as three can often understand simple safety instructions and help to protect themselves when needed.

Earthquakes

Earthquakes most typically occur on the West Coast from Alaska to southern California. The region that skirts the Mississippi River is also at higher risk of earthquake. Although scientists have studied earthquakes for years, and more information has been gathered, earthquakes cannot be predicted or pinpointed with any great accuracy. Be prepared for earthquakes in your motorhome. Many injuries in RV accidents are caused by loose objects flying around during sudden stops. The same effect can happen during earth-quakes. Always secure items in your motorhome.

If you do find yourself rocking and rolling in your RV while camping in an RV park, stay put until the shaking stops. You are safer inside your rig away from falling branches and power lines.

If you are driving when an earthquake strikes, slow your speed to help retain control of the vehicle (the quake may cause a towed travel trailer to sway violently) and pull over when it is safe to do so. Stay inside the vehicle until it is safe to exit. Afterward, open closet and cupboard doors carefully, as heavy items may have shifted.

Earthquakes can also trigger land and rock slides. If you are camping in an area that is prone to these, you may be advised to pack up and leave quickly by park personnel or police. If you are told to leave, do so as quickly as possible even if it means leaving your RV. Possessions can be replaced, but human lives cannot.

Floods

Floods are among the most common and dangerous natural disasters that RVers may encounter. Heavy rainfall will warn you that flooding is possible, but many campers have been surprised by flooding in an area that has not seen rainfall. Heavy rains in other areas can cause rivers to rise above flood stage in areas many miles downriver. These conditions can occur anywhere but are especially common in the desert Southwest, which is subject to monsoonal rains.

You should always keep an eye on the weather and weather forecasts. Listen to the radio or watch the local news for forecasts and warnings. If a flash flood warning is issued, pack up and get out. Move to higher ground as soon as possible.

Hurricanes and Tornadoes

These greatest of nature's storms have one thing in common: high winds. Hurricanes are also accompanied by heavy rains and possible flooding (mentioned earlier). If a tornado warning is sounded, unhook from electrical power and turn off the propane.

If you are staying in an RV park, try to get to the office or another built shelter if there is time. These structures will offer more protection in high winds.

If you are on the road, seek the shelter of a highway overpass or a truck stop if one is close enough. Find a low spot to lie down in if you are in the open and a tornado is approaching.

If you are traveling and you approach an area of bad weather with thunderstorms that have the potential of spawning tornadoes, find a place to pull over and stop for a while. If you have enough time, try to locate a rest stop or truck stop with a permanent structure. This will provide a place for you to stretch your legs and possibly get a meal or snack while you wait out the bad weather with more protection than what your RV can provide.

Hurricanes generally provide more warning time for evacuation. If you are advised to leave, do so as soon as possible. Many hurricane-prone areas also have limited access with evacuation routes quickly turning into parking lots. You will find evacuation routes marked with the symbol illustrated here.

EVACUATION ROUTE SIGN

Fire

Fire is a danger in most national parks and heavily forested areas. Southern California also has a high fire danger, even in heavily populated areas. Stay alert for fires. Wildfires can move quickly and change direction without warning. If there is a fire in the area, pack up and move to another area. Don't wait until you are ordered to evacuate. At that time, you may only get out with the clothes on your back.

 QUESTION?

Where can I find information on the natural disasters in areas I want to visit?
FEMA (Federal Emergency Management Agency) has the information you need. Besides information on risks, they also have tips and precautions you can take to help protect your loved ones in case of disaster. Go online at ✎*www.fema.gov*.

RV Park and Campground Directory: The United States and Southern Canada

THE FOLLOWING GUIDE PROVIDES DETAILED information on campgrounds and parks that are well suited for RV travel in forty-nine U.S. states (Hawaii is not included) and seven Canadian provinces. Each state has dozens (and, for the most popular travel states, hundreds) of other places where you might stay during your RV adventure. These campgrounds and parks were chosen for having a good combination of services (water, sewer, electric); locations near desired tourist destinations or large cities; and as many "extras" as possible on site, such as washer/dryers, Internet access, etc.

The price you will pay to stay at these parks and campgrounds can vary, depending on many factors such as the season of the year and the number of people you are traveling with. As a general guide, we have indicated the price for an average night's stay at each park with this code:

$	under $20
$$	$20 to $29
$$$	$30 to $39
$$$$	$40 and above

It is always a good idea to call ahead to parks and campgrounds (before you leave on your trip if possible) to verify prices, availability, services, and amenities.

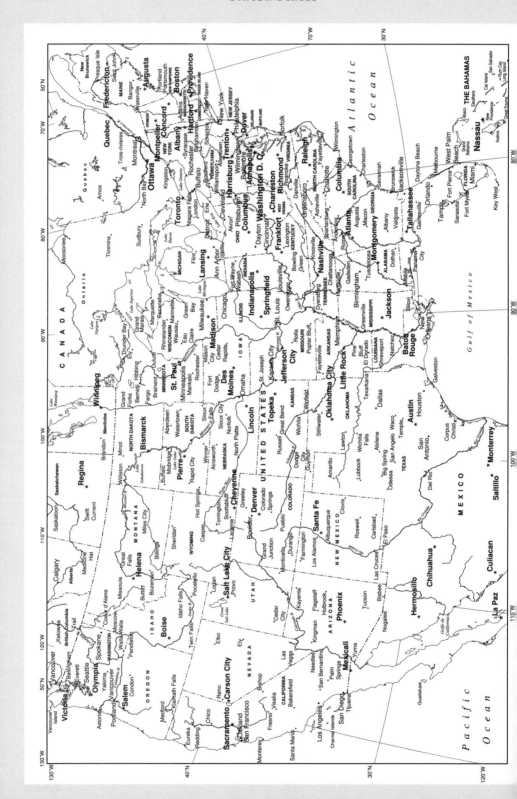

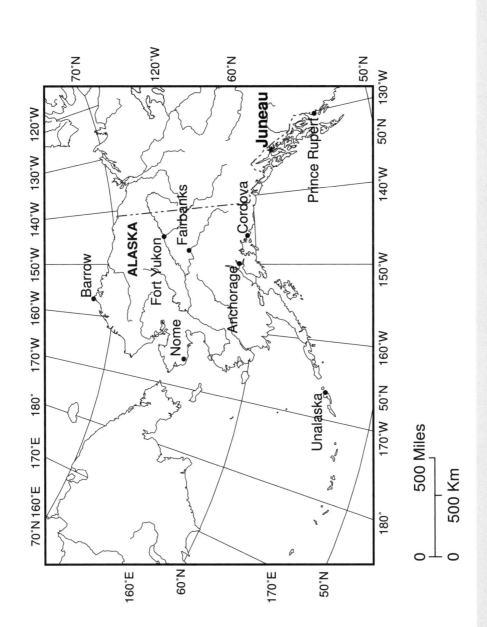

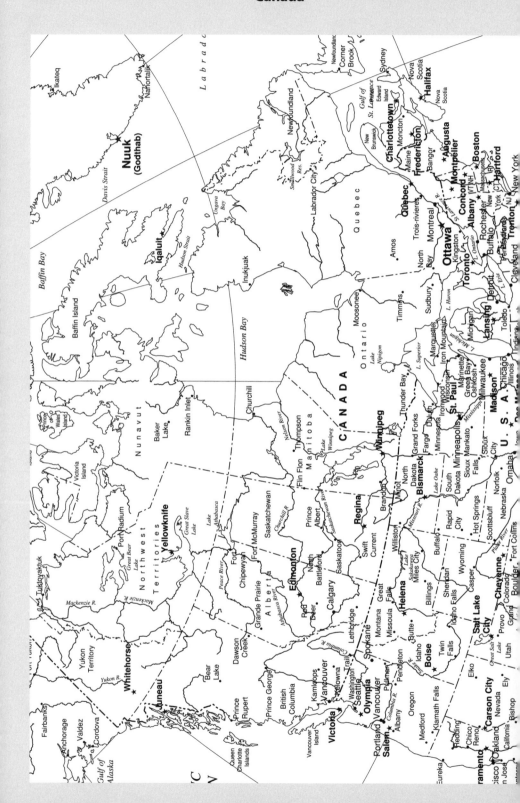

The section of campgrounds and parks for each state and province begins on the pages indicated.

United States

Southern Canada

ALABAMA

Logan Landing RV Resort & Campground
TALLADEGA (Talladega)
Phone: 888-564-2671
Web site: *www.loganlanding.com*

Directions: From I-20 (eastbound exit 158, westbound exit 158-B): Go 3½ mi. S on US 231, then 5½ mi. E on Hwy 34 (Mays Dr), then 6¾ S on CR 207 (Stemley Rd.), then ¾ mi. W on CR 54. Follow signs to PB Bryant Rd.

Description: An RV PARK with shaded, level sites on Logan Martin Lake.

Rates: $$

Number of Sites: 140

Seasonal Sites: Some Seasonal Sites

Number of Full Hookups: 110

Number of Water/Electric Hookups: 30

Number of Pull-Thru Sites: 19

Typical Site Width: 25 ft.

Services: Dump Station, LP Gas by Meter, LP Gas by Weight, Partial Handicap Access

Hookup Information: 20 amps, 30 amps, 50 amps

Amenities: A/C Allowed, Fire Rings, Grills, Heater Allowed, Ice, Laundry, Phone or Modem Hookup—Central Location, Phone or Modem Hookups at Site (need activation), Public Phone, Traffic Control Gate, Wood

Recreation: Badminton, Basketball, Boating, Canoe Rentals, Canoeing, Dock, Electric Motors Only, Fishing, Fishing Supplies, Hiking Trails, Kayaking, Lake Fishing, Lake Swimming, Pavilion, Pedal Boat Rentals, Planned Activities (Weekends Only), Play Equipment, Playground, Ramp, Recreation Hall, Rowboat Rentals, Sports Field, Volleyball

Credit Cards Accepted: MasterCard, Visa

Ozark Travel Park
OZARK (Dale)
Phone: 800-359-3218
Web site: *www.trav-l-park.com*

Directions: From jct. US 231 & Hwy 27: Go 3 mi. N on US 231 (mile marker 47-east side).

Description: RV PARK with level, paved sites.

Rates: $$

Number of Sites: 50

Number of Full Hookups: 50

Number of Pull-Thru Sites: 33

Typical Site Width: 20 ft.

Services: Dump Station, LP Gas by Meter, LP Gas by Weight, Non-Guest Dumping, Non-Guest Dumping Fee

Open: All Year

Hookup Information: 20 amps, 30 amps, 50 amps

Amenities: A/C Allowed, Cable TV, Fire Rings, Grills, Groceries, Heater Allowed, Heater Fee, Ice, Laundry, Phone or Modem Hookup—Central Location, Phone or Modem Hookups at Site (need activation), Public Phone, RV Supplies, Wood

Recreation: Badminton, Coin Games, Fishing, Fishing Supplies, Play Equipment, Pond Fishing, Pool, Recreation Hall, Recreation Room/Area, Volleyball

Credit Cards Accepted: American Express, Discover, MasterCard, Visa

Island Retreat RV Park
GULF SHORES (Baldwin)
Phone: 251-967-1666
Web site: *www.islandretreatrv.com*

Directions: From jct. I-10 and Hwy 59 (Loxley exit #44): Go 35 mi. S on Hwy 59, then 1½mi. W on Hwy 180 W.

Description: RV PARK with level & some shaded sites.

Rates: $$

Number of Sites: 172

Number of Full Hookups: 172

Number of Pull-Thru Sites: 16

Services: LP Gas by Meter

Open: All Year

Pets: Pet Restrictions

Hookup Information: 20 amps, 30 amps, 50 amps

Amenities: A/C Allowed, Cable TV, Fire Rings, Heater Allowed, Ice, Laundry, Limited Groceries, Phone or Modem Hookup—Central Location, Phone or Modem Hookups at Site (need activ.), Public Phone, RV Supplies

Recreation: Playground, Pool, Recreation Hall

Credit Cards Accepted: MasterCard, Visa

ALASKA

Golden Nugget Camper Park

ANCHORAGE (Anchorage)

Phone: 800-449-2012

Web site: *www.alaskan.com/camperpark*

Directions: From jct. Glenn Hwy 1 & Boniface Pkwy: Go 1 mi. S on Boniface Pkwy, then ½ mi. W on DeBarr, then S on Hoyt.

Description: In town RV PARK with level, open, gravel sites. Partially shaded.

Rates: $–$$

Number of Sites: 224

Seasonal Sites: Some Seasonal Sites

Number of Full Hookups: 190

Number of Electric Hookups: 25

Number of Sites with No Hookups: 9

Number of Pull-Thru Sites: 43

Max RV Length: 42

Services: Partial Handicap Access

Amenities: A/C Allowed, Heater Allowed, Laundry, Phone or Modem Hookup—Central Location, Phone or Modem Hookups at Site (need activation), Public Phone

Recreation: Equipped Pavilion, Horseshoes, Local Tours, Volleyball

Credit Cards Accepted: American Express, Discover, MasterCard, Visa
Facility Fully Operational: May–Sept.

Denali Rainbow Village RV Park & Country Mall
DENALI NATIONAL PARK (Denali)
Phone: 907-683-7777
Web site: *www.denalirvrvpark.com*

Directions: From Denali National Park entrance: Go 1 mi. N on George Parks Hwy (Hwy 3).

Description: An RV PARK with open, gravel sites.

Rates: $$$

Number of Sites: 85

Number of Full Hookups: 16

Number of Water/Electric Hookups: 43

Number of Electric Hookups: 17

Number of Sites with No Hookups: 9

Open: May 20

Close: Sep 20

Number of Pull-Thru Sites: 45

Max RV Length: 42

Typical Site Width: 18 ft.

Services: Dump Station, Non-Guest Dumping, Non-Guest Dumping Fee

Hookup Information: 20 amps, 30 amps, 50 amps

Amenities: A/C Allowed, Fire Rings, Heater Allowed, Hot Shower Fee, Laundry, Phone or Modem Hookup—Central Location, Public Phone, RV Supplies, Wood

Recreation: Fishing, Local Tours

Credit Cards Accepted: ATM On site, MasterCard, Visa

Chena Lake Recreation Area (Fairbanks North Star Borough)
FAIRBANKS (Fairbanks North Star)

Directions: From jct. Richardson Hwy 2 & Laurence Rd S of North Pole: Go E on Laurence Rd.

Number of Sites: 82

Typical Site Width: 18 ft.

Number of Sites with No Hookups: 82

Number of Pull-Thru Sites: 22

Rates: $

Phone: 907-488-1655

Services: Dump Station

Open All Year

Amenities: Fire Rings, Grills, Marine/Rec Only, Non-Flush Only, Public Phone, Wood

Recreation: Basketball, Boating, Canoe Rentals, Canoeing, Dock, Equipped Pavilion, Fishing, Hiking Trails, Horseshoes, Lake Fishing, Lake Swimming, Pedal Boat Rentals, Playground, Pontoon Rentals, Ramp, River Fishing, River Swimming, Rowboat Rentals, Volleyball

Season Exceptions: No showers.

Eagle's Rest RV Park & Cabins
VALDEZ
Phone: 907-835-2373
Web site: *www.eaglesrestrvpark.com*

Directions: At jct. Richardson Hwy 4 & Pioneer Dr in town.

Description: A level, open, & gravel-surfaced RV park.

Rates: $–$$

Number of Sites: 233

Number of Full Hookups: 165

Number of Water/Electric Hookups: 35

Number of Sites with No Hookups: 33

Number of Pull-Thru Sites: 30

Typical Site Width: 20 ft.

Services: Dump Station, LP Gas by Meter, Non-Guest Dumping

Open All Year

Amenities: A/C Allowed, Cable TV, Cable TV Fee, Fire Rings, Heater Allowed, Ice, Laundry, Limited Groceries, Phone or Modem Hookup—Central Location, Phone or Modem Hookups at Site (need activation), Public Phone, RV Supplies, Wood

Recreation: Fishing Guides, Fishing Supplies, Horseshoes, Local Tours

Discounts: FMCA Discount

Credit Cards Accepted: American Express, Discover, MasterCard, Visa

Facility Fully Operational: May–Oct.

ARIZONA

Sundance 1 RV Resort
CASA GRANDE (Pinal)
Phone: 888-332-5335

Directions: From jct. I-10 (exit 194) & Hwy 287: Go 4 mi. W on Hwy 287 (Florence Blvd), then continue 1 mi. W on Hwy 84, then 1 mi. N on Thornton.

Description: Luxury resort RV PARK.

Rates: $$

Number of Sites: 711

Seasonal Sites: Some Seasonal Sites

Number of Full Hookups: 711

Open: Sept. 15

Close: April

Number of Pull-Thru Sites: 17

Typical Site Width: 40 ft.

Services: Partial Handicap Access

Pets: Pet Restrictions

Hookup Information: 30 amps, 50 amps, Accepts Full Hookup Units Only

Additional Facilities: A/C Allowed, Cable TV, Heater Allowed, Laundry, Phone or Modem, Hookup—Central Location, Phone or Modem Hookups at Site (on arrival), Public Phone, Traffic Control Gate

Recreation: Horseshoes

Planned Activities: Pool, Recreation Hall, Recreation Room/Area, Shuffleboard, Whirlpool

Credit Cards Accepted: MasterCard

Las Quintas Oasis RV Park
YUMA (Yuma)
Phone: 877-975-9005
Web site: *www.lasquintasresort.com*

Directions: From jct. I-8 (exit 12) & Fortuna Rd: Go ½ mi. W on north frontage road.

Description: Resort RV PARK with large, spacious sites.

Rates: $$

Number of Sites: 460

Seasonal Sites: Some Seasonal Sites

Number of Full Hookups: 460

Number of Pull-Thru Sites: 38

Typical Site Width: 38 ft.

Services: Partial Handicap Access

Open All Year

Pets: Pet Restrictions

Hookup Information: 30 amps, 50 amps, Accepts Full Hookup Units Only

Amenities: A/C Allowed, Cable TV, Heater Allowed, Laundry, Phone or Modem Hookup—Central Location, Phone or Modem Hookups at Site (need activ.), Public Phone

Recreation: Horseshoes, Local Tours, Planned Activities, Pool, Recreation Hall, Recreation Room/Area, Shuffleboard, Volleyball, Whirlpool

Credit Cards Accepted: MasterCard, Visa

Grand Canyon-KOA
WILLIAMS (Coconino)
Phone: 800-KOA-5771

Directions: From jct. I-40 & Hwy 64: Go 4 mi. N on Hwy 64.

Description: A CAMPGROUND with open, level, partly shaded sites.

Rates: $$–$$$

Number of Sites: 62

Number of Full Hookups: 6

Number of Water/Electric Hookups: 56

Number of Sites with No Hookups: 34

Open: March 1

Close: Oct.

Number of Pull-Thru Sites: 25

Typical Site Width: 18 ft.

Services: Dump Station, LP Gas by Meter, Non-Guest Dumping, Non-Guest Dumping Fee, Partial Handicap Access

Hookup Information: 20 amps, 30 amps, 50 amps, 50 amps Fee

Amenities: A/C Allowed, Cable TV, Cable TV Fee, Fire Rings, Grills, Groceries, Heater Allowed, Ice, Laundry, Phone or Modem Hookup— Central Location, Public Phone, RV Supplies, Wood

Recreation: Coin Games, Equipped Pavilion, Local Tours, Playground, Pool, Recreation Room/Area, Whirlpool

Discounts: KOA 10% Value Card Discount

Credit Cards Accepted: American Express, Discover, MasterCard, Visa

ARKANSAS

KOA-Hot Springs

HOT SPRINGS (Garland)

Phone: 501-624-5912

Web site: *www.hotspringskoa.com*

Directions: On US 70 at east city limits (exit 4), follow signs.

Description: A rolling CAMPGROUND with level, shaded, or open sites.

Rates: $$–$$$

Number of Sites: 82

Number of Full Hookups: 76

Number of Water/Electric Hookups: 6

Number of Pull-Thru Sites: 13

Typical Site Width: 25 ft.

Services: Dump Station, LP Gas by Meter, LP Gas by Weight, Partial Handicap Access

Open All Year

Hookup Information: 20 amps, 30 amps, 50 amps, 50 amps Fee

Amenities: A/C Allowed, Cable TV, Cable TV Fee, Fire Rings,

Full-Service Store, Grills, Heater Allowed, Ice, Laundry, Phone or Modem Hookup—Central Location

Phone or Modem Hookups at Site (need activ.), Public Phone, RV Supplies, Wood

Recreation: Badminton, Basketball, Coin Games, Fishing, Local Tours, Playground, Pond Fishing, Pool, Recreation Hall, Recreation Room/Area, Shuffleboard, Sports Field, Volleyball

Discounts: KOA 10% Value Card Discount

Credit Cards Accepted: American Express, Discover, MasterCard, Visa

---

KOA-Little Rock North
NORTH LITTLE ROCK (Pulaski)
Phone: 501-758-4598

Directions: From jct. I-40 (exit 148) & Crystal Hill Rd: Go 1 mi. SW on Crystal Hill Rd., enter right or from jct. I-430 (exit 12) & Crystal Hill Rd.: Go ½ mi NE on Crystal Hill Rd. Enter left.

Description: Semi-wooded, family oriented CAMPGROUND with shaded & open sites.

Rates: $$–$$$

Number of Sites: 89

Seasonal Sites: Some Seasonal Sites

Number of Full Hookups: 71

Number of Water/Electric Hookups: 17

Number of Sites with No Hookups: 1

Number of Pull-Thru Sites: 50

Typical Site Width: 30 ft.

Services: Dump Station, LP Gas by Meter, LP Gas by Weight, Non-Guest Dumping, Non-Guest Dumping Fee

Open All Year

Pets: Pet Restrictions

Hookup Information: 20 amps, 30 amps, 50 amps, 50 amps Fee

Amenities: A/C Allowed, Cable TV, Cable TV Fee, Grills, Groceries, Heater Allowed, Ice, Laundry, Phone or Modem Hookup—Central Location, Phone or Modem Hookups at Site (need activ.), Phone/Modem Hookups at Site (on arrival), Public Phone, RV Supplies, Traffic Control Gate

Recreation: Basketball, Horseshoes, Playground, Pool, Recreation Room/Area, Volleyball, Whirlpool

Discounts: KOA 10% Value Card Discount

Credit Cards Accepted: American Express, Discover, MasterCard, Visa

White River Campground & Cottages
COTTER (Marion)
Phone: 870-453-2299

Directions: From jct. US 62 & US 62B: From west jct. go ½ mi. E on US 62B.

Description: Riverside family CAMPGROUND with shaded & open sites.

Rates: $–$$

Number of Sites: 95

Number of Full Hookups: 78

Number of Water/Electric Hookups: 17

Number of Pull-Thru Sites: 24

Typical Site Width: 30 ft.

Services: Dump Station, LP Gas by Meter, LP Gas by Weight, Non-Guest Dumping, Non-Guest Dumping Fee

Open All Year

Hookup Information: 20 amps, 30 amps, 50 amps

Amenities: A/C Allowed, Cable TV, Fire Rings, Grills, Heater Allowed, Heater Fee, Ice, Laundry, Limited Groceries, Marine Gas, Phone or Modem Hookup—Central Location, Phone/Modem Hookups at Site (on arrival), Public Phone, RV Supplies, Wood

Recreation: Boating, Canoe Rentals, Canoeing, Dock, Equipped Pavilion, Fishing, Fishing Guides, Fishing Supplies, Float Trips, Horseshoes, Play Equipment, Pool, Ramp, Recreation Room/Area, River Fishing, River Swimming, Rowboat Rentals, Shuffleboard, Sports Field, Volleyball

Credit Cards Accepted: American Express, ATM On site, Diners Club, Discover, MasterCard, Visa

CALIFORNIA

Anaheim Resort RV Park
ANAHEIM (Orange)
Phone: 714-774-3860
Web site: *www.anaheimharborrvpark.com*

Directions: From jct. Hwy 91 & I-5: Go 5 mi. S on I-5, then ½ mi. E on Ball Rd., then ¼ mi. S on Anaheim Blvd, then 1 block W on Midway Dr.

Description: RV SPACES in a mobile home park in a metro area with paved sites. Good Sam Park, Disneyland Shuttle.

Rates: $$$

Number of Sites: 151

Seasonal Sites: Some Seasonal Sites

Number of Full Hookups: 151

Number of Pull-Thru Sites: 5

Typical Site Width: 25 ft.

Services: Dump Station, Non-Guest Dumping, Non-Guest Dumping Fee, Partial Handicap Access

Open All Year

Hookup Information: 20 amps, 30 amps, 50 amps

Amenities: A/C Allowed, Cable TV, Heater Allowed, Ice, Laundry, Phone or Modem Hookup—Central Location, Phone or Modem Hookups at Site (need activ.), Public Phone, RV Supplies

Recreation: Local Tours, Pool, Recreation Hall, Whirlpool

Discounts: FMCA Discount

Credit Cards Accepted: American Express, Discover, MasterCard, Visa

San Francisco RV Resort (formerly Pacific Park)
PACIFICA (San Mateo)
Phone: 800-822-1250
Web site: *www.sanfranciscorvresort.com*

Directions: From south jct. I-280 & Hwy 1: Go 2½ mi. S on Hwy 1 (Manor Dr. exit), then 3 blocks S on Palmetto Ave.

Description: Open, paved sites at an ocean-side RV PARK.

Rates: $$$$

Number of Sites: 182

Seasonal Sites: Some Seasonal Sites

Number of Full Hookups: 182

Number of Pull-Thru Sites: 105

Max RV Length: 45

Typical Site Width: 12 ft.

Services: Dump Station, LP Gas by Meter, Non-Guest Dumping, Non-Guest Dumping Fee, Partial Handicap Access

Open All Year

Pets: Pet Restrictions

Hookup Information: 20 amps, 30 amps, 50 amps

Amenities: A/C Allowed, Cable TV, Fire Rings, Groceries, Heater Allowed, Ice, Laundry, Phone or Modem Hookup—Central Location, Public Phone, RV Supplies

Recreation: Coin Games, Fishing, Playground, Pool, Recreation Room/Area, Saltwater Fishing, Saltwater Swimming, Whirlpool

Credit Cards Accepted: MasterCard, Visa

La Pacifica RV Resort
SAN DIEGO (San Diego)
Phone: 619-428-4411

Directions: From jct. I-5 & Dairy Mart: Go 1 block E on Dairy Mart, then 1 block N on San Ysidro Blvd.

Description: RV PARK with paved, level sites.

Rates: $$

Number of Sites: 177

Seasonal Sites: Mostly Seasonal Sites

Number of Full Hookups: 177

Number of Pull-Thru Sites: 64

Max RV Length: 50

Services: Dump Station, Non-Guest Dumping, Non-Guest Dumping Fee, Partial Handicap Access

Open All Year

Hookup Information: 20 amps, 30 amps, 50 amps

Amenities: A/C Allowed, A/C Fee, Cable TV, Heater Allowed, Heater Fee, Laundry, Phone or Modem Hookup—Central Location, Phone or Modem Hookups at Site (need activ.), Public Phone, Traffic Control Gate

Recreation: Local Tours, Pool, Recreation Room/Area, Whirlpool

Discounts: FMCA Discount

Credit Cards Accepted: American Express, Discover, MasterCard, Visa

Tahoe Valley Campground
SOUTH LAKE TAHOE (El Dorado)
Phone: 530-541-2222

Directions: From north jct. Hwy 89 & US 50: Go 1/4 mi. SW on US 50.

Description: Level, shaded, natural sites in a pine-wooded area near town.

Rates: $$$–$$$$

Number of Sites: 413

Seasonal Sites: Some Seasonal Sites

Number of Full Hookups: 306

Number of Water/Electric Hookups: 33

Number of Sites with No Hookups: 74

Number of Pull-Thru Sites: 40

Max RV Length: 45

Typical Site Width: 20 ft.

Services: Dump Station, LP Gas by Meter, Non-Guest Dumping, Non-Guest Dumping Fee

Open All Year

Hookup Information: 15 amps, 20 amps, 30 amps, 50 amps

Amenities: A/C Allowed, Cable TV, Grills, Groceries, Heater Allowed, Ice, Laundry, Phone or Modem Hookup—Central Location, Public Phone, RV Supplies, Wood

Recreation: Badminton, Basketball, Coin Games, Equipped Pavilion, Fishing, Hiking Trails, Horseshoes, Local Tours, Playground, Pool, Recreation Hall, Recreation Room/Area, River Fishing, Tennis, Volleyball

Credit Cards Accepted: American Express, Discover, MasterCard, Visa

Season Exceptions: Pool open Memorial Day through Sept. 30.

COLORADO

Tiger Run RV Resort
BRECKENRIDGE (Summit)
Phone: 970-453-9690

Directions: From jct. I-70 (exit 203) & Hwy 9: Go 6½ mi. S on Hwy 9.

Description: RV PARK with level sites with landscaped paved pads by a river in a scenic mountain setting.

Rates: $$$$

Number of Sites: 365

Number of Full Hookups: 365

Number of Pull-Thru Sites: 27

Typical Site Width: 50 ft.

Services: LP Gas by Meter, LP Gas by Weight, Partial Handicap Access

Open All Year

Hookup Information: 30 amps, 50 amps

Amenities: A/C Allowed, Cable TV, Grills, Heater Allowed, Ice, Laundry, Limited Groceries, Phone or Modem Hookup—Central Location, Phone or Modem Hookups at Site (need activ.), Public Phone, RV Supplies, Traffic Control Gate, Wood

Recreation: Badminton, Basketball, Coin Games, Equipped Pavilion, Fishing, Fishing Guides, Float Trips, Hiking Trails, Lake Fishing, Local Tours, Planned Activities, Playground, Pool, Recreation Hall, Recreation Room/Area, River Fishing, Tennis, Volleyball, Whirlpool

Credit Cards Accepted: American Express, Discover, MasterCard, Visa

Alpen-Rose RV Park
DURANGO (La Plata)
Phone: 877-259-5791

Directions: From West jct. US 160/550: Go 6½ mi. N on US 550.

Description: An RV PARK with grassy shaded sites in a beautiful mountain setting.

Rates: $$$–$$$$

Number of Sites: 100

Seasonal Sites: Some Seasonal Sites

Number of Full Hookups: 100

Open: April 1

Close: Oct. 31

Number of Pull-Thru Sites: 76

Typical Site Width: 28 ft.

Services: Dump Station, LP Gas by Weight, Partial Handicap Access

Hookup Information: 30 amps, 50 amps, 50 amps Fee

Amenities: A/C Allowed, Cable TV, Grills, Heater Allowed, Ice, Laundry, Limited Groceries, Phone or Modem Hookup—Central Location, Phone or Modem Hookups at Site (need activ.), Public Phone, RV Supplies

Recreation: Badminton, Basketball, Coin Games, Fishing, Fishing Supplies, Horseshoes, Local Tours, Pavilion, Planned Activities, Play Equipment, Pond Fishing, Pool, Putting Green, Recreation Hall, Recreation Room/Area, Volleyball

Credit Cards Accepted: MasterCard, Visa

Season Exceptions: Weather permitting.

Denver Meadows RV Park

AURORA (Adams)

Phone: 800-364-9487

Web site: *www.denvermeadows.com*

Directions: From jct. I-70 (exit 282) & I-225: Go 2 mi. S on I-225 (exit 10), then 1 block W on Colfax, then ¼ mi. N on Potomac St.

Description: RV PARK with open and shaded sites.

Rates: $$$

Number of Sites: 287

Seasonal Sites: Some Seasonal Sites

Number of Full Hookups: 287

Max RV Length: 40

Typical Site Width: 16 ft.

Services: Dump Station

Open All Year

Pets: Pet Restrictions

Hookup Information: 20 amps, 30 amps, 50 amps

Amenities: A/C Allowed, Cable TV, Grills, Heater Allowed, Ice, Laundry, Phone or Modem Hookups at Site (need activ.), Public Phone

Recreation: Pavilion, Pool, Recreation Hall, Whirlpool

Credit Cards Accepted: MasterCard, Visa

CONNECTICUT

Brialee RV & Tent Park
ASHFORD (Windham)
Phone: 800-303-CAMP

Directions: From jct. US 44 & Hwy 89: Go 1 mi. N on Hwy 89, then ½ mi. W on Perry Hill Rd., then ¾ mi. N on Laurel Lane.

Description: Wooded CAMPGROUND with well-spaced sites

Rates: $$$–$$$$

Number of Sites: 215

Number of Full Hookups: 20

Number of Water/Electric Hookups: 185

Number of Sites with No Hookups: 10

Hookup Information: 20 amps, 30 amps, 50 amps, 50 amps Fee

Open: April 1

Close: Dec.1

Number of Pull-Thru Sites: 10

Average Site Width: 40 ft.

Services: Dump Station, LP Gas by Meter, LP Gas by Weight, Non-Guest Dumping, Non-Guest Dumping Fee, Portable Dump

Amenities: Laundry, Phone or Modem Hookup—Central Location, Phone or Modem Hookups at Site (need activ.), Public Phone

Recreation: Badminton, Boating, Canoe Rentals, Canoeing, Fishing, Hiking Trails, Pavilion, Pedal Boat Rentals, Planned Activities, Playground, Pond Fishing, Pond Swimming, Pool, Recreation Hall, Recreation Room/Area, Rowboat Rentals, Shuffleboard, Sports Field, Volleyball

Aces High RV Park
EAST LYME (New London)
Phone: 860-739-8858

Directions: From jct. I-95 (exit 74) & Hwy 161: Go 3 mi. N on Hwy 161.

Description: Level, open, pull-thru RV sites.

Rates: $$$

Number of Sites: 70

Number of Full Hookups: 70

Number of Water/Electric Hookups: 70

Number of Sites with No Hookups: 0

Hookup Information: 20 amps, 30 amps, 50 amps

Open: All year

Number of Pull-Thru Sites: 70

Average Site Width: 45 ft.

Services: Dump Station, LP Gas by Meter, LP Gas by Weight, Non-Guest Dumping, Non-Guest Dumping Fee

Amenities: A/C Allowed, Cable TV, Fire Rings, Grills, Heater Allowed, Hot Shower Fee, Ice, Laundry, Limited Groceries, Phone or Modem Hookup—Central Location, Phone or Modem Hookups at Site (need activ.), Public Phone, RV Supplies, Traffic Control Gate, Wood

Recreation: Badminton, Basketball, Bike Rentals, Boating, Canoeing, Coin Games, Fishing, Fishing Supplies, Hiking Trails, Pedal Boat Rentals, Planned Activities (Weekends Only), Playground, Pond Fishing, Pond Swimming, Recreation Room/Area, Rowboat Rentals, Sports Field, Stream Fishing, Volleyball

Credit Cards: MasterCard, Visa

Highland Orchards Resort Park
NORTH STONINGTON (New London)
Phone: 800-624-0829

Directions: Southbound: From jct. I-95 & Hwy 49: Go ¼ mi. N on Hwy 49. Northbound: From jct. I-95 (exit 92) & Hwy 2: Go ¼ mi. W on Hwy 2, then 1 mi. NE on Service Rd, then ¼ mi. N on Hwy 49. From Hartford or Foxwoods: Go E on Rt. 2, then E on Rt. 184, then S on Rt. 49.

Description: CAMPGROUND with open or shaded grassy sites & wooded tent sites.

Rates: $$$–$$$$

Number of Sites: 278

Number of Full Hookups: 109

Number of Water/Electric Hookups: 151

Number of Sites with No Hookups: 18

Hookup Information: 20 amps, 30 amps, 50 amps, 50 amps Fee

Open: All Year

Number of Pull-Thru Sites: 96

Average Site Width: 35 ft.

Services: Dump Station, LP Gas by Meter, LP Gas by Weigh, Non-Guest Dumping, Non-Guest Dumping Fee, Portable Dump, Partial Handicap Access

Amenities: A/C Allowed, Cable TV, Fire Rings, Groceries, Heater Allowed, Ice, Laundry, Phone or Modem Hookup—Central Location, Phone or Modem Hookups at Site (need activ.), Public Phone, RV Supplies, Traffic Control Gate, Wood

Recreation: Basketball, Coin Games, Fishing, Fishing Supplies, Horseshoes, Mini-Golf, Pavilion, Planned Activities (Weekends Only), Playground, Pond Fishing, Pool, Recreation Hall, Recreation Room/Area, Shuffleboard, Sports Field, Volleyball

Discounts: FMCA Discount

Credit Cards: American Express, Discover, MasterCard, Visa

DELAWARE

Tall Pines
LEWES (Sussex)
Phone: 302-684-0300

Directions: From jct. Hwy 1 & US 9: Go 2¾ mi. SW on US 9, then ¾ mi. SW on service road.

Description: An RV PARK with open & shaded sites

Rates: $$–$$$$

Number of Sites: 512
Number of Full Hookups: 463
Number of Water/Electric Hookups: 49
Number of Sites with No Hookups: 0
Hookup Information: 20 amps, 30 amps
Open All Year
Number of Pull-Thru Sites: 5
Average Site Width: 50 ft.
Services: Dump Station, LP Gas by Meter, LP Gas by Weight
Amenities: A/C Allowed, A/C Fee, Fire Rings, Groceries, Heater Allowed, Heater Fee, Ice, Laundry, Public Phone, Wood
Recreation: Basketball, Coin Games, Pavilion, Playground, Pool, Shuffleboard, Volleyball
Credit Cards: MasterCard, Visa

Big Oaks Family Campground
REHOBOTH BEACH
Phone: 302-645-6838
Directions: From jct. Hwy 1 & Hwy 24 & CR 270: Go ½ mi. E on CR 270.
Description: Level, wooded, and open sites
Rates: $$$
Number of Sites: 150
Number of Full Hookups: 125
Number of Water/Electric Hookups: 25
Number of Sites with No Hookups: 0
Hookup Information: 20 amps, 30 amps, 50 amps, 50 amps Fee
Open: May 1
Close: Oct. 1
Number of Pull-Thru Sites: 0
Average Site Width: 30 ft.
Services: Dump Station
Amenities: A/C Allowed, Cable TV, Cable TV Fee, Fire Rings, Grills, Groceries, Ice, Laundry, Phone or Modem Hookup—Central Location, Public Phone, RV Supplies, Wood

Recreation: Basketball, Coin Games, Horseshoes, Local Tours, Pavilion, Planned Activities (Weekends Only), Playground, Pool, Recreation Hall, Recreation Room/Area, Shuffleboard

Restrictions: Pet Restrictions

FLORIDA

Space Coast RV Resort
COCOA (Brevard)
Phone: 800-982-4233
Web site: *www.spacecoastrv.net*

Directions: Southbound from I-95 (exit 195): Go 200 yd. N on Fiske Blvd, then 200 yd. E on Barnes Blvd. Northbound from I-95 (exit 195): Go 300 yd. straight ahead from light.

Description: Wooded, quiet, RV RESORT.

Rates: $$$

Number of Sites: 273

Number of Full Hookups: 267

Number of Sites with No Hookups: 6

Number of Pull-Thru Sites: 85

Typical Site Width: 35 ft.

Services: Dump Station, LP Gas by Meter, LP Gas by Weight, Non-Guest Dumping, Non-Guest Dumping Fee

Policies: Age Restrictions May Apply

Open All Year

Hookup Information: 20 amps, 30 amps, 50 amps, 50 amps Fee

Amenities: A/C Allowed, Grills, Heater Allowed, Laundry, Phone or Modem Hookup—Central Location, Phone or Modem Hookups at Site (need activ.), Public Phone, RV Supplies

Recreation: Equipped Pavilion, Fishing, Horseshoes, Planned Activities, Play Equipment, Pond Fishing, Pool, Recreation Hall, Recreation Room/Area, Shuffleboard, Wading Pool

Discounts: FCRV 10% Discount, FMCA Discount

Credit Cards Accepted: American Express, Discover, MasterCard, Visa

Southern Comfort RV Resort
HOMESTEAD (Dade)
Phone: 888-477-6909

Directions: From jct. Hwy 27, US 1 & Southern Terminus of Florida Turnpike: Go 1 block E of US 1 on Palm Dr (344 St).

Description: Grassy, semi-shaded CAMPGROUND.

Rates: $$

Number of Sites: 356

Seasonal Sites: Some Seasonal Sites

Number of Full Hookups: 350

Number of Water/Electric Hookups: 6

Number of Pull-Thru Sites: 52

Typical Site Width: 26 ft.

Services: Dump Station, LP Gas by Meter, LP Gas by Weight, Non-Guest Dumping, Non-Guest Dumping Fee

Open All Year

Pets: Pet Restrictions

Hookup Information: 20 amps, 30 amps, 50 amps

Amenities: A/C Allowed, Heater Allowed, Ice, Laundry, Limited Groceries, Phone or Modem, Hookup—Central Location, Phone or Modem Hookups at Site (need activ.), Public Phone, RV Supplies, Traffic Control Gate

Recreation: Equipped Pavilion, Local Tours, Planned Activities, Pool, Recreation Hall, Shuffleboard

Credit Cards Accepted: MasterCard, Visa

Mouse Mountain RV Camping Resort
KISSIMMEE (Polk)
Phone: 800-347-6388
Web site: *www.mousemountainrv.com*

Directions: From jct. I-4 (exit 58) & Hwy 532: Go 1½ mi. E on Hwy 532.

Description: Shaded, rolling, grassy sites in an RV PARK.

Rates: $$

Number of Sites: 279

Seasonal Sites: Many Seasonal Sites
Number of Full Hookups: 260
Number of Sites with No Hookups: 19
Number of Pull-Thru Sites: 25
Typical Site Width: 35 ft.
Services: LP Gas by Meter, LP Gas by Weight, Partial Handicap Access
Open All Year
Hookup Information: 20 amps, 30 amps, 50 amps,
Amenities: A/C Allowed, Cable TV, Cable TV Fee, Heater Allowed, Laundry, Phone or Modem Hookup—Central Location, Phone or Modem Hookups at Site (need activ.), Public Phone, RV Supplies
Recreation: Basketball, Horseshoes, Planned Activities, Playground, Pool, Putting Green, Recreation Hall, Recreation Room/Area, Shuffleboard,
Credit Cards Accepted: American Express, MasterCard, Visa

KOA-Miami/Everglades
MIAMI (Dade)
Phone: 800-562-7732

Directions: From jct. US 1 & SW 216 St.: Go 4¾ mi. W on SW 216 St., then ¼ mi. N on 162nd Ave.
Description: Semi-wooded, quiet, secluded CAMPGROUND.
Rates: $$$–$$$$
Number of Sites: 297
Seasonal Sites: Many Seasonal Sites
Number of Full Hookups: 215
Number of Water/Electric Hookups: 65
Number of Sites with No Hookups: 17
Number of Pull-Thru Sites: 241
Typical Site Width: 22 ft.
Services: Dump Station, LP Gas by Meter, LP Gas by Weight, Non-Guest Dumping, Non-Guest Dumping Fee
Open All Year
Hookup Information: 20 amps, 30 amps, 50 amps, 50 amps Fee
Amenities: A/C Allowed, Cable TV, Full-Service Store, Heater Allowed, Ice, Laundry, Phone, or Modem Hookup—Central Location,

Phone or Modem Hookups at Site (need activ.), Public Phone, RV Supplies, Traffic Control Gate

Recreation: Badminton, Basketball, Bike Rentals, Hiking Trails, Horseshoes, Planned Activities, Playground, Pool, Recreation Hall, Shuffleboard, Sports Field, Volleyball, Whirlpool

Discounts: KOA 10% Value Card Discount

Credit Cards Accepted: MasterCard, Visa

GEORGIA

Atlanta North Family Campground
KENNESAW (Cobb)
Phone: 770-427-2406

Directions: From jct. I-75 (exit 269) & Barrett Pkwy: Go 2 mi. W on Barrett Pkwy. (to second light past US 41), then ½ mi. N on Old US 41.

Description: Rolling, Semi-wooded CAMPGROUND with shaded & open paved sites.

Rates: $$–$$$

Number of Sites: 230

Seasonal Sites: Many Seasonal Sites

Number of Full Hookups: 220

Number of Water/Electric Hookups: 10

Number of Pull-Thru Sites: 110

Typical Site Width: 30 ft.

Services: Dump Station, LP Gas by Meter, LP Gas by Weight, Non-Guest Dumping, Non-Guest Dumping Fee

Open All Year

Hookup Information: 20 amps, 30 amps, 50 amps

Amenities: A/C Allowed, Groceries, Heater Allowed, Ice, Laundry, Phone or Modem Hookup—Central Location, Phone or Modem Hookups at Site (need activ.), Public Phone, RV Supplies

Recreation: Basketball, Coin Games, Playground, Pool, Recreation Room

Discounts: KOA 10% Value Card Discount

Credit Cards Accepted: American Express, Discover, MasterCard, Visa

Jekyll Island Campground
JEKYLL ISLAND (Glynn)
Web site: *www.jekyllisland.com*

Directions: From jct. I-95 (exit 29) & US 17N: Go 5 mi. E on US 17N, then 6 mi. SE on Hwy 520 (Jekyll Island Causeway), then 4½ mi. N on Beach View Dr/Riverview Dr.

Rates: Call for information

Number of Sites: 208

Typical Site Width: 20 ft.

Number of Full Hookups: 162

Number of Water/Electric Hookups: 2

Number of Sites with No Hookups: 44

Number of Pull-Thru Sites: 40

Phone: 866-658-3021

Services: Dump Station, LP Gas by Meter, LP Gas by Weight, Non-Guest Dumping, Non-Guest, Dumping Fee, Partial Handicap Access

Open All Year

Hookup Information: 30 amps, 50 amps

Amenities: A/C Allowed, Cable TV, Fire Rings, Heater Allowed, Ice, Laundry, Limited, Groceries, Phone or Modem Hookup—Central Location, Public Phone, RV Supplies, Traffic Control Gate, Wood

Recreation: Bike Rentals, Fishing, Fishing Supplies, Hiking Trails, Lake Fishing, Saltwater Fishing, Saltwater Swimming

Credit Cards Accepted: Discover, MasterCard, Visa

Bellaire Woods Campground
SAVANNAH (Chatham)
Phone: 800-851-0717

Directions: From jct. I-95 (exit 94) & Hwy 204: Go 2½ mi. W on Hwy 204.

Description: Shaded sites in a wooded, family-oriented park.

Rates: $$$

Number of Sites: 139

Number of Full Hookups: 98

Number of Water/Electric Hookups: 41

Number of Pull-Thru Sites: 70

Typical Site Width: 30 ft.

Services: Dump Station, LP Gas by Meter, LP Gas by Weight, Non-Guest Dumping, Non-Guest, Dumping Fee, Partial Handicap Access

Open All Year

Hookup Information: 30 amps, 50 amps

Amenities: A/C Allowed, Cable TV, Grills, Groceries, Heater Allowed, Ice, Laundry, Phone or Modem Hookup—Central Location, Phone or Modem Hookups at Site (need activ.), Public Phone, RV Supplies, Traffic Control Gate, Wood

Recreation: Boating, Canoeing, Coin Games, Dock, Fishing, Kayaking, Pavilion, Playground, Pond Fishing, Pool, Ramp, Recreation Room/Area, River Fishing

Discounts: FMCA Discount

Credit Cards Accepted: Discover, MasterCard, Visa

IDAHO

Blackwell Island RV Resort

COEUR D'ALENE (Kootenai)

Phone: 888-571-2900

Web site: *www.idahorvpark.com*

Directions: From I-90 & US 95: Go 1½ mi. S on US 95.

Description: Wide, long, & level sites on the water.

Rates: $$–$$$

Number of Sites: 122

Number of Full Hookups: 122

Open: April 1

Close: Oct. 31

Number of Pull-Thru Sites: 100

Typical Site Width: 40 ft.

Services: LP Gas by Meter, Partial Handicap Access

Hookup Information: 30 amps, 50 amps

Amenities: A/C Allowed, Cable TV, Heater Allowed, Ice, Laundry,

Limited Groceries, Phone or Modem Hookup—Central Location, Public Phone, RV Supplies

Recreation: Boating, Canoe Rentals, Canoeing, Dock, Fishing, Kayak Rentals, Kayaking, Local Tours, Motorboat Rentals, Pavilion, Pedal Boat Rentals, Playground, Pontoon Rentals, Ramp, Recreation Hall, River Fishing, River Swimming, Volleyball

Credit Cards Accepted: MasterCard, Visa

KOA-Idaho Falls
IDAHO FALLS (Bonneville)
Phone: 208-523-3362

Directions: From jct. I-15 (exit 119) & US 20: Go 1 block E on US 20, then ½ mi. N on Lindsay Blvd.

Description: CAMPGROUND with open and shaded sites.

Rates: $$–$$$

Number of Sites: 167

Number of Full Hookups: 57

Number of Water/Electric Hookups: 76

Number of Sites with No Hookups: 34

Number of Pull-Thru Sites: 48

Typical Site Width: 35 ft.

Services: Dump Station, LP Gas by Meter, LP Gas by Weight, Non-Guest Dumping, Non-Guest Dumping Fee

Open All Year

Hookup Information: 30 amps, 50 amps, 50 amps Fee

Amenities: A/C Allowed, Grills, Groceries, Heater Allowed, Ice, Laundry, Phone or Modem Hookup—Central Location, Phone or Modem Hookups at Site (need activ.), Public Phone, RV Supplies

Recreation: Basketball, Coin Games, Fishing, Hiking Trails, Mini-Golf, Mini-Golf Fee, Planned Activities, Playground, Pool, Recreation Room/Area, Stream Fishing, Whirlpool

Discounts: KOA 10% Value Card Discount

Credit Cards Accepted: MasterCard, Visa

Kellogg/Silver Valley KOA
PINEHURST (Shoshone)
Phone: 800-562-0799

Directions: From I-90 (exit 45 Pinehurst): Go ¼ mi. S on Division St.

Description: Shaded streamside CAMPGROUND.

Rates: $$–$$$

Number of Sites: 35

Number of Full Hookups: 27

Number of Water/Electric Hookups: 8

Open: April 15

Close: Oct. 15

Number of Pull-Thru Sites: 22

Services: Dump Station

Hookup Information: 30 amps, 50 amps, 50 amps Fee

Amenities: A/C Allowed, Cable TV, Cable TV Fee, Grills, Heater Allowed, Ice, Laundry, Limited Groceries, Phone or Modem Hookup—Central Location, Phone or Modem Hookups at Site (need activ.), Public Phone, RV Supplies, Traffic Control Gate, Wood

Recreation: Bike Rentals, Coin Games, Fishing, Fishing Supplies, Hiking Trails, Mini-Golf, Mini-Golf Fee, Pavilion, Pedal Boat Rentals, Planned Activities (Weekends Only), Playground, Pond Fishing, Pool, Recreation Room/Area, Stream Fishing, Whirlpool

Discounts: KOA 10% Value Card Discount

Credit Cards Accepted: American Express, Discover, MasterCard, Visa

Anderson Camp
EDEN (Jerome)
Phone: 888-480-9400
Web site: *www.andersoncamp.com*

Directions: From jct. US 93 & I-84: Go 9 mi. E on I-84 (exit 182), then 100 yd. N on Hwy 50, then ½ mi. E on Tripperary Rd.

Description: CAMPGROUND with open and shaded sites.

Rates: $$

Number of Sites: 125

Number of Full Hookups: 90
Number of Water/Electric Hookups: 18
Number of Sites with No Hookups: 17
Number of Pull-Thru Sites: 72
Typical Site Width: 25 ft.
Services: Dump Station, LP Gas by Meter, LP Gas by Weight, Partial Handicap Access
Open All Year
Hookup Information: 20 amps, 30 amps, 50 amps, 50 amps Fee
Amenities: A/C Allowed, Fire Rings, Grills, Heater Allowed, Ice, Laundry, Limited Groceries, Phone or Modem Hookup—Central Location, Phone or Modem Hookups at Site (need activ.), Public Phone, RV Supplies, Wood
Recreation: Basketball, Coin Games, Mini-Golf, Mini-Golf Fee, Pavilion, Planned Activities, Playground, Pool, Recreation Hall, Recreation Room/Area, Volleyball, Wading Pool
Credit Cards Accepted: American Express, Discover, MasterCard, Visa

ILLINOIS

Shady Lakes Camping & Recreation
ALPHA (Mercer)
Phone: 309-667-2709

Directions: From jct. I-74 (exit 32) & Hwy 17: Go 2½ mi. W on Hwy 17, then ½ mi. S on Hwy 150, then 3¾ mi. W on Oxford Rd.
Description: CAMPGROUND in a rural location with level, open, & shaded sites.
Rates: $$
Number of Sites: 253
Seasonal Sites: Many Seasonal Sites
Number of Full Hookups: 243
Number of Water/Electric Hookups: 10
Open: Mid-April
Close: Mid-Oct.

Number of Pull-Thru Sites: 32

Typical Site Width: 30 ft.

Services: Dump Station, LP Gas by Meter, LP Gas by Weight, Non-Guest Dumping, Non-Guest Dumping Fee, Partial Handicap Access

Hookup Information: 30 amps, 50 amps, 50 amps Fee

Amenities: A/C Allowed, Fire Rings, Heater Allowed, Ice, Laundry, Limited Groceries, Phone or Modem Hookup—Central Location, Public Phone, RV Supplies, Traffic Control Gate, Wood

Recreation: Badminton, Basketball, Bike Rentals, Boating, Canoeing, Coin Games, Dock, Electric Motors Only, Fishing, Fishing Supplies, Hiking Trails, Lake Fishing, Mini-Golf, Mini-Golf Fee, Motorboat Rentals, Pavilion, Pedal Boat Rentals, Playground, Pool, Ramp, Recreation Hall, Recreation Room/Area, Rowboat Rentals, Sports Field, Volleyball, Wading Pool

Discounts: FCRV 10% Discount, FMCA Discount

Credit Cards Accepted: Discover, MasterCard, Visa

O'Connell's Yogi Bear's Jellystone Park Camp-Resort
AMBOY (Lee)
Phone: 815-857-3860
Web site: *www.jellystoneamboy.com*

Directions: From jct. Hwy 52 & Main St.: Go 1½ mi. E on Main St., then 2½ mi. SE on Shaw Rd., then 1 mi. N on Green Wing Rd.

Description: A rolling grassy CAMPGROUND with shaded and open sites.

Rates: $$$–$$$$

Number of Sites: 747

Seasonal Sites: Some Seasonal Sites

Number of Full Hookups: 493

Number of Water/Electric Hookups: 154

Number of Sites with No Hookups: 100

Number of Pull-Thru Sites: 173

Typical Site Width: 40 ft.

Services: Dump Station, LP Gas by Meter, LP Gas by Weight, Non-Guest Dumping, Non-Guest Dumping Fee, Portable Dump

Open All Year

Hookup Information: 20 amps, 30 amps, 50 amps,

Additional Facilities: A/C Allowed, Fire Rings, Groceries, Heater Allowed, Ice, Laundry, Phone or Modem Hookup—Central Location, Phone or Modem Hookups at Site (on arrival), Public Phone, RV Supplies, Traffic Control Gate, Wood

Recreation: Basketball, Boating, Canoeing, Coin Games, Electric Motors Only, Equipped Pavilion, Fishing, Fishing Supplies, Hiking Trails, Horseshoes, Kayak Rentals, Kayaking, Lake Fishing, Lake Swimming, Mini-Golf, Mini-Golf Fee, Pavilion, Pedal Boat Rentals, Planned Activities, Play Equipment, Playground, Pool, Recreation Hall, Recreation Room/Area, River Fishing, Sports Field, Volleyball, Wading Pool, Whirlpool

Credit Cards Accepted: Discover, MasterCard, Visa

Facility Fully Operational: Mid-April, mid-Oct.

Yogi Bear Jellystone Camp-Resort Chicago-Millbrook
MILLBROOK (Kendall)
Phone: 800-438-9644

Directions: From jct. Hwy 47 & Hwy 71: Go 6 mi. SW on Hwy 71, then 1 mi. W on Millbrook Rd.

Description: Level, grassy, shaded sites in a resort RV PARK.

Rates: $$$$

Number of Sites: 413

Seasonal Sites: Some Seasonal Sites

Number of Full Hookups: 224

Number of Water/Electric Hookups: 132

Number of Pull-Thru Sites: 2

Typical Site Width: 40 ft.

Services: Dump Station, LP Gas by Meter, LP Gas by Weight

Open All Year

Hookup Information: 20 amps, 30 amps, 50 amps

Amenities: A/C Allowed, Fire Rings, Grills, Groceries, Heater Allowed, Ice, Laundry, Phone or Modem Hookup—Central Location, Public Phone, RV Supplies, Traffic Control Gate, Wood

Recreation: Badminton, Basketball, Bike Rentals, Coin Games, Fishing, Fishing Supplies, Hiking Trails, Pavilion, Planned Activities, Play Equipment, Playground, Pond Fishing, Pond Swimming, Pool, Recreation Room/Area, Sports Field, Stream Fishing, Volleyball, Wading Pool, Whirlpool

Credit Cards Accepted: American Express, Discover, MasterCard, Visa

INDIANA

Lake Rudolph Campground & RV Resort
SANTA CLAUS (Spencer)
Phone: 877-478-3657
Web site: *www.lakerudolph.com*

Directions: From jct. I-64 (exit 63) & Hwy 162: Go 7¼ mi. S on Hwy 162, then 1 block N on Hwy 245.

Description: A CAMPGROUND with wooded sites in a rural area.

Rates: $$–$$$

Number of Sites: 245

Number of Full Hookups: 195

Number of Water/Electric Hookups: 50

Open: April 1

Close: Dec. 1

Number of Pull-Thru Sites: 2

Typical Site Width: 30 ft.

Services: Dump Station, LP Gas by Meter, LP Gas by Weight, Partial Handicap Access

Pets: Pet Restrictions

Hookup Information: 30 amps, 50 amps

Amenities: A/C Allowed, Fire Rings, Grills, Groceries, Heater Allowed, Ice, Laundry, Phone or Modem Hookup—Central Location, Public Phone, RV Supplies, Traffic Control Gate, Wood

Recreation: Basketball, Coin Games, Equipped Pavilion, Fishing, Fishing Supplies, Hiking Trails, Horseshoes, Lake Fishing, Mini-Golf, Pavilion, Pedal Boat Rentals, Planned Activities (Weekends Only),

Playground, Pool, Recreation Hall, Recreation Room/Area, Row Boat Rentals, Volleyball, Wading Pool

Credit Cards Accepted: Discover, MasterCard, Visa

KOA-South Bend East
SOUTH BEND (St. Joseph)
Phone: 574-277-1335

Directions: From jct. I-80/90/Indiana Turnpike (exit 83): Go ½ mi. to Hwy 23, then 2 mi. N on Hwy 23, then ³⁄₁₀ mi. N on Princess Way.

Description: CAMPGROUND with level, shaded sites.

Rates: $$–$$$

Number of Sites: 95

Number of Full Hookups: 41

Number of Water/Electric Hookups: 44

Number of Sites with No Hookups: 10

Open: March 15

Close: Nov. 15

Number of Pull-Thru Sites: 40

Typical Site Width: 30 ft.

Services: Dump Station, LP Gas by Meter, LP Gas by Weight, Non-Guest Dumping, Non-Guest Dumping Fee, Partial Handicap Access

Hookup Information: 30 amps, 50 amps

Amenities: A/C Allowed, Cable TV, Fire Rings, Grills, Groceries, Heater Allowed, Ice, Laundry, Phone or Modem Hookup—Central Location, Public Phone, RV Supplies, Traffic Control Gate, Wood

Recreation: Badminton, Basketball, Bike Rentals, Coin Games, Equipped Pavilion, Horseshoes, Local Tours, Mini-Golf, Mini-Golf Fee, Pavilion, Planned Activities, Playground, Pool, Recreation Room/Area, Sports Field, Volleyball

Discounts: KOA 10% Value Card Discount

Credit Cards Accepted: American Express, Discover, MasterCard, Visa

Elkhart Campground
ELKHART (Elkhart)
Phone: 574-264-2914

Directions: From jct. I-80/90 (Exit 92) & Hwy 19: Go ¼ mi. N on Hwy 19, then ¾ mi. E on CR4.

Description: CAMPGROUND with grassy sites.

Rates: $–$$

Number of Sites: 450

Number of Full Hookups: 115

Number of Water/Electric Hookups: 335

Open: April 1

Close: Nov. 25

Number of Pull-Thru Sites: 357

Typical Site Width: 30 ft.

Services: Dump Station, LP Gas by Meter, LP Gas by Weight, Non-Guest Dumping, Non-Guest Dumping Fee, Partial Handicap Access

Hookup Information: 30 amps, 50 amps

Amenities: A/C Allowed, Fire Rings, Heater Allowed, Ice, Laundry, Limited Groceries, Phone or Modem Hookup—Central Location, Public Phone, RV Supplies, Wood

Recreation: Basketball, Coin Games, Horseshoes, Mini-Golf, Mini-Golf Fee, Pavilion, Playground, Pool, Recreation Hall, Recreation Room/Area, Sports Field, Tennis, Volleyball

Discounts: FMCA Discount

Credit Cards Accepted: MasterCard, Visa

IOWA

Skip-A-Way RV Park & Campground
CLERMONT (Fayette)
Phone: 800-728-1167
Web site: *www.skipawayresort.com*

Directions: On US 18 at west end of Clermont.

Description: Riverside CAMPGROUND with level gravel and grassy sites in conjunction with a restaurant on a private lake.

Rates: $–$$

Number of Sites: 172

Seasonal Sites: Some Seasonal Sites

Number of Full Hookups: 121

Number of Water/Electric Hookups: 38

Number of Sites with No Hookups: 13

Number of Pull-Thru Sites: 13

Typical Site Width: 30 ft.

Services: Dump Station, Non-Guest Dumping, Non-Guest Dumping Fee

Open All Year

Hookup Information: 30 amps, 50 amps

Amenities: A/C Allowed, A/C Fee, Cable TV, Cable TV Fee, Fire Rings, Grills, Heater Allowed, Heater Fee, Ice, Laundry, Limited Groceries, Phone or Modem Hookup—Central Location, Public Phone, RV Supplies, Wood

Recreation: Badminton, Basketball, Canoe Rentals, Canoeing, Coin Games, Equipped Pavilion, Fishing, Fishing Supplies, Float Trips, Hiking Trails, Horseshoes, Lake Fishing, Lake Swimming, Local Tours, Mini-Golf, Mini-Golf Fee, Pedal Boat Rentals, Planned Activities (Weekends Only), Play Equipment, Playground, Pontoon Rentals, Recreation Room/Area, River Fishing, Sports Field, Volleyball

Credit Cards Accepted: Discover, MasterCard, Visa

Facility Fully Operational: May 1 through Oct. 15

Timberline Campground
DES MOINES (Dallas)
Phone: 515-987-1714

Directions: From west jct. I-35 & I-80: Go 6 mi. W on I-80 (exit 117), then 1 mi. N on CR R22, then ½ mi. E on CR F64.

Description: A rural, family-oriented CAMPGROUND with shaded sites.

Rates: $–$$

Number of Sites: 103

Seasonal Sites: Some Seasonal Sites

Number of Full Hookups: 38

Number of Water/Electric Hookups: 58
Number of Sites with No Hookups: 7
Open: April 1
Close: Nov. 1
Number of Pull-Thru Sites: 76
Typical Site Width: 25 ft.
Services: Dump Station, LP Gas by Meter, LP Gas by Weight, Non-Guest Dumping, Non-Guest Dumping Fee
Hookup Information: 30 amps, 50 amps
Amenities: A/C Allowed, Fire Rings, Grills, Heater Allowed, Ice, Laundry, Limited Groceries, Phone or Modem Hookup—Central Location, Phone or Modem Hookups at Site (need activ.), Public Phone, RV Supplies, Wood
Recreation: Badminton, Basketball, Coin Games, Hiking Trails, Horseshoes, Pavilion, Planned Activities (Weekends Only), Playground, Pool, Recreation Hall, Sports Field, Volleyball
Credit Cards Accepted: Discover, MasterCard, Visa

Sleepy Hollow RV Park & Campground
OXFORD (Johnson)
Phone: 319-828-4900

Directions: From jct. I-80 (exit 230) & CR W38: Go 1 block N on Black Hawk Ave.
Description: Prepared sites in a CAMPGROUND on a private lake.
Rates: $$
Number of Sites: 143
Number of Full Hookups: 60
Number of Water/Electric Hookups: 45
Number of Sites with No Hookups: 38
Number of Pull-Thru Sites: 62
Typical Site Width: 35 ft.
Services: Dump Station, LP Gas by Meter, LP Gas by Weight
Open All Year
Hookup Information: 30 amps, 50 amps, 50 amps Fee
Amenities: A/C Allowed, A/C Fee, Fire Rings, Grills, Groceries,

Heater Allowed, Heater Fee, Ice, Laundry, Phone or Modem Hookup—
Central Location, Phone or Modem Hookups at Site (need activ.),
Public Phone, RV Supplies, Wood

Recreation: Badminton, Basketball, Fishing, Fishing Supplies, Lake
Fishing, Planned Activities (Weekends Only), Playground, Pool,
Recreation Room/Area, Sports Field, Volleyball

Credit Cards Accepted: Discover, MasterCard, Visa

Facility Fully Operational: April 1 through Nov. 1

KANSAS

Gunsmoke Trav-L-Park
DODGE CITY (Ford)
Phone: 620-227-8247

Directions: From jct. Business US 50 & 2nd Ave (in town): Go 3 mi.
W on Business US 50.

Description: Open, level sites with shaded park area & western-
style buildings.

Rates: $$

Number of Sites: 100

Number of Full Hookups: 85

Number of Sites with No Hookups: 15

Open: March 1

Close: Oct. 31

Number of Pull-Thru Sites: 58

Typical Site Width: 22 ft.

Services: Dump Station, Non-Guest Dumping, Non-Guest Dumping Fee

Hookup Information: 15 amps, 20 amps, 30 amps, 50 amps, 50 amps Fee

Amenities: A/C Allowed, Cable TV, Fire Rings, Grills, Heater
Allowed, Ice, Laundry, Limited Groceries, Phone or Modem Hookup—
Central Location, Phone or Modem Hookups at Site (need activ.),
Public Phone, RV Supplies, Wood

Recreation: Coin Games, Equipped Pavilion, Playground, Pool,
Recreation Hall, Volleyball

Credit Cards Accepted: Discover, MasterCard, Visa

Spring Lake RV Resort
HALSTEAD (Harvey)
Phone: 316-835-3443

Directions: From jct. I-135 (exit 30) & Hwy 50: Go 12 mi. W on Hwy 50.
Description: Level, open, and shaded sites by a natural creek
Rates: $$
Number of Sites: 180
Number of Full Hookups: 62
Number of Water/Electric Hookups: 118
Number of Pull-Thru Sites: 20
Services: Dump Station, Non-Guest Dumping, Non-Guest Dumping Fee
Open All Year
Hookup Information: 20 amps, 30 amps, 50 amps
Amenities: A/C Allowed, Fire Rings, Heater Allowed, Ice, Laundry, Phone or Modem Hookup—Central Location, Public Phone, RV Supplies
Recreation: Basketball, Fishing, Mini-Golf, Pavilion, Planned Activities (Weekends Only), Playground, Pond Fishing, Pool, Recreation Hall, Recreation Room/Area, Stream Fishing
Discounts: FMCA Discount
Credit Cards Accepted: MasterCard, Visa

Lawrence/Kansas City KOA
LAWRENCE (Douglas)
Phone: 800-562-3708

Directions: From jct. I-70 (exit 204) & US 59/40: Go ½ mi. N on US 59/40, then ¼ mi. E on US 24/40.
Description: Large, grassy spaces in a CAMPGROUND at the edge of town.
Rates: $$
Number of Sites: 91
Seasonal Sites: Some Seasonal Sites
Number of Full Hookups: 61
Number of Water/Electric Hookups: 10
Number of Sites with No Hookups: 20

Number of Pull-Thru Sites: 62

Typical Site Width: 22 ft.

Services: Dump Station, LP Gas by Meter, LP Gas by Weight, Non-Guest Dumping, Non-Guest Dumping Fee

Open All Year

Hookup Information: 20 amps, 30 amps, 50 amps, 50 amps Fee

Amenities: A/C Allowed, Cable TV, Cable TV Fee, Fire Rings, Grills, Heater Allowed, Ice, Laundry, Limited Groceries, Phone or Modem Hookup—Central Location, Phone or Modem Hookups at site (need activ.), Public Phone, RV Supplies, Wood

Recreation: Badminton, Basketball, Canoeing, Coin Games, Float Trips, Horseshoes, Kayaking, Planned Activities (Weekends Only), Playground, Pool, Recreation Room/Area, Sports Field, Volleyball

Discounts: KOA 10% Value Card Discount

Credit Cards Accepted: Discover, MasterCard, Visa

KENTUCKY

KOA-Bowling Green
BOWLING GREEN (Warren)
Phone: 270-843-1919
Web site: *www.bgkoa.com*

Directions: From jct. I-65 (exit 22) & Hwy 231: Go 1,000 ft. W on Hwy 231, then 1½ mi. S on Hwy 884.

Description: CAMPGROUND with level, open sites in the countryside.

Rates: $$–$$$

Number of Sites: 150

Number of Full Hookups: 43

Number of Water/Electric Hookups: 72

Number of Sites with No Hookups: 35

Number of Pull-Thru Sites: 81

Max RV Length: 70

Typical Site Width: 30 ft.

Services: Dump Station, LP Gas by Meter, LP Gas by Weight, Non-Guest

Dumping, Non-Guest Dumping Fee, Partial Handicap Access

Open All Year

Hookup Information: 30 amps, 50 amps

Amenities: A/C Allowed, Cable TV, Fire Rings, Grills, Groceries, Heater Allowed, Ice, Laundry, Phone or Modem Hookup—Central Location, Phone or Modem Hookups at Site (need activ.), Public Phone, RV Supplies, Wood

Recreation: Badminton, Bike Rentals, Coin Games, Equipped Pavilion, Fishing, Fishing Supplies, Hiking Trails, Horseshoes, Lake Fishing, Pedal Boat Rentals, Planned Activities (Weekends Only), Playground, Pool, Recreation Room/Area, Sports Field, Volleyball

Discounts: KOA 10% Value Card Discount

Credit Cards Accepted: Discover, MasterCard, Visa

Facility Fully Operational: Swimming: Memorial Day, Labor Day

Prizer Point Marina & Resort
CADIZ (Trigg)
Phone: 270-522-3762
Web site: *www.prizerpoint.com*

Directions: From jct. I-24 (exit 56) & Hwy 139: Go 1½ mi. S on Hwy 139, then 6 mi. W on Hwy 276, then ¼ mi. S on Hwy 274, then 1 mi. W on Prizer Point Rd. (follow signs).

Description: Secluded, lakeside, shaded CAMPGROUND adjacent to a full-service marina.

Rates: $$–$$$

Number of Sites: 120

Number of Full Hookups: 47

Number of Water/Electric Hookups: 63

Number of Sites with No Hookups: 10

Open: March 1

Close: Nov. 1

Number of Pull-Thru Sites: 15

Max RV Length: 70

Typical Site Width: 40 ft.

Services: Dump Station, LP Gas by Meter, LP Gas by Weight, Partial Handicap Access

Hookup Information: 30 amps, 50 amps, 50 amps Fee

Amenities: A/C Allowed, A/C Fee, Cable TV, Cable TV Fee, Fire Rings, Heater Allowed, Heater Fee, Ice, Laundry, Limited Groceries, Marine Gas, Phone or Modem Hookup—Central Location, Public Phone, RV Supplies, Wood

Recreation: Badminton, Basketball, Bike Rentals, Boating, Canoe Rentals, Canoeing, Dock, Equipped Pavilion, Fishing, Fishing Guides, Fishing Supplies, Hiking Trails, Kayaking, Lake Fishing, Mini-Golf, Mini-Golf Fee, Motorboat Rentals, Pedal Boat Rentals, Planned Activities, Play Equipment, Playground, Pontoon Rentals, Pool, Ramp, Recreation Hall, Sports Field, Volleyball

Credit Cards Accepted: American Express, ATM On site, Discover, MasterCard, Visa

Mammoth Cave Jellystone Park Camp Resort
CAVE CITY (Barren)
Phone: 800-523-1854
Web site: *www.jellystonemammothcave.com*

Directions: From jct. I-65 (Exit 53) & Hwy 70: Go ¾ mi. W on Hwy 70.

Description: Rolling, grassy family CAMPGROUND with shaded & open sites.

Rates: $–$$$

Number of Sites: 191

Number of Full Hookups: 61

Number of Water/Electric Hookups: 80

Number of Sites with No Hookups: 50

Number of Pull-Thru Sites: 100

Typical Site Width: 30 ft.

Services: Dump Station, LP Gas by Meter, LP Gas by Weight, Non-Guest Dumping, Non-Guest Dumping Fee, Partial Handicap Access

Open All Year

Pets: Pet Restrictions

Hookup Information: 30 amps, 50 amps

Amenities: A/C Allowed, A/C Fee, Fire Rings, Grills, Groceries, Heater Allowed, Heater, Ice, Laundry, Phone or Modem Hookup—Central

Location, Public Phone, RV Supplies, Wood

Recreation: Badminton, Basketball, Coin Games, Equipped Pavilion, Fishing, Hiking Trails, Mini-Golf, Mini-Golf Fee, Pavilion, Planned Activities, Playground, Pond Fishing, Pool, Recreation Hall, Recreation Room/Area, Sports Field, Volleyball, Wading Pool

Credit Cards Accepted: Discover, MasterCard, Visa

Facility Fully Operational: Memorial Day, Labor Day

Season Exceptions: Limited facilities Nov. through Feb.

LOUISIANA

Cajun Country Campground
BATON ROUGE (West Baton Rouge)
Phone: 800-264-8554

Directions: From jct. I-10 (exit 151) & Hwy 415: Go ¾ mi. N on Hwy 415, then ½ mi. W on Hwy 76 (Rosedale Rd), then ½ mi. W on Rebelle Lane.

Description: Campground with open, level sites.

Rates: $–$$

Number of Sites: 77

Number of Full Hookups: 77

Number of Pull-Thru Sites: 54

Typical Site Width: 35 ft.

Services: LP Gas by Meter, LP Gas by Weight, No Camping Motorcyclists, Partial Handicap Access

Open All Year

Hookup Information: 20 amps, 30 amps, 50 amps, 50 amps Fee

Amenities: A/C Allowed, Heater Allowed, Ice, Laundry, Limited Groceries, Phone or Modem Hookup—Central Location, Phone or Modem Hookups at Site (need activ.), Public Phone, RV Supplies, Wood

Recreation: Basketball, Coin Games, Fishing, Hiking Trails, Pavilion, Pond Fishing, Pool, Recreation Room/Area, Volleyball

Discounts: FCRV 10% Discount, FMCA Discount

Credit Cards Accepted: MasterCard, Visa

KOA-New Orleans East
SLIDELL (St. Tammany)
Phone: 800-562-2128
Web site: *www.koa.com*

Directions: From jct. I-10: Go 4 mi. SW on I-10 (exit 263), then ¾ mi. E on Hwy 433.

Description: Open, shaded, level CAMPGROUND with gravel sites.

Rates: $$

Number of Sites: 126

Seasonal Sites: Some Seasonal Sites

Number of Full Hookups: 99

Number of Water/Electric Hookups: 27

Number of Pull-Thru Sites: 92

Typical Site Width: 20 ft.

Services: Dump Station, LP Gas by Meter, LP Gas by Weight, Non-Guest Dumping, Non-Guest Dumping Fee, Partial Handicap Access

Open All Year

Hookup Information: 15 amps, 20 amps, 30 amps, 50 amps

Amenities: A/C Allowed, Heater Allowed, Ice, Laundry, Limited Groceries, Phone or Modem Hookup—Central Location, Phone or Modem Hookups at Site (need activ.), Public Phone, RV Supplies

Recreation: Badminton, Coin Games, Fishing, Fishing Supplies, Local Tours, Mini-Golf, Pool, Recreation Hall, Stream Fishing, Volleyball

Discounts: KOA 10% Value Card Discount

Credit Cards Accepted: Discover, MasterCard, Visa

Yogi Bear's Jellystone Park Camp-Resort
LAKE CHARLES (Calcasieu)
Phone: 877-433-2400

Directions: From east jct. I-210 Bypass & I-10: Go 2½ mi. E on I-10 (exit 36), then 2 mi. N on Pujol Rd., then 1 mi. W & ¼ mi. N on Luke Powers Rd.

Description: CAMPGROUND with level sites in a wooded area.

Rates: $$–$$$

Number of Sites: 63
Number of Full Hookups: 63
Number of Pull-Thru Sites: 20
Typical Site Width: 25 ft.
Services: Dump Station, Non-Guest Dumping, Non-Guest Dumping Fee, Partial Handicap Access
Hookup Information: 20 amps, 30 amps, 50 amps
Amenities: Fire Rings, Ice, Laundry, Limited Groceries, Phone or Modem Hookup—Central Location, RV Supplies, Wood
Recreation: Canoe Rentals, Canoeing, Coin Games, Fishing, Lake Fishing, Mini-Golf, Mini-Golf Fee, Pavilion, Pedal Boat Rentals, Planned Activities, Playground, Pool, Recreation Room/Area
Credit Cards Accepted: American Express, Discover, MasterCard, Visa

MAINE

Paul Bunyan Campground
BANGOR (Penobscot)
Phone: 207-941-1177
Directions: From jct. I-95 (exit 47) & Hwy 222: Go 2½ mi. W on Hwy 222.
Description: Spacious, open & shaded sites on a rolling terrain.
Rates: $–$$
Number of Sites: 52
Number of Full Hookups: 12
Number of Water/Electric Hookups: 40
Open: April
Close: Oct.
Number of Pull-Thru Sites: 19
Average Site Width: 30 ft.
Services: Dump Station, LP Gas by Meter, Non-Guest Dumping Fee
Amenities: A/C Allowed, Fire Rings, Heater Allowed, Ice, Laundry, Limited Groceries, Phone or Modem Hookup—Central Location, Phone or Modem Hookups at Site (need activ.), Public Phone, RV Supplies, Wood

Recreation: Badminton, Basketball, Boating, Coin Games, Equipped Pavilion, Fishing, Fishing Supplies, Hiking Trails, Horseshoes, Pedal Boat Rentals, Planned Activities (Weekends Only), Playground, Pond Fishing, Pool, Recreation Hall, Sports Field, Volleyball

Credit Cards: Discover, MasterCard, Visa

Pleasant Hill RV Park & Campground

BANGOR (Penobscot)

Phone: 207-848-5127

Directions: From jct. I-95 (exit 47) & Hwy 222: Go 5 mi. W on Hwy 222.

Description: Family-oriented CAMPGROUND with open and shaded sites.

Rates: $–$$

Number of Sites: 106

Number of Full Hookups: 34

Number of Water/Electric Hookups: 62

Number of Sites with no Hookups: 10

Open: May 1l

Close: Columbus Day

Number of Pull-Thru Sites: 40

Average Site Width: 35 ft.

Services: Dump Station, LP Gas by Meter, LP Gas by Weight, Non-Guest Dumping Fee, Portable Dump

Amenities: A/C Allowed, Cable TV, Fire Rings, Heater Allowed, Ice, Laundry, Limited Groceries, Phone or Modem Hookup—Central Location, Phone or Modem Hookups at Site (need activ.), Public Phone, RV Supplies, Wood

Recreation: Badminton, Basketball, Boating, Coin Games, Horseshoes, Mini-Golf, Mini-Golf Fee, Pavilion, Playground, Pool, Recreation Room/Area, Sports Field, Volleyball

Credit Cards: Discover, MasterCard, Visa

Bar Harbor KOA
BAR HARBOR (Hancock)
Phone: 888-562-5605

Directions: At jct. Hwy 3 & Hwy 102 at head of island

Description: Grassy CAMPGROUND with shaded & open sites. Some sites are waterfront.

Rates: $$$–$$$$

Number of Sites: 200

Number of Full Hookups: 38

Number of Water/Electric Hookups: 137

Number of Sites with no Hookups: 25

Open: Early May

Close: Mid-Oct.

Number of Pull-Thru Sites: 75

Average Site Width: 28 ft.

Services: Dump Station, LP Gas by Meter, LP Gas by Weight, Fee, Portable Dump

Amenities: A/C Allowed, Fire Rings, Grills, Groceries, Heater Allowed, Hot Shower Fee, Ice, Laundry, Phone or Modem Hookup—Central Location, Phone or Modem Hookups at Site (need activ.), Public Phone, RV Supplies, Wood

Recreation: Badminton, Basketball, Bike Rentals, Boating, Canoeing, Coin Games, Fishing, Fishing Supplies, Horseshoes, Kayak Rentals, Kayaking, Local Tour, Planned Activities (Weekends Only), Playground, Ramp, Recreation Hall, Saltwater Fishing, Saltwater Swimming, Sports Field, Volleyball

Discounts: KOA 10% Value Card Discount

Credit Cards: Discover, MasterCard, Visa

Hadley's Point Campground
BAR HARBOR (Hancock)
Phone: 207-288-4808

Directions: From jct. Hwy 102 & Hwy 3: Go 3 mi. SE on Hwy 3, then ⅛ mi. N on Hadley Point Rd.

Description: Spacious, grassy, open and shaded sites near the ocean beach and Acadia National Park.

Rates: $$

Number of Sites: 180

Number of Full Hookups: 15

Number of Water/Electric Hookups: 117

Open: May 15

Close: Oct. 15

Number of Pull-Thru Sites: 99

Average Site Width: 26 ft.

Services: Dump Station, LP Gas by Meter, Portable Dump

Amenities: A/C Allowed, Fire Rings, Heater Allowed, Hot Shower Fee, Ice, Laundry, Limited Groceries, Phone or Modem Hookup—Central Location, Public Phone, RV Supplies, Wood

Recreation: Basketball, Horseshoes, Local Tours, Playground, Pool, Shuffleboard Sports Field

Credit Cards: MasterCard, Visa

Mt. Desert Narrows Camping Resort

BAR HARBOR (Hancock)

Phone: 207-288-4782

Web site: *www.narrowscamping.com*

Directions: From jct. Hwy 102 & Hwy 3: Go 1½ mi. SE on Hwy 3.

Description: An ocean-side location with tree-shaded and open sites.

Rates: Call for information

Number of Sites: 235

Number of Full Hookups: 62

Number of Water/Electric Hookups: 120

Number of Sites with No Hookups: 53

Open: May 15

Close: Oct. 25

Number of Pull-Thru Sites: 75

Average Site Width: 24 ft.

Services: Dump Station, LP Gas by Meter, Portable Dump

Amenities: A/C Allowed, A/C Fee, Cable TV, Fire Rings, Full-Service

Store, Heater Allowed, Heater Fee, Ice, Laundry, Phone or Modem Hookup—Central Location Phone/Modem Hookups at Site (on arrival), Public Phone, RV Supplies, Wood

Recreation: Basketball, Canoe Rentals, Canoeing, Coin Games, Fishing, Fishing Supplies, Kayak Rentals, Kayaking, Local Tours, Planned Activities, Playground, Pool, Recreation Hall, Recreation Room/Area, Saltwater Fishing, Volleyball

Credit Cards: Discover, MasterCard, Visa, ATM Onsite

MARYLAND

Bar Harbor RV Park & Marina
ABINGDON (Harford)
Phone: 800-351-2267
Web site: *www.barharborrvpark.com*

Directions: From jct. I-95 (exit 80) & Hwy 543: Go 1⁴/₁₀ mi. S on Hwy 543, then 1⁷/₁₀ mi. W on US 40, then ¾ mi. S on Long Bar Rd., then ½ mi. E on Baker Ave.

Description: Wooded sites on Chesapeake Bay.

Rates: $$$

Number of Sites: 93

Seasonal Sites: Some Seasonal Sites

Number of Full Hookups: 93

Number of Pull-Thru Sites: 7

Typical Site Width: 30 ft.

Services: Dump Station, LP Gas by Meter, LP Gas by Weight, No Camping Motorcyclists

Open All Year

Hookup Information: 30 amps, 50 amps

Amenities: A/C Allowed, Cable TV, Fire Rings, Grills, Heater Allowed, Ice, Laundry, Limited Groceries, Phone or Modem Hookup—Central Location, Phone or Modem Hookups at Site (need activ.), Public Phone, RV Supplies, Traffic Control Gate, Wood

Recreation: Boating, Canoeing, Coin Games, Dock, Fishing, Fishing

Supplies, Kayak Rentals, Kayaking, Pedal Boat Rentals, Play Equipment, Playground, Pool, Ramp, Recreation Hall, Recreation Room/Area, River Fishing, Saltwater Fishing

Credit Cards Accepted: ATM On site, MasterCard, Visa

Season Exceptions: Dec. 31 through March 1, self-contained units only.

Capitol KOA/Washington D.C. Northeast
MILLERSVILLE (Anne Arundel)
Phone: 800-562-0248

Directions: Northbound from jct. Hwy 32/I-97/Hwy 3: Go ½ mi. N on Veterans Hwy, then follow blue campground signs. Southbound from jct. I-695 & I-97 (exit 4): Go 8½ mi. S on I-97 (exit 10A), then S on Veterans Hwy & follow blue campground signs.

Description: CAMPGROUND with open and wooded sites.

Rates: $$$–$$$$

Number of Sites: 156

Number of Full Hookups: 68

Number of Water/Electric Hookups: 56

Number of Sites with No Hookups: 32

Open: March 25

Close: Oct. 31

Number of Pull-Thru Sites: 69

Typical Site Width: 40 ft.

Services: Dump Station, LP Gas by Meter, Partial Handicap Access

Pets: Pet Restrictions

Hookup Information: 20 amps, 30 amps, 50 amps, 50 amps Fee

Amenities: A/C Allowed, Fire Rings, Grills, Groceries, Heater Allowed, Ice, Laundry, Phone or Modem Hookup—Central Location, Public Phone, RV Supplies, Wood

Recreation: Badminton, Coin Games, Equipped Pavilion, Hiking Trails, Horseshoes, Local Tours, Planned Activities, Playground, Pool, Recreation Room/Area, Sports Field, Volleyball

Discounts: KOA 10% Value Card Discount

Credit Cards Accepted: Discover, MasterCard, Visa

Ramblin' Pines Family Campground & RV Park
WOODBINE (Carroll)
Phone: 800-550-8733

Directions: From jct. I-70 (exit 76) & Hwy 97: Go 2½ mi. N on Hwy 97, then ½ mi. NW on Hoods Mill Rd.

Description: CAMPGROUND with wooded & open sites.

Rates: $$$

Number of Sites: 200

Number of Full Hookups: 200

Number of Pull Thru Sites: 15

Typical Site Width: 42 ft.

Services: Dump Station, LP Gas by Meter, LP Gas by Weight, Non-Guest Dumping, Non-Guest Dumping Fee, Partial Handicap Access

Open All Year

Pets: Pet Restrictions

Hookup Information: 20 amps, 30 amps, 50 amps

Amenities: A/C Allowed, Fire Rings, Heater Allowed, Ice, Laundry, Limited Groceries, Phone or Modem Hookup—Central Location, Phone or Modem Hookups at Site (need activ.), Public Phone, RV Supplies, Traffic Control Gate, Wood

Recreation: Basketball, Coin Games, Equipped Pavilion, Fishing, Fishing Supplies, Hiking Trails, Horseshoes, Mini-Golf, Mini-Golf Fee, Planned Activities (Weekends Only), Playground, Pond Fishing, Pool, Recreation Hall, Recreation Room/Area, Shuffleboard, Sports Field, Volleyball

Discounts: FCRV 10% Discount, FMCA Discount

Credit Cards Accepted: MasterCard, Visa

MASSACHUSETTS

Circle CG Farm Adult RV Park
BELLINGHAM (Norfolk)
Phone: 508-966-1136

Directions: From jct. Hwy 495 & Hwy 126 (exit 18): Go 1 mi. S on Hwy 126.

Description: Level, grassy or graveled, semi-wooded sites in well-developed RV park with western theme.

Rates: $$$

Number of Sites: 150

Number of Full Hookups: 90

Number of Water/Electric Hookups: 60

Number of Sites with No Hookups: 0

Hookup Information: 20 amps, 30 amps, 50 amps, 50 amps Fee

Open: All year

Pets: Pet Restrictions

Number of Pull-Thru Sites: 20

Average Site Width: 30 ft.

Services: Dump Station, LP Gas by Meter, LP Gas by Weight, Portable Dump

Amenities: A/C Allowed, A/C Fee, Fire Rings, Groceries, Heater Allowed, Heater Fee, Ice, Laundry, Phone or Modem Hookup—Central Location, Public Phone, RV Supplies, Traffic, Control Gate, Wood

Recreation: Recreation Pond, Freshwater Fishing, Tackle, Heated Pool, Horseshoes, Recreation Hall, Game Room, Planned Activities, Recreation Field

Credit Cards: Visa, MasterCard

Normandy Farm Family Campground
FOXBORO
Phone: 508-543-7600
Web site: www.NormandyFarms.com

Directions: From Boston, take I-95 S or I-93 then exit I-95 S (Providence, RI) to Exit 9 onto Hwy 1, then 6.7 mi. Son Hwy 1 (fifth Traffic Light) turn left onto Thurston St. for 1.3 mi. to Normandy Farm

Description: Rolling terrain with mostly wooded, level sites.

Rates: $$–$$$$

Number of Sites: 410

Number of Full Hookups: 133

Number of Water/Electric Hookups: 252

Number of Sites with No Hookups: 25

Hookup Information: 20 amps, 30 amps, 50 amps

Open: All Year

Number of Pull-Thru Sites: 225

Average Site Width: 35 ft.

Services: Dump Station, LP Gas by Meter, LP Gas by Weight, Non-Guest Dumping, Non-Guest Dumping Fee, Portable Dump

Amenities: A/C Allowed, Fire Rings, Full-Service Store, Grills, Heater Allowed, Ice, Laundry, Phone or Modem Hookup—Central Location, Phone or Modem Hookups at Site (need activ.), Public Phone, RV Supplies, Traffic Control Gate, Wood

Recreation: Badminton, Basketball, Coin Games, Fishing, Hiking Trails, Local Tours, Pavilion, Planned Activities, Playground, Pond Fishing, Pool, Recreation Hall, Recreation Room/Area, Shuffleboard, Sports Field, Volleyball, Wading Pool, Whirlpool

Credit Cards: ATM Onsite, Discover, MasterCard, Visa

Peters Pond Park
SANDWICH (Barnstable)
Phone: 508-477-1775
Web site: *www.campcapecod.com*

Directions: From jct. US 6 (exit 2) & Hwy 130: Go 3$\frac{1}{10}$ mi. S on Hwy 130, then ¾ mi. E on Quaker Meeting House Rd., then ¾ mi. S on Cotuit Rd.

Description: A lakeside wooded CAMPGROUND on a 137-acre pond.

Rates: $$$–$$$$

Number of Sites: 466

Number of Full Hookups:350

Number of Water/Electric Hookups: 100

Number of Sites with No Hookups: 16

Hookup Information: 20 amps, 30 amps, 50 amps

Open: April 16

Close: Oct. 12

Number of Pull-Thru Sites: 3

Average Site Width: 40 ft.

Services: Dump Station, LP Gas by Meter, LP Gas by Weight

Amenities: A/C Allowed, Cable TV, Full-Service Store, Heater Allowed, Hot Shower Fee, Ice, Laundry, Phone or Modem Hookup—Central Location, Phone or Modem Hookups at Site (need activ.), Public Phone, RV Supplies, Traffic Control Gate

Recreation: Badminton, Basketball, Boating, Canoeing, Coin Games, Dock, Fishing, Fishing Supplies, Hiking Trails, Horseshoes, Kayak Rentals, Kayaking, Lake Fishing, Lake Swimming, Pedal Boat Rentals, Planned Activities, Playground, Ramp, Recreation Hall, Recreation Room/Area, Rowboat Rentals, Shuffleboard, Sports Field, Volleyball

Credit Cards: Discover, MasterCard, Visa

MICHIGAN

Camper's Cove RV & Canoe Livery
ALPENA (Alpena)
Phone: 989-356-3708

Directions: From jct. US 23 & Long Rapids Rd.: Go 6 mi. W on Long Rapids Rd. (Johnson St.).

Description: Level shaded CAMPGROUND on a lake.

Rates: $–$$$

Number of Sites: 89

Seasonal Sites: Some Seasonal Sites

Number of Full Hookups: 16

Number of Water/Electric Hookups: 49

Number of Electric Hookups: 15

Number of Sites with No Hookups: 9

Open: Mid-May

Close: Mid-Nov.

Number of Pull-Thru Sites: 8

Typical Site Width: 50 ft.

Services: Dump Station, LP Gas by Meter, LP Gas by Weight, Non-Guest Dumping, Non-Guest Dumping Fee, Portable Dump, Partial Handicap Access

Hookup Information: 20 amps, 30 amps, 50 amps, 50 amps Fee

Amenities: A/C Allowed, A/C Fee, Cable TV, Fire Rings, Heater Allowed, Heater Fee, Ice, Laundry, Limited Groceries, Phone or Modem Hookup—Central Location, Phone or Modem Hookups at Site (need activ.), Public Phone, RV Supplies, Wood

Recreation: Badminton, Basketball, Bike Rentals, Boating, Canoe Rentals, Canoeing, Dock, Fishing, Fishing Supplies, Horseshoes, Kayak Rentals, Kayaking, Lake Fishing, Mini-Golf, Mini-Golf Fee, Pavilion, Pedal Boat Rentals, Playground, Pond Fishing, Pontoon Rentals, Pool, Ramp, Recreation Room/Area, River Fishing, Rowboat Rentals, Shuffleboard, Volleyball

Credit Cards Accepted: MasterCard, Visa

Facility Fully Operational: Memorial Day through Labor Day

KOA-Mackinaw City/Mackinac Island
MACKINAW CITY (Emmet)
Phone: 800-KOA-1738

Directions: Northbound: From jct. I-75 (exit 337) & Hwy 108: Go 1 block S to Trailsend Rd., then ½ mi. W on Trailsend Rd. Southbound: From jct. I-75 (exit 338) & Hwy 108: Go 1 mi. S to Trailsend Rd, then ½ mi. W.

Description: A CAMPGROUND with level, mostly shaded sites.

Rates: $$–$$$

Number of Sites: 110

Number of Full Hookups: 33

Number of Water/Electric Hookups: 58

Number of Sites with No Hookups: 19

Open: May 1

Close: Oct. 15

Number of Pull-Thru Sites: 63

Typical Site Width: 35 ft.

Services: Dump Station, Non-Guest Dumping, Non-Guest Dumping Fee

Hookup Information: 20 amps, 30 amps, 50 amps

Amenities: A/C Allowed, A/C Fee, Fire Rings, Groceries, Heater Allowed, Ice, Laundry, Phone or Modem Hookup—Central Location, Public Phone, RV Supplies, Wood

Recreation: Coin Games, Hiking Trails, Horseshoes, Local Tours, Playground, Pool, Recreation Room/Area

Discounts: KOA 10% Value Card Discount

Credit Cards Accepted: Discover, MasterCard, Visa

Frankenmuth Jellystone Park Camp-Resort

FRANKENMUTH (Saginaw)

Phone: 989-652-6668

Web site: *www.frankenmuthjellystone.com*

Directions: Southbound from I-75 (Bridgeport exit 144) and Nouthbound from I-75 (Birch Run exit 136): Follow signs to Frankenmuth to south end of city at 1339 Weiss St.

Description: Open, level, grassy sites in an RV PARK in a tourist area.

Rates: $$$–$$$$

Number of Sites: 260

Number of Full Hookups: 160

Number of Water/Electric Hookups: 100

Number of Pull-Thru Sites: 48

Typical Site Width: 30 ft.

Services: Dump Station, LP Gas by Meter, LP Gas by Weight, Non-Guest Dumping, Non-Guest Dumping Fee, Partial Handicap Access

Open All Year

Hookup Information: 20 amps, 30 amps, 50 amps

Amenities: A/C Allowed, Groceries, Heater Allowed, Ice, Laundry, Phone or Modem Hookup Central Location, Public Phone, RV Supplies, Traffic Control Gate, Wood

Recreation: Badminton, Basketball, Bike Rentals, Coin Games, Horseshoes, Mini-Golf, Mini-Golf Fee, Planned Activities, Playground, Pool, Recreation Hall, Recreation Room/Area, Sports Field, Volleyball, Whirlpool

Credit Cards Accepted: MasterCard, Visa

MINNESOTA

Minneapolis NW/Maple Grove KOA

MINNEAPOLIS (Hennepin)

Phone: 763-420-2255

Directions: From west jct. I-494 & I-94: Go 3 mi NW on I-94 (exit 213), turn right to west CR 30 after McDonalds, then 2 mi. W on CR 30, then 1 mi, N on CR 101 (15 mi. NW of Minneapolis).

Description: Level, open and shaded, grassy sites in a rural CAMPGROUND.

Rates: $$–$$$

Number of Sites: 170

Seasonal Sites: Some Seasonal Sites

Number of Full Hookups: 40

Number of Water/Electric Hookups: 110

Number of Sites with No Hookups: 20

Open: April 1

Close: Oct. 15

Number of Pull-Thru Sites: 50

Typical Site Width: 35 ft.

Services: Dump Station, LP Gas by Meter, LP Gas by Weight, Non-Guest Dumping, Non-Guest Dumping Fee, Portable Dump

Hookup Information: 20 amps, 30 amps, 50 amps, 50 amps Fee,

Amenities: A/C Allowed, Fire Rings, Grills, Groceries, Heater Allowed, Ice, Laundry, Phone or Modem Hookup—Central Location, Phone or Modem Hookups at Site (need activ.), Public Phone, RV Supplies, Wood

Recreation: Basketball, Coin Games, Equipped Pavilion, Horseshoes, Mini-Golf, Mini-Golf Fee, Playground, Pool, Recreation Room/Area, Shuffleboard, Sports Field

Discounts: KOA 10% Value Card Discount

Credit Cards Accepted: MasterCard, Visa

St. Cloud Campground & RV Park
ST CLOUD (Benton)
Phone: 320-251-4463

Directions: From jct. US 10 & Hwy 23: Go ¼ mi. E on Hwy 23, then 1 block S on 14th Ave. SE, then 1 mi. E on CR 8.

Description: Private, shaded & open sites in a rural location.

Rates: $$

Number of Sites: 105

Seasonal Sites: Some Seasonal Sites

Number of Full Hookups: 72

Number of Water/Electric Hookups: 16

Number of Sites with No Hookups: 17

Number of Pull-Thru Sites: 40

Typical Site Width: 30 ft.

Services: Dump Station, LP Gas by Meter, LP Gas by Weight, Non-Guest Dumping, Non-Guest Dumping Fee

Policies: Age Restrictions May Apply

Hookup Information: 20 amps, 30 amps, 50 amps, 50 amps Fee

Amenities: A/C Allowed, Fire Rings, Heater Allowed, Ice, Laundry, Limited Groceries, Phone or Modem Hookup—Central Location, Phone or Modem Hookups at Site (need activ.), Public Phone, RV Supplies, Wood

Recreation: Badminton, Basketball, Coin Games, Hiking Trails, Horseshoes, Planned Activities (Weekends Only), Playground, Pool, Recreation Hall, Recreation Room/Area, Sports Field, Volleyball

Discounts: FMCA Discount

Credit Cards Accepted: Discover, MasterCard, Visa

Facility Fully Operational: April 25 through Oct. 15

Stony Point Resort Trailer Park & Campground
CASS LAKE (Cass)
Phone: 800-332-6311
Web site: *www.stonyptresortcasslake.com*

Directions: From jct. Hwy 371 & US 2: Go 2 mi. E on US 2.

Description: Lakeside CAMPGROUND with shaded, level, grassy sites.

Rates: $$

Number of Sites: 160

Seasonal Sites: Many Seasonal Sites

Number of Full Hookups: 135

Number of Water/Electric Hookups: 15

Number of Sites with No Hookups: 10

Open: May 1

Close: Oct. 15

Number of Pull-Thru Sites: 29

Typical Site Width: 35 ft.

Services: Dump Station, LP Gas by Meter, LP Gas by Weight, Non-Guest Dumping, Non-Guest Dumping Fee

Hookup Information: 20 amps, 30 amps, 50 amps

Amenities: A/C Allowed, A/C Fee, Fire Rings, Grills, Heater Allowed, Ice, Laundry, Limited Groceries, Marine Gas, Phone or Modem Hookup—Central Location, Public Phone, RV Supplies, Wood

Recreation: Badminton, Basketball, Boating, Canoe Rentals, Canoeing, Coin Games, Dock, Fishing, Fishing Guides, Fishing Supplies, Horseshoes, Kayak Rentals, Kayaking, Lake Fishing, Lake Swimming, Motorboat Rentals, Pavilion, Pedal Boat Rentals, Play Equipment, Playground, Pond Fishing, Pontoon Rentals, Ramp, Recreation Hall, Sports Field, Volleyball

Credit Cards Accepted: American Express, Discover, MasterCard, Visa

MISSISSIPPI

Cajun RV Park
BILOXI (Harrison)
Phone: 877-225-8699
Web site: *www.cajunrvpark.com*

Directions: From jct. I-10 & I-110: Go 4 mi. S on I-110, then 3 mi. W on US 90.

Description: Grassy RV PARK across the highway from the Gulf.

Rates: $$

Number of Sites: 116

Number of Full Hookups: 88

Number of Water/Electric Hookups: 28

Number of Pull-Thru Sites: 53

Typical Site Width: 26 ft.

Services: LP Gas by Meter, LP Gas by Weight

Open All Year

Hookup Information: 30 amps, 50 amps

Amenities: A/C Allowed, Heater Allowed, Ice, Laundry, Phone or

Modem Hookup—Central Location, Public Phone, RV Supplies
   Recreation: Pavilion, Play Equipment, Pool, Recreation Room/Area
   Credit Cards Accepted: MasterCard, Visa

Memphis South Campground & RV Park
COLDWATER (Tate)
Phone: 662-622-0056
   Directions: From I-55 (exit 271) & Hwy 306: Go 200 ft. W on Hwy 306 (turn before gas station).
   Description: Open prepared site near a major highway.
   Rates: $–$$
   Number of Sites: 82
   Seasonal Sites: Some Seasonal Sites
   Number of Full Hookups: 82
   Number of Pull-Thru Sites: 82
   Typical Site Width: 50 ft.
   Open All Year
   Service: Partial Handicap Access
   Hookup Information: 20 amps, 30 amps, 50 amps
   Amenities: A/C Allowed, Heater Allowed, Laundry, Phone or Modem Hookups at Site (need activ.), Public Phone, RV Supplies
   Recreation: Play Equipment, Pool
   Credit Cards Accepted: American Express, Discover, MasterCard, Visa

Baywood RV Park and Campground, Inc.
GULFPORT (Harrison)
Phone: 888-747-4840
   Directions: From jct. I-10 (exit 38) & Lorraine/Cowen Rd.: Go 3 mi. S on Lorraine/Cowen Rd.
   Description: A CAMPGROUND in town & near the Gulf with mostly paved, level sites.
   Rates: $$
   Number of Sites: 114
   Seasonal Sites: Some Seasonal Sites
   Number of Full Hookups: 114

Number of Pull-Thru Sites: 8

Typical Site Width: 25 ft.

Services: Dump Station, LP Gas by Meter, LP Gas by Weight, Open All Year

Hookup Information: 15 amps, 30 amps, 50 amps,

Amenities: A/C Allowed, Cable TV, Groceries, Heater Allowed, Ice, Laundry, Phone or Modem Hookups at Site (need activ.), Public Phone, RV Supplies

Recreation: Fishing, Fishing Supplies, Planned Activities (Weekends Only), Playground, Pond Fishing, Pool, Recreation Hall

Discounts: FMCA Discount

Credit Cards Accepted: MasterCard, Visa

MISSOURI

Compton Ridge Campground

BRANSON (Stone)

Phone: 417-338-2911

Web site: *www.comptonridge.com*

Directions: From jct. US 65 & Hwy 76: Go 8 mi. W on Hwy 76, then 1 mi. S on Hwy 265.

Description: Wooded with level sites and many activities.

Rates: $$–$$$

Number of Sites: 227

Seasonal Sites: Some Seasonal Sites

Number of Full Hookups: 186

Number of Water/Electric Hookups: 41

Open: April 1

Close: Nov. 30

Number of Pull-Thru Sites: 53

Typical Site Width: 30 ft.

Services: Dump Station, LP Gas by Weight, Partial Handicap Access

Hookup Information: 20 amps, 30 amps, 50 amps, 50 amps Fee

Amenities: A/C Allowed, Cable TV, Fire Rings, Full-Service Store,

Grills, Heater Allowed, Ice, Laundry, Phone or Modem Hookup—Central Location, Public Phone, RV Supplies, Wood

Recreation: Badminton, Basketball, Coin Games, Equipped Pavilion, Hiking Trails, Local Tours, Planned Activities, Playground, Pool, Recreation Hall, Recreation Room/Area, Tennis, Volleyball, Wading Pool

Credit Cards Accepted: Discover, MasterCard, Visa

Yogi Bear's Jellystone Park Resort at Six Flags
EUREKA (St. Louis)
Phone: 800-861-3020

Directions: From jct. I-270 & I-44: Go 15 mi. W on I-44 to Six Flags/Allenton exit (exit 261), then ½ mi. W on Fox Creek Rd. (N service road).

Description: Level, grassy shaded sites in a wooded setting.

Rates: $$–$$$

Number of Sites: 110

Number of Full Hookups: 28

Number of Water/Electric Hookups: 82

Open: March 1

Close: Oct. 1

Number of Pull-Thru Sites: 10

Max RV Length: 42

Typical Site Width: 25 ft.

Services: Dump Station, LP Gas by Meter, LP Gas by Weight, Non-Guest Dumping, Non-Guest Dumping Fee, Partial Handicap Access

Hookup Information: 30 amps, 50 amps, 50 amps Fee

Amenities: A/C Allowed, A/C Fee, Fire Rings, Grills, Groceries, Heater Allowed, Heater Fee, Ice, Laundry, Phone or Modem Hookup—Central Location, Phone or Modem Hookups at Site (need activ.), Public Phone, RV Supplies, Wood

Recreation: Badminton, Coin Games, Equipped Pavilion, Float Trips, Hiking Trails, Mini-Golf, Mini-Golf Fee, Planned Activities, Playground, Pool, Recreation Hall, Shuffleboard, Volleyball

Credit Cards Accepted: Discover, MasterCard, Visa

Ozark Trails RV Park
LINN CREEK (Camden)
Phone: 573-346-5490

Directions: From jct. Hwy 5 & US 54: Go 4 mi. E on US 54.

Description: Level, shaded sites in a terraced campground in a tourist area.

Rates: $–$$

Number of Sites: 58

Seasonal Sites: Some Seasonal Sites

Number of Full Hookups: 30

Number of Water/Electric Hookups: 5

Number of Sites with No Hookups: 23

Number of Pull-Thru Sites: 23

Typical Site Width: 30 ft.

Services: Dump Station, LP Gas by Meter, LP Gas by Weight

Open All Year

Hookup Information: 20 amps, 30 amps, 50 amps

Amenities: A/C Allowed, Cable TV, Fire Rings, Groceries, Heater Allowed, Ice, Laundry, Phone or Modem Hookup—Central Location, Public Phone, Wood

Recreation: Coin Games, Hiking Trails, Horseshoes, Playground, Pool, Recreation Hall, Recreation Room/Area

Discounts: FMCA Discount

Credit Cards Accepted: Discover, MasterCard, Visa

Season Exceptions: Facilities limited Nov. 15 through March 15.

MONTANA

Bear Canyon Campground
BOZEMAN (Gallatin)
Phone: 800-438-1575
Web site: *www.bearcanyoncampground.com*

Directions: From I-90 (exit 313): Go S 1 block to entrance.

Description: Level gravel sites overlooking town with a view of the Gallatin Mountains.

Rates: $–$$

Number of Sites: 78

Seasonal Sites: Some Seasonal Sites

Number of Full Hookups: 31

Number of Water/Electric Hookups: 32

Number of Sites with No Hookups: 15

Open: May

Close: Oct.

Number of Pull-Thru Sites: 31

Services: Dump Station

Hookup Information: 20 amps, 30 amps, 50 amps

Amenities: A/C Allowed, Grills, Heater Allowed, Ice, Laundry, Limited Groceries, Phone or Modem Hookups at Site (need activ.), Public Phone, RV Supplies

Recreation: Coin Games, Pavilion, Playground, Pool, Recreation Room/Area, Sports Field

Credit Cards Accepted: Discover, MasterCard, Visa

Helena Campground and RV Park

HELENA (Lewis & Clark)

Phone: 406-458-4714

Directions: From jct. I-15 (exit 193) & US 12 (Cedar St.): Go ¾ mi. W on Cedar St., then 3½ mi. N on Montana. From jct. I-15 (exit 200): Go W ¼ mi. to Montana, then S 3½ mi. Entrance on west side.

Description: CAMPGROUND in metro area with mature shade trees & view of the Elkhorn Mountains.

Rates: $$

Number of Sites: 98

Number of Full Hookups: 47

Number of Water/Electric Hookups: 51

Open: April 1

Close: Sept. 30

Number of Pull-Thru Sites: 26

Max RV Length: 40

Typical Site Width: 25 ft.

Services: Dump Station, Partial Handicap Access

Hookup Information: 20 amps, 30 amps, 50 amps

Amenities: A/C Allowed, A/C Fee, Fire Rings, Grills, Groceries, Heater Allowed, Heater Fee, Ice, Laundry, Phone or Modem Hookup—Central Location, Public Phone, RV Supplies, Wood

Recreation: Badminton, Basketball, Coin Games, Planned Activities, Playground, Pool, Recreation, Room/Area, Sports Field, Volleyball, Whirlpool

Discounts: FMCA Discount

Credit Cards Accepted: Discover, MasterCard, Visa

Yellowstone Holiday Resort RV Campground & Marina
WEST YELLOWSTONE (Gallatin)
Phone: 877-646-4242

Directions: From jct. US 287 & US 191: Go 5¼ mi. N on Hwy 287 to mile marker 17.

Description: CAMPGROUND with level gravel sites adjacent to a marina on Hebgen Lake in Gallatin National Forest.

Rates: $$$

Number of Sites: 27

Seasonal Sites: Some Seasonal Sites

Number of Full Hookups: 27

Open: May 15

Close: Sept. 15

Number of Pull-Thru Sites: 7

Max RV Length: 90

Typical Site Width: 30 ft.

Services: Partial Handicap Access

Hookup Information: 20 amps, 30 amps, 50 amps

Amenities: A/C Allowed, Fire Rings, Grills, Heater Allowed, Ice, Laundry, Limited Groceries, Marine Gas, Phone or Modem Hookup—Central Location, Public Phone, RV Supplies, Wood

Recreation: Bike Rentals, Boating, Canoe Rentals, Canoeing, Dock, Fishing, Kayak Rentals, Kayaking, Lake Fishing, Lake Swimming, Motorboat Rentals, Pavilion, Pedal Boat Rentals, Ramp

Credit Cards Accepted: MasterCard, Visa

NEBRASKA

Holiday Park
NORTH PLATTE (Lincoln)
Phone: 800-424-4531

Directions: From jct. I-80 (exit 177) & US 83: Go 1 block N on US 83, then ½ mi. S & E on Halligan Dr. (frontage road).

Description: Level spaces in a CAMPGROUND.

Rates: $–$$

Number of Sites: 90

Number of Full Hookups: 70

Number of Water/Electric Hookups: 20

Number of Pull-Thru Sites: 84

Typical Site Width: 30 ft.

Services: Dump Station, Non-Guest Dumping, Non-Guest Dumping Fee

Open All Year

Hookup Information: 30 amps, 50 amps, 50 amps Fee

Amenities: A/C Allowed, Cable TV, Cable TV Fee, Grills, Heater Allowed, Ice, Laundry, Limited Groceries, Phone or Modem Hookup—Central Location, Phone or Modem Hookups at Site (need activ.), Public Phone, RV Supplies

Recreation: Equipped Pavilion, Play Equipment, Playground, Pool, Recreation Room/Area, Sports Field

Discounts: FMCA Discount

Credit Cards Accepted: Discover, MasterCard, Visa

Facility Fully Operational: April 15 through Oct. 15

West Omaha KOA
OMAHA (Sarpy)
Phone: 402-332-3010

Directions: From jct. I-80 (exit 432) & Hwy 31 & US 6: Go 100 ft. N on US 6, then ¾ mi. W on US 6.

Description: CAMPGROUND with shaded sites.

Rates: $–$$

Number of Sites: 96

Number of Full Hookups: 31

Number of Water/Electric Hookups: 43

Number of Electric Hookups: 12

Number of Sites with No Hookups: 9

Open: April 1

Close: Oct. 31

Number of Pull-Thru Sites: 65

Services: Dump Station, LP Gas by Meter, Non-Guest Dumping, Non-Guest Dumping Fee

Hookup Information: 30 amps, 50 amps, 50 amps Fee

Amenities: A/C Allowed, Fire Rings, Grills, Heater Allowed, Ice, Laundry, Limited Groceries, Phone or Modem Hookup—Central Location, Phone or Modem Hookups at Site (need activ.), Public Phone, RV Supplies, Wood

Recreation: Basketball, Coin Games, Mini-Golf, Pavilion, Playground, Pool, Recreation Hall, Shuffleboard, Sports Field, Volleyball, Whirlpool

Discounts: KOA 10% Value Card Discount

Credit Cards Accepted: American Express, Discover, MasterCard, Visa

NEVADA

Oasis Las Vegas RV Resort
LAS VEGAS (Clark)
Phone: 702-260-2000

Directions: From jct. I-15 (exit 33) & Hwy 160 (Blue Diamond): Go ¼ mi. E on Blue Diamond, then ¼ mi. S on Las Vegas Blvd., then 1 block W on Windmill Lane.

Description: Walled resort RV PARK with level, paved landscaped sites in a desert area.

Rates: $$–$$$

Number of Sites: 700

Seasonal Sites: Some Seasonal Sites

Number of Full Hookups: 700

Number of Pull-Thru Sites: 320

Typical Site Width: 25 ft.

Services: Dump Station, LP Gas by Meter, Non-Guest Dumping, Non-Guest Dumping Fee, Partial Handicap Access

Open All Year

Pets: Pet Restrictions

Hookup Information: 15 amps, 20 amps, 30 amps, 50 amps

Amenities: A/C Allowed, Cable TV, Groceries, Heater Allowed, Ice, Laundry, Phone or Modem Hookup—Central Location, Phone or Modem Hookups at Site (on arrival), Public Phone, RV Supplies

Recreation: Coin Games, Local Tours, Planned Activities, Pool, Putting Green, Recreation Hall, Recreation Room/Area, Whirlpool

Discounts: FMCA Discount

Credit Cards Accepted: American Express, ATM Onsite, Discover, MasterCard, Visa

Avi RV Resort
LAUGHLIN (Clark)
Phone: 800-284-2946
Web site: *www.avicasino.com*

Directions: From jct. Hwy 163 & Needles Hwy (west of Laughlin): Go 9 mi. S on Needles Hwy, then 4½ mi. SE on Aha Macau Pkwy.

Description: RV PARK adjacent to Avi Hotel & Casino. Recreational facilities at hotel may be used by campers.

Rates: $–$$$

Number of Sites: 260

Number of Full Hookups: 260

Number of Pull-Thru Sites: 191

Services: Dump Station, Non-Guest Dumping, Non-Guest Dumping Fee, Partial Handicap Access

Open All Year

Hookup Information: 20 amps, 30 amps, 50 amps, 50 amps Fee

Amenities: A/C Allowed, Cable TV, Groceries, Heater Allowed, Ice, Laundry, Marine Gas, Phone or Modem Hookup—Central Location, Phone/Modem Hookups at Site (on arrival), Public Phone

Recreation: Boating, Canoeing, Coin Games, Dock, Equipped Pavilion, Fishing, Kayaking, Local Tours, Pavilion, Planned Activities, Pool, Ramp, River Fishing, River Swimming, Whirlpool

Credit Cards Accepted: American Express, ATM Onsite, Discover, MasterCard, Visa

Boomtown RV Park

RENO (Washoe)

Phone: 877-626-6686

Web site: *www.boomtownreno.com*

Directions: From jct. I-80 (exit 4) & Boomtown/Garson Rd.: Go ¼ mi. N on Boomtown/Garson Rd.

Description: RV PARK adjacent to casino with paved sites and grassy area in the Sierra Foothills.

Rates: $$–$$$$

Number of Sites: 203

Number of Full Hookups: 203

Number of Pull-Thru Sites: 132

Typical Site Width: 28 ft.

Services: Dump Station, LP Gas by Meter, Non-Guest Dumping, Non-Guest Dumping Fee

Ammenities: Cable TV, Message and Mail, Center, Outdoor Swimming Pool & Spas, Private Showers, Picnic Area, Coin-Operated Laundromat, Casino

NEW HAMPSHIRE

Chocorua Camping Village
CHOCORUA (Carroll)
Phone: 888-237-8642
Web site: *www.chocoruacamping.com*

Directions: From north jct. Hwy 25 & Hwy 16: Go 3 mi. N on Hwy 16.

Description: CAMPGROUND along Moore's Pond and Chocorua River on hilly terrain with level, shaded, prepared sites.

Rates: $$$

Number of Sites: 143

Number of Full Hookups: 95

Number of Water/Electric Hookups: 35

Number of Sites with No Hookups: 13

Hookup Information: 20 amps, 30 amps, 50 amps

Open: May 1

Close: Oct. 15

Number of Pull-Thru Sites: 15

Average Site Width: 50 ft.

Services: Dump Station, LP Gas by Meter, LP Gas by Weight, Non-Guest Dumping, Non-Guest Dumping Fee, Portable Dump

Amenities: A/C Allowed, Cable TV, Cable TV Fee, Fire Rings, Grills, Heater Allowed, Hot Shower Fee, Ice, Laundry, Limited Groceries, Phone or Modem Hookup—Central Location, Phone or Modem Hookups at Site (need activ.), Public Phone, RV Supplies, Traffic Control Gate, Wood

Recreation: Badminton, Basketball, Boating, Canoe Rentals, Canoeing, Coin Games, Dock, Electric Motors Only, Fishing, Fishing Supplies, Hiking Trails, Horseshoes, Kayak Rentals, Kayaking, Lake Fishing, Lake Swimming, Pedal Boat Rental, Planned Activities, Playground, Recreation Hall, Recreation Room/Area, River Fishing, Rowboat Rentals, Sports Field, Volleyball

Credit Cards: MasterCard, Visa

Circle 9 Ranch
EPSOM (Merrimack)
Phone: 603-736-9656

Directions: From jct. US 4/202/Hwy 9 & Hwy 28 (Epsom Traffic Circle): Go ¼ mi. S on Hwy 28, then ¼ mi. W on Windymere Dr.

Description: CAMPGROUND with open, prepared sites & shaded sites in a forest setting.

Rates: $$–$$$$
Number of Sites: 144
Number of Full Hookups: 95
Number of Water/Electric Hookups: 49
Number of Sites with No Hookups: 0
Hookup Information: 20 amps, 30 amps, 50 amps
Open All Year
Number of Pull-Thru Sites: 21
Average Site Width: 20 ft.
Services: Dump Station, Portable Dump, Partial Handicap Access
Amenities: A/C Allowed, A/C Fee, Cable TV, Cable TV Fee, Fire Rings, Heater Allowed, Heater Fee, Hot Shower Fee, Ice, Laundry, Limited Groceries, Phone or Modem Hookup—Central Location, Phone or Modem Hookups at Site (need activ.), Phone/Modem Hookups at Site (on arrival), Public Phone, RV Supplies, Traffic Control Gate, Wood
Recreation: Basketball, Coin Games, Fishing, Fishing Supplies, Horseshoes, Play Equipment, Pond Fishing, Pool, Recreation Hall, Recreation Room/Area, Stream Fishing, Whirlpool
Credit Cards: American Express, Discover, MasterCard, Visa

Twin Tamarack Family Camping and RV Resort
MEREDITH (Belknap)
Phone: 603-279-4387

Directions: From jct. I-93 (exit 23) & Hwy104: Go 2½ mi. E on Hwy104.

Description: A CAMPGROUND on Pemigewasset Lake with spacious, shaded sites.

Rates: $$$

Number of Sites: 247
Number of Full Hookups: 147
Number of Water/Electric Hookups: 100
Number of Sites with No Hookups: 0
Hookup Information: 30 amps, 50 amps, 50 amps Fee
Open: Memorial Day
Close: Columbus Day
Number of Pull-Thru Sites: 30
Average Site Width: 40 ft.
Services: Dump Station
Amenities: A/C Allowed, Cable TV, Cable TV Fee, Fire Rings, Heater Allowed, Ice, Laundry, Limited Groceries, Phone or Modem Hookup—Central Location, Public Phone, RV Supplies, Wood
Recreation: Badminton, Basketball, Boating, Canoe Rentals, Canoeing, Coin Games, Dock, Fishing, Kayak Rentals, Kayaking, Lake Fishing, Lake Swimming, Pedal Boat Rentals, Planned Activities (Weekends Only), Playground, Pool, Ramp, Recreation Room/Area, Rowboat Rentals, Sports Field, Volleyball, Whirlpool
Credit Cards: Discover, MasterCard, Visa

NEW JERSEY

Timberlane Campground
CLARKSBORO (Gloucester)
Phone: 856-423-6677
Web site: *www.timberlanecampground.com*

Directions: Northbound from I-295 (exit 18): Go ¾ mi. E on Timberlane Rd. Entrance on right. Southbound from I-295 (exit 18): Go 1 mi. SE on Hwy 667, then right ¼ mi. on Friendship Rd., then right ¼ mi. on Timberlane Rd. Entrance on left.

Description: Resort, open & wooded, grassy sites in a suburban location.
Rates: $$$
Number of Sites: 96
Number of Full Hookups: 82

Number of Water/Electric Hookups: 0
Number of Sites with No Hookups: 14
Open All Year
Number of Pull-Thru Sites: 51
Average Site Width: 30 ft.

Services: Dump Station, LP Gas by Meter, LP Gas by Weight, Non-Guest Dumping, Non-Guest Dumping Fee, Partial Handicap Access

Amenities: A/C Allowed, A/C Fee, Cable TV, Fire Rings, Heater Allowed, Heater Fee, Ice, Laundry, Phone or Modem Hookup—Central Location, Phone or Modem, Hookups at Site (need activ.), Public Phone, RV Supplies, Wood

Recreation: Basketball, Coin Games, Fishing, Fishing Supplies, Horseshoes, Pavilion, Playground, Pond Fishing, Pool, Recreation Room/Area, Shuffleboard, Volleyball, Wading Pool

Credit Cards: MasterCard, Visa

Best Holiday Trav-L-Park/Holly Acres
EGG HARBOR CITY (Atlantic)
Phone: 609-965-2287
Web site: *www.kiz.com/bestholiday*

Directions: From jct. Hwy 50 & US 30: Go 2 mi. E on US 30, then 1½ mi. N on Frankfurt Ave. Entrance on right. From Southbound Garden State Pkwy (exit 44): Make 2 hard rights, then 4½ mi. W on Alt 561, then ½ mi. S on Frankfurt Ave.

Description: Flat terrain with wooded and open, grassy sites.
Rates: $$$
Number of Sites: 175
Number of Full Hookups: 125
Number of Water/Electric Hookups: 50
Number of Sites with No Hookups: 0
Hookup Information: 30 amps, 50 amps, 50 amps Fee
Open: May 1
Close: Sept. 30
Number of Pull-Thru Sites: 8
Average Site Width: 35 ft.

Amenities: A/C Allowed, Cable TV, Fire Rings, Heater Allowed, Ice, Laundry, Limited Groceries, Phone or Modem Hookup—Central Location, Public Phone, Traffic Control Gate, Wood

Recreation: Badminton, Coin Games, Equipped Pavilion, Fishing, Mini-Golf, Mini-Golf Fee, Planned Activities (Weekends Only), Playground, Pond Fishing, Pool, Recreation Hall, Shuffleboard, Volleyball, Wading Pool.

Credit Cards: MasterCard, Visa

Cape Island Campground
CAPE MAY (Cape May)
Phone: 609-884-5777
Web site: *www.capeisland.com*

Directions: From jct. Hwy 109 & US 9: Go ½ mi. N on US 9.

Description: Sites well separated by high shrubbery.

Rates: $$$$

Number of Sites: 465

Number of Full Hookups: 310

Number of Water/Electric Hookups: 127

Number of Sites with No Hookups: 18

Hookup Information: 20 amps, 30 amps, 50 amps

Open: May 1

Close: Nov. 1

Number of Pull-Thru Sites: 17

Average Site Width: 37 ft.

Services: Dump Station, LP Gas by Weight, Non-Guest Dumping, Non-Guest Dumping Fee, Partial Handicap Access, No Motorcycles

Amenities: A/C Allowed, Cable TV, Cable TV Fee, Fire Rings, Groceries, Heater Allowed, Hot Shower Fee, Ice, Laundry, Phone or Modem Hookups at Site (need activ.), Public Phone, RV Supplies, Traffic Control Gate, Wood

Recreation: Basketball, Coin Games, Equipped Pavilion, Mini-Golf, Mini-Golf Fee, Planned Activities, Playground, Pool, Recreation Hall, Recreation Room/Area, Shuffleboard, Sports Field, Tennis, Volleyball, Wading Pool, Whirlpool

Credit Cards: MasterCard, Visa

NEW MEXICO

Enchanted Trails Camping Resort
ALBUQUERQUE (Bernalillo)
Phone: 800-326-6317

Directions: From jct I-40 (exit 149) & Paseo del Volcan Ave.: Go 700 ft. N on Paseo del Volcan Ave., then 1½ mi. W on north frontage road.

Description: RV PARK with open & shaded sites in a rural area on the west edge of town.

Rates: $–$$
Number of Sites: 135
Seasonal Sites: Some Seasonal Sites
Number of Full Hookups: 115
Number of Water/Electric Hookups: 20
Number of Pull-Thru Sites: 127
Typical Site Width: 22 ft.
Services: Dump Station, LP Gas by Meter, LP Gas by Weight, Non-Guest Dumping, Non-Guest Dumping Fee, Partial Handicap Access
Open All Year
Hookup Information: 30 amps, 50 amps, 50 amps Fee
Amenities: A/C Allowed, Heater Allowed, Ice, Laundry, Phone or Modem Hookup—Central Location, Phone or Modem Hookups at Site (need activ.), Public Phone, RV Supplies
Recreation: Pavilion, Planned Activities, Pool, Recreation Hall, Recreation Room/Area, Whirlpool
Credit Cards Accepted: American Express, Discover, MasterCard, Visa
Season Exceptions: Pool open Memorial Day through Oct. 31.

Rancheros de Santa Fe Campground
SANTA FE (Santa Fe)
Phone: 800-426-9259

Directions: From I-25 (exit 290): Go ³/₁₀ mi. N on frontage road, then 1 mi. E on Old Las Vegas Hwy.

Description: Rustic, wooded, secluded CAMPGROUND with level sites in a resort setting.

Rates: $$

Number of Sites: 124

Number of Full Hookups: 43

Number of Water/Electric Hookups: 41

Number of Sites with No Hookups: 40

Open: March 15

Close: Nov. 1

Number of Pull Thrus: 69

Typical Site Width: 22 ft.

Services: Dump Station, LP Gas by Meter, LP Gas by Weight, Non-Guest Dumping, Non-Guest Dumping Fee

Hookup Information: 30 amps, 50 amps

Amenities: A/C Allowed, Cable TV, Fire Rings, Grills, Heater Allowed, Ice, Laundry, Limited Groceries, Phone or Modem Hookup—Central Location, Phone or Modem Hookups at Site (need activ.), Public Phone, RV Supplies, Wood

Recreation: Coin Games, Hiking Trails, Pavilion, Planned Activities, Playground, Pool, Recreation Hall, Recreation Room/Area

Discounts: FMCA Discount, KOA 10% Value Card Discount

Credit Cards Accepted: American Express, Discover, MasterCard, Visa

Stagecoach Stop Resort RV Park
RIO RANCHO (Sandoval)
Phone: 505-867-1000

Directions: From jct I-25 (exit 242) & Hwy 44: Go 2½ mi. W on Hwy 44, then ½ mi. S on Hwy 528.

Description: Level, paved sites in open location at edge of metro area.

Rates: $$–$$$

Number of Sites: 85

Seasonal Sites: Some Seasonal Sites

Number of Full Hookups: 85

Number of Pull-Thru Sites: 85

Typical Site Width: 30 ft.

Services: Dump Station, Non-Guest Dumping, Non-Guest Dumping Fee, Partial Handicap Access

Open All Year

Hookup Information: 30 amps, 50 amps

Amenities: Laundry, Phone or Modem Hookup—Central Location, Phone or Modem Hookups at Site (need activ.), Public Phone

Recreation: Pavilion, Planned Activities, Play Equipment, Playground, Pool, Recreation Hall, Recreation Room/Area, Tennis

Discounts: FMCA Discount

NEW YORK

KOA-Niagara Falls North

LEWISTON (Niagara)

Phone: 716-754-8013

Directions: From north jct. I-190 (exit 25B) & Robert Moses Pkwy: Go 3 mi. N on Robert Moses Pkwy, then 1¾ mi. E on Pletcher Rd.

Description: CAMPGROUND with open and shaded sites

Rates: $$–$$$$

Number of Sites: 92

Number of Full Hookups:18

Number of Water/Electric Hookups: 56

Number of Sites with No Hookups: 18

Hookup Information: 20 amps, 30 amps, 50 amps, 50 amps Fee

Open: April 1

Close: Oct. 15

Number of Pull-Thru Sites: 40

Average Site Width: 24 ft.

Services: Dump Station, LP Gas by Meter, LP Gas by Weight, Non-Guest Dumping, Non-Guest Dumping Fee

Amenities: A/C Allowed, Fire Rings, Groceries, Heater Allowed, Ice, Laundry, Phone or Modem Hookup—Central Location, Public Phone, RV Supplies, Wood

Recreation: Basketball, Bike Rentals, Coin Games, Horseshoes, Local Tours, Playground, Pool, Recreation Room/Area, Volleyball

Discounts: KOA 10% Value Card Discount

Credit Cards Accepted: Discover, MasterCard, Visa

Adirondack 1000 Islands Camping
NATURAL BRIDGE (Lewis)
Phone: 315-644-4880

Directions: From jct. I-81 (exit 48) & Hwy 342: Go 7 mi. E on Hwy 342, then 7 mi. E on Hwy 3, then 5 mi. E on Hwy 3A, then 6 mi. E on Hwy 3.

Description: Semi-wooded CAMPGROUND with shaded & some open sites.

Rates: $$–$$$

Number of Sites: 67

Number of Full Hookups: 29

Number of Water/Electric Hookups: 26

Number of Sites with No Hookups: 12

Hookup Information: 20 amps, 30 amps, 50 amps

Open: April 1

Close: Nov. 1

Number of Pull-Thru Sites: 37

Services: Dump Station, LP Gas by Meter, LP Gas by Weight, Partial Handicap Access

Amenities: A/C Allowed, Fire Rings, Grills, Groceries, Heater Allowed, Ice, Laundry, Phone or Modem Hookup—Central Location, Public Phone, RV Supplies, Wood

Recreation: Badminton, Basketball, Bike Rentals, Coin Games, Equipped Pavilion, Hiking, Trails, Horseshoes, Planned Activities (Weekends Only), Playground, Pool, Recreation Hall, Recreation Room/Area, Sports Field, Volleyball

Discounts: KOA 10% Value Card Discount

Credit Cards Accepted: Discover, MasterCard, Visa

Rip Van Winkle Campground
SAUGERTIES (Ulster)
Phone: 845-246-8114

Directions: Southbound from I-87 (exit 20-Saugerties) & Hwy 32: Go ⅛ mi. S on Hwy 32, 2 mi. W on Hwy 212, then ½ mi. N at Centerville Fork on CR 35. Northbound from jct. I-87 (exit

20—Saugerties) & Hwy 212: Go 2 mi. W on Hwy 212, then ½ mi. N at Centerville Fork on CR 35.

Description: Wooded sites in a rural area.

Rates: $$$

Number of Sites: 125

Number of Full Hookups: 36

Number of Water/Electric Hookups: 47

Number of Sites with No Hookups: 42

Hookup Information: 20 amps, 30 amps, 50 amps

Open: May

Close: Oct. 15

Number of Pull-Thru Sites: 37

Average Site Width: 60 ft.

Services: Dump Station, LP Gas by Meter, LP Gas by Weight, Partial Handicap Access

Amenities: A/C Allowed, Fire Rings, Heater Allowed, Hot Shower Fee, Ice, Laundry, Limited Groceries, Phone or Modem Hookup—Central Location, Public Phone, RV Supplies, Traffic Control Gate, Wood

Recreation: Badminton, Fishing, Hiking Trails, Horseshoes, Playground, River Fishing, River Swimming, Sports Field, Volleyball

Discounts: FMCA Discount

Credit Cards Accepted: Discover MasterCard, Visa

NORTH CAROLINA

Asheville-Bear Creek RV Park and Campground
ASHEVILLE (Buncombe)
Phone: 828-253-0798

Web site: *www.ashevillebearcreek.com*

Directions: From jct. I-40 (exit 47) & Hwy 191: Westbound, go ¼ mi. W across Hwy 191, then ¼ mi. W on S Bear Creek Rd. Eastbound: Go ¼ mi. N on Hwy 191, then ¼ mi. W on S Bear Creek Rd.

Description: A developed, hilltop CAMPGROUND with level, open & shaded, prepared sites in an urban area.

Rates: $$
Number of Sites: 106
Number of Full Hookups: 90
Number of Water/Electric Hookups: 16
Number of Pull-Thru Sites: 45
Typical Site Width: 30 ft.
Services: Dump Station, Partial Handicap Access
Open All Year
Hookup Information: 15 amps, 20 amps, 30 amps, 50 amps, 50 amps Fee
Amenities: A/C Allowed, Cable TV, Cable TV Fee, Heater Allowed, Ice, Laundry, Limited Groceries, Phone or Modem Hookup—Central Location, Phone or Modem Hookups at Site (need activ.), Public Phone, RV Supplies
Recreation: Basketball, Bike Rentals, Coin Games, Playground, Pool, Recreation Hall, Recreation Room/Area, Volleyball
Discounts: FMCA Discount

Hatteras Sands Resort
HATTERAS (Dare)
Phone: 252-986-2422
Web site: *www.hatterassands.com*
Directions: From the Ocracoke-Hatteras Ferry: Go ¹/₁₀ mi. N on Hwy 12, then ¼ mi. E on Eagle Pass Rd.
Description: Open & shaded, paved & grassy sites at a family-oriented CAMPGROUND along saltwater canals.
Rates: $$$–$$$$
Number of Sites: 128
Number of Full Hookups: 54
Number of Water/Electric Hookups: 53
Number of Sites with No Hookups: 21
Open: March 1
Close: Dec. 1
Number of Pull-Thru Sites: 26
Typical Site Width: 30 ft.
Services: Dump Station, Non-Guest Dumping, Non-Guest

Dumping Fee, Portable Dump, Partial Handicap Access

Pets: Pet Restrictions

Hookup Information: 15 amps, 20 amps, 30 amps, 50 amps, 50 amps Fee

Amenities: A/C Allowed, Cable TV, Heater Allowed, Ice, Laundry, Limited Groceries, Phone or Modem Hookup—Central Location, Phone/Modem Hookups at Site (need activ.), Public Phone, RV Supplies, Traffic Control Gate

Recreation: Badminton, Basketball, Bike Rentals, Canoeing, Coin Games, Fishing, Fishing Guides, Fishing Supplies, Kayaking, Pavilion, Pedal Boat Rentals, Planned Activities, Playground, Pool, Recreation Room/Area, Saltwater Fishing, Volleyball, Wading Pool, Whirlpool

Credit Cards Accepted: MasterCard, Visa

Twin Lakes Camping Resort and Yacht Basin
WASHINGTON (Beaufort)
Phone: 252-946-5700

Directions: From jct. US 264 & US 17: Go 1¾ mi. S on US 17, then 1½ mi. SE on Whichards Beach Rd.

Description: A CAMPGROUND with shaded, grassy sites on a peninsula between the Pamlico River & Chocowinity Bay.

Rates: $$–$$$

Number of Sites: 379

Seasonal Sites: Many Seasonal Sites

Number of Full Hookups: 354

Number of Water/Electric Hookups: 25

Number of Pull-Thru Sites: 64

Typical Site Width: 34 ft.

Services: LP Gas by Meter, LP Gas by Weight, Portable Dump

Open All Year

Hookup Information: 20 amps, 30 amps, 50 amps

Amenities: A/C Allowed, A/C Fee, Fire Rings, Groceries, Heater Allowed, Heater Fee, Ice, Laundry, Marine Gas, Phone or Modem Hookup—Central Location, Phone or Modem Hookups at Site (need activ.), Public Phone, RV Supplies, Wood

Recreation: Basketball, Boating, Canoeing, Coin Games, Dock,

Equipped Pavilion, Fishing, Fishing Supplies, Hiking Trails, Kayaking, Lake Fishing, Planned Activities (Weekends Only), Playground, Pool, Ramp, Recreation Hall, Recreation Room/Area, River Fishing, Volleyball, Wading Pool

Credit Cards Accepted: Discover, MasterCard, Visa

NORTH DAKOTA

Grand Forks Campground
GRAND FORKS (Grand Forks)
Phone: 701-772-6108

Directions: From jct. US 2 & I-29 (exit 141): Go 3 mi. S on I-29 to exit 138, then 1 mi. S on west frontage gravel road.

Description: CAMPGROUND with mostly gravel, well-shaded sites

Rates: $

Number of Sites: 188

Number of Full Hookups: 88

Number of Water/Electric Hookups: 87

Number of Sites with No Hookups: 13

Open: April 1

Close: Nov. 1

Number of Pull-Thru Sites: 68

Typical Site Width: 28 ft.

Services: Dump Station, LP Gas by Meter, LP Gas by Weight

Hookup Information: 20 amps, 30 amps, 50 amps, 50 amps Fee

Amenities: Laundry, Phone or Modem Hookup—Central Location, Public Phone

Recreation: Playground, Pool, Recreation Room/Area

Jamestown Campground
JAMESTOWN (Stutsman)
Phone: 800-313-6262

Directions: From I-94 (exit 256): Go 1 mi. W on S Frontage Rd.

Description: Open, rural CAMPGROUND with grassy sites & trees.

Rates: $$

Number of Sites: 68

Number of Full Hookups: 29

Number of Water/Electric Hookups: 19

Number of Sites with No Hookups: 20

Open: April 15

Close: Oct. 15

Number of Pull-Thru Sites: 42

Typical Site Width: 35 ft.

Services: Dump Station

Hookup Information: 20 amps, 30 amps, 50 amps, 50 amps Fee

Amenities: A/C Allowed, Cable TV, Fire Rings, Grills, Heater Allowed, Ice, Laundry, Limited Groceries, Phone or Modem Hookup—Central Location, Public Phone, RV Supplies, Wood

Recreation: Basketball, Coin Games, Hiking Trails, Horseshoes, Playground, Pool, Recreation Room/Area, Sports Field

Discounts: FMCA Discount

Credit Cards Accepted: Discover, MasterCard, Visa

OHIO

Shelby/Mansfield KOA (Wagon Wheel Campground)

SHELBY (Crawford)

Phone: 419-347-1392

Web site: *www.wagonwheelcampground.com*

Directions: From jct. Hwy 61 & Hwy 39: Go 4 mi. W on Hwy 39, then 4½ mi. N on Baker 47.

Description: Open & shaded sites in a rural area.

Rates: $$–$$$$

Number of Sites: 198

Seasonal Sites: Some Seasonal Sites

Number of Full Hookups: 144

Number of Water/Electric Hookups: 54

Open: May 1

Close: Oct. 15

Number of Pull-Thru Sites: 49

Max RV Length: 85

Typical Site Width: 35 ft.

Services: Dump Station, LP Gas by Meter, LP Gas by Weight, Non-Guest Dumping, Non-Guest Dumping Fee, Partial Handicap Access

Hookup Information: 20 amps, 30 amps, 50 amps

Amenities: A/C Allowed, Fire Rings, Grills, Groceries, Heater Allowed, Ice, Laundry, Phone or Modem Hookup—Central Location, Phone or Modem Hookups at Site (on arrival), Public Phone, RV Supplies, Traffic Control Gate, Wood

Recreation: Badminton, Basketball, Bike Rentals, Coin Games, Equipped Pavilion, Fishing, Fishing Supplies, Hiking Trails, Horseshoes, Lake Fishing, Mini-Golf, Mini-Golf Fee, Pavilion, Pedal Boat Rentals, Planned Activities (Weekends Only), Playground, Pool, Recreation Hall, Recreation Room/Area, Shuffleboard, Sports Field, Tennis, Volleyball, Wading Pool, Whirlpool

Discounts: KOA 10% Value Card Discount

Credit Cards Accepted: ATM Onsite, Discover, MasterCard, Visa

Lazy J Family Campground
BELLEVUE (Huron)
Phone: 800-305-9644

Directions: From jct. Ohio Tpk I-80/90 (exit 110) & Hwy 4: Go 4 mi. S on Hwy 4, then 1 mi. E on US 20.

Description: A CAMPGROUND with open and tree-shaded sites.

Rates: $$

Number of Sites: 129

Number of Water/Electric Hookups: 129

Open: April 15

Close: Oct. 15

Number of Pull-Thru Sites: 64

Typical Site Width: 30 ft.

Services: Dump Station, LP Gas by Meter, LP Gas by Weight, Non-Guest Dumping, Non-Guest Dumping Fee, Portable Dump, Partial Handicap Access

Pets: Pet Restrictions

Hookup Information: 20 amps, 30 amps, 50 amps, 50 amps Fee

Amenities: A/C Allowed, A/C Fee, Fire Rings, Grills, Groceries, Heater Allowed, Ice, Laundry, Phone or Modem Hookup—Central Location, Phone or Modem Hookups at Site (need activ.), Public Phone, RV Supplies, Wood

Recreation: Badminton, Basketball, Coin Games, Fishing, Horseshoes, Mini-Golf, Pavilion, Pedal Boat Rentals, Planned Activities (Weekends Only), Playground, Pond Fishing, Pool, Recreation Hall, Recreation Room/Area, Sports Field, Volleyball, Wading Pool

Credit Cards Accepted: Discover, MasterCard, Visa

KOA-Bear Creek Resort Ranch
CANTON (Stark)
Phone: 330-484-3901
Web site: *www.bearcreek.us*

Directions: From jct. I-77 (exit 99) & Fohl Rd.: Go ½ mi. W on Fohl Rd, then 3 mi. S on Sherman Church Rd., then 1 mi. E on Haut Rd.

Description: A hilly CAMPGROUND in a western setting.

Rates: $$–$$$

Number of Sites: 92

Number of Full Hookups: 49

Number of Water/Electric Hookups: 35

Number of Sites with No Hookups: 8

Number of Pull Thrus: 50

Typical Site Width: 35 ft.

Services: Dump Station, LP Gas by Meter, LP Gas by Weight, Non-Guest Dumping

Non-Guest Dumping Fee

Open All Year

Hookup Information: 20 amps, 30 amps, 50 amps

Amenities: A/C Allowed, A/C Fee, Fire Rings, Grills, Groceries, Heater Allowed, Heater Fee, Ice, Laundry, Phone or Modem Hookup—Central Location, Public Phone, RV Supplies, Wood

Recreation: Badminton, Basketball, Coin Games, Fishing, Hiking

Trails, Horseshoes, Lake Fishing, Mini-Golf, Mini-Golf Fee, Pavilion, Pedal Boat Rentals, Planned Activities (Weekends Only), Playground, Pool, Recreation Hall, Recreation Room/Area, Sports Field, Volleyball

Discounts: KOA 10% Value Card Discount

Credit Cards Accepted: American Express, Discover, MasterCard, Visa

OKLAHOMA

Checotah/Henryetta KOA
CHECOTAH (McIntosh)
Phone: 800-562-7510

Directions: From jct. US 69 & I-40: Go 10 mi. W on I-40 (exit 255), then ½ mi. W on N service road.

Description: A rural, lakeside CAMPGROUND with open & shaded sites.

Rates: $$

Number of Sites: 76

Seasonal Sites: Some Seasonal Sites

Number of Full Hookups: 35

Number of Water/Electric Hookups: 34

Number of Sites with No Hookups: 7

Number of Pull-Thru Sites: 31

Typical Site Width: 33 ft.

Services: Dump Station, LP Gas by Meter, LP Gas by Weight, Partial Handicap Access

Open All Year

Hookup Information: 15 amps, 20 amps, 30 amps, 50 amps

Amenities: A/C Allowed, Grills, Groceries, Heater Allowed, Ice, Laundry, Phone or Modem Hookup—Central Location, Public Phone, RV Supplies, Wood

Recreation: Badminton, Canoe Rentals, Canoeing, Coin Games, Fishing, Hiking Trails, Kayak Rentals, Kayaking, Lake Fishing, Pavilion, Pedal Boat Rentals, Play Equipment, Playground, Pool, Recreation Hall, Recreation Room/Area, Sports Field, Volleyball

Discounts: KOA 10% Value Card Discount

Credit Cards Accepted: MasterCard, Visa

A-OK RV Park
OKLAHOMA CITY (Oklahoma)
Phone: 405-787-7356

Directions: From west jct. I-44 & I-40: Go 3 mi. W on I-40 to exit 143, then ⅛ mi. S on Rockwell Ave.

Description: Level, mostly shaded, grassy sites next to a motel.

Rates: $

Number of Sites: 34

Seasonal Sites: Some Seasonal Sites

Number of Full Hookups: 34

Number of Pull-Thru Sites: 20

Typical Site Width: 25 ft.

Policies: Big Rigs Welcome

Open All Year

Hookup Information: 20 amps, 30 amps, 50 amps, 50 amps Fee

Amenities: A/C Allowed, Heater Allowed, Ice, Laundry, Limited Groceries, Phone or Modem Hookup—Central Location, Public Phone

Recreation: Play Equipment, Pool,

Credit Cards Accepted: American Express, Discover, MasterCard, Visa

KOA-Tulsa
TULSA (Rogers)
Phone: 918-266-4227

Directions: From jct. US 66 & I-44: Go ½ mi. W on I-44 (193 E Ave exit 240A), then 1 block N on 193 E Ave.

Description: CAMPGROUND with level, mostly shady sites. Has storm shelter.

Rates: $$

Number of Sites: 190

Seasonal Sites: Some Seasonal Sites

Number of Full Hookups: 77

Number of Water/Electric Hookups: 113

Number of Pull-Thru Sites: 190

Typical Site Width: 20 ft.

Services: Dump Station, LP Gas by Meter, LP Gas by Weight

Open All Year

Hookup Information: 30 amps, 50 amps

Amenities: A/C Allowed, Heater Allowed, Ice, Laundry, Limited Groceries, Phone or Modem Hookup—Central Location, Phone or Modem Hookups at Site (need activ.), Public Phone, RV Supplies

Recreation: Coin Games, Playground, Pool, Recreation Room/Area, Volleyball

Discounts: KOA 10% Value Card Discount

Credit Cards Accepted: MasterCard, Visa

OREGON

Astoria-Warrenton-Seaside-KOA

ASTORIA

Phone: 503-861-2606

Web site: *www.astoriakoa.com*

Directions: From US 101, 3 mi. S of Astoria: Go 4½ mi. W on Alt US 101, then follow state park signs.

Description: Level, terraced sites in a rural, wooded setting.

Rates: $$$–$$$$

Number of Sites: 259

Number of Full Hookups: 116

Number of Water/Electric Hookups: 116

Number of Sites with No Hookups: 27

Number of Pull-Thru Sites: 98

Typical Site Width: 35 ft.

Services: LP Gas by Meter, Non-Guest Dumping, Non-Guest Dumping Fee

Open All Year

Pets: Pet Restrictions

Hookup Information: 20 amps, 30 amps, 50 amps

Amenities: A/C Allowed, Cable TV, Cable TV Fee, Fire Rings, Full-Service Store, Grills, Heater Allowed, Ice, Laundry, Phone or Modem Hookup—Central Location, Phone or Modem Hookups at Site (on arrival), Public Phone, RV Supplies, Wood

Recreation: Badminton, Basketball, Bike Rentals, Coin Games, Equipped Pavilion, Hiking Trails, Local Tours, Mini-Golf, Mini-Golf Fee, Planned Activities, Play Equipment, Playground, Pool, Recreation Room/Area, Sports Field, Volleyball, Whirlpool

Discounts: KOA 10% Value Card Discount

Credit Cards Accepted: Discover, MasterCard, Visa

Premier RV Resorts of Eugene
EUGENE (Lane)
Phone: 541-686-3152
Web site: *www.premierrvresorts.com*

Directions: From I-5 (exit 199, Coburg): Go 2 blocks E on Van Duyn Rd.

Description: RV PARK resort in a scenic, rural setting.

Rates: $$

Number of Sites: 154

Seasonal Sites: Some Seasonal Sites

Number of Full Hookups: 154

Number of Pull-Thru Sites: 132

Typical Site Width: 22 ft.

Open All Year

Hookup Information: 20 amps, 30 amps, 50 amps

Amenities: A/C Allowed, Cable TV, Grills, Heater Allowed, Ice, Laundry, Phone or Modem Hookup—Central Location, Phone or Modem Hookups at Site (need activ.), Phone/Modem Hookups at Site (on arrival), Public Phone, RV Supplies

Recreation: Basketball, Fishing, Planned Activities, Pond Fishing, Pool, Recreation Hall

Discounts: FMCA Discount, KOA 10% Value Card Discount

Credit Cards Accepted: MasterCard, Visa

Holiday RV Park
MEDFORD (Jackson)
Phone: 800-452-7970

Directions: From I-5 (exit 24): Go ⅛ mi. W on Fern Valley Rd.

Description: RV PARK on the banks of Bear Creek.

Rates: $$

Number of Sites: 110

Number of Full Hookups: 110

Number of Pull-Thru Sites: 80

Typical Site Width: 25 ft.

Services: LP Gas by Meter

Open All Year

Hookup Information: 15 amps, 20 amps, 30 amps, 50 amps

Amenities: A/C Allowed, Cable TV, Heater Allowed, Hot Shower Fee, Ice, Laundry, Limited Groceries, Phone or Modem Hookup—Central Location, Public Phone, RV Supplies

Recreation: Basketball, Equipped Pavilion, Horseshoes, Pool, Recreation Room/Area

Credit Cards Accepted: MasterCard, Visa

PENNSYLVANIA

KOA-Allentown-Lehigh Valley Kampground

ALLENTOWN (Lehigh)

Phone: 610-298-2160

Directions: From jct. PA Tpk (exit 56/33) & US 22: Go 3 mi. W on US 22, then 6½ mi. N on Hwy 100, then ½ mi. W on Narris Rd.

Description: Grassy, streamside CAMPGROUND.

Rates: $$–$$$

Number of Sites: 103

Number of Full Hookups: 36

Number of Water/Electric Hookups: 64

Number of Sites with No Hookups: 3

Hookup Information: 20 amps, 30 amps, 50 amps

Open: April 1

Close: Nov. 1

Number of Pull-Thru Sites: 24

Average Site Width: 28 ft.

Services: Dump Station, LP Gas by Meter, LP Gas by Weight, Non-Guest Dumping, Non-Guest Dumping Fee, Portable Dump, Partial Handicap Access

Amenities: A/C Allowed, A/C Fee, Cable TV, Cable TV Fee, Fire Rings, Groceries, Heater Allowed, Heater Fee, Ice, Laundry, Phone or Modem Hookup—Central Location, Phone or Modem Hookups at Site (need activ.), Public Phone, RV Supplies, Wood

Recreation: Basketball, Coin Games, Fishing, Hiking Trails, Horseshoes, Pavilion, Planned Activities (Weekends Only), Playground, Pool, Recreation Hall, Recreation Room/Area, Stream Fishing, Volleyball, Wading Pool

Credit Cards: Discover, MasterCard, Visa

Discounts: KOA 10% Value Card

Drummer Boy Camping Resort
GETTYSBURG (Adams)
Phone: 800-293-2808
Web site: *www.drummerboycamping.com*

Directions: From jct. Bypass US 15 & Hwy 116: Go 100 yd. E on Hwy 116, then ⅛ mi. N on Rocky Grove Rd.

Description: Wooded CAMPGROUND in a natural setting with shaded sites in historic area.

Rates: $$–$$$$
Number of Sites: 286
Number of Full Hookups: 125
Number of Water/Electric Hookups: 110
Number of Sites with No Hookups: 50
Hookup Information: 20 amps, 30 amps, 50 amps
Open: April 2
Close: Oct. 31
Number of Pull-Thru Sites: 51
Average Site Width: 32 ft.

Services: Dump Station, Non-Guest Dumping, Non-Guest Dumping Fee, Portable Dump, Partial Handicap Access

Amenities: A/C Allowed, Cable TV, Fire Rings, Full-Service Store, Heater Allowed, Ice, Laundry, Phone or Modem Hookup—Central Location, Public Phone, RV Supplies, Wood

Recreation: Badminton, Basketball, Coin Games, Fishing, Hiking Trails, Horseshoes, Local Tours, Mini-Golf, Mini-Golf Fee, Pavilion, Planned Activities, Playground, Pond Fishing, Pool, Recreation Hall, Recreation Room/Area, Volleyball, Whirlpool

Discounts: FMCA Discount

Credit Cards: Discover, MasterCard, Visa

KOA-Philadelphia/West Chester

WEST CHESTER (Chester)

Phone: 610-486-0447

Web site: *www.philadelphiakoa.com*

Directions: From jct. US 202 & US 1: Go 9 mi. S on US 1, then 3 mi. NW on Hwy 82, then 3 mi. E on Hwy 162.

Description: Grassy CAMPGROUND with open & wooded sites.

Rates: $$$

Number of Sites: 104

Number of Full Hookups: 40

Number of Water/Electric Hookups: 25

Number of Electric Hookups: 9

Number of Sites with No Hookups: 30

Hookup Information: 20 amps, 30 amps, 50 amps, 50 amps Fee

Open: April 1

Close: Oct. 31

Number of Pull-Thru Sites: 8

Average Site Width: 28 ft.

Services: Dump Station, LP Gas by Meter, LP Gas by Weight, Partial Handicap Access

Amenities: A/C Allowed, Fire Rings, Groceries, Heater Allowed, Ice, Laundry, Phone or Modem Hookup—Central Location, Public Phone, RV Supplies, Wood

Recreation: Badminton, Canoe Rentals, Canoeing, Coin Games, Fishing, Kayaking, Local Tours, Mini-Golf, Mini-Golf Fee, Pavilion, Planned Activities (Weekends Only), Playground, Pool, Recreation Room/Area, River Fishing, Volleyball, Wading Pool

Discounts: KOA 10% Value Card Discount

Credit Cards: American Express, Discover, MasterCard, Visa

RHODE ISLAND

Holiday Acres Camping Resort
HARMONY (Providence)
Phone: 401-934-0780

Directions: From jct. I-295 & Hwy 44: Go 2½ mi. W on Hwy 44, then 1½ mi. S on Hwy 116 (Smith Ave), then at Knight's Farm go straight on Snake Hill Rd for 2¾ mi.

Description: Hilly terrain with open & wooded sites adjacent to a reservoir.

Rates: $$–$$$

Number of Sites: 225

Number of Full Hookups: 165

Number of Water/Electric Hookups: 60

Number of Sites with No Hookups: 0

Open All Year

Number of Pull-Thru Sites: 30

Average Site Width: 50 ft.

Services: Dump Station, LP Gas by Meter, LP Gas by Weight, Non-Guest Dumping, Non-Guest Dumping Fee, Portable Dump

Amenities: A/C Allowed, A/C Fee, Fire Rings, Heater Allowed, Heater Fee, Ice, Laundry, Limited Groceries, Phone or Modem Hookup—Central Location, Phone or Modem Hookups at Site (need activ), Public Phone, Wood

Recreation: Badminton, Basketball, Boating, Canoe Rentals, Canoeing, Coin Games, Electric Motors Only, Fishing, Fishing Supplies, Hiking Trails, Kayak Rentals, Kayaking, Lake Fishing, Lake Swimming, Mini-Golf, Mini-Golf Fee, Pavilion, Pedal Boat Rentals, Planned Activities (Weekends Only), Playground, Ramp, Recreation Hall, Recreation Room/Area, Rowboat Rentals, Shuffleboard, Sports Field, Volleyball

Discounts: FMCA Discount

Ginny-B Family Campground
FOSTER (Providence)
Phone: 401-397-9477

Directions: From jct. Hwy 94 & US 6: Go 3¼ mi. W on US 6, then

3½ mi. S on Cucumber Hill Rd., then ½ mi. E on Harrington Rd.

Description: CAMPGROUND with large, grassy sites adjacent to a golf course.

Rates: Call for information

Number of Sites: 200

Number of Full Hookups: 50

Number of Water/Electric Hookups: 150

Number of Sites with No Hookups: 0

Hookup Information: 20 amp, 30 amp

Open: May 1

Close: Sept. 30

Number of Pull-Thru Sites: 35

Average Site Width: 35 ft.

Services: Dump Station, Non-Guest Dumping, Non-Guest Dumping Fee, Portable Dump

Amenities: Fire Rings, Ice, Laundry, Limited Groceries, Phone or Modem Hookups at Site (need activ.), Public Phone, Wood

Recreation: Basketball, Fishing, Horseshoes, Planned Activities (Weekends Only), Playground, Pond Fishing, Pond Swimming, Recreation Hall, Sports Field, Stream Fishing, Volleyball

SOUTH CAROLINA

Lake Aire RV Park and Campground

CHARLESTON (Charleston)

Phone: 843-571-1271

Web site: *www.lakeairerv.com*

Directions: (N) from jct. I-526 W & US 17: Go 7½ mi. S on US 17, then 1,000 ft. S on Hwy 162. (S) from Ravenel: Go 8 mi. N on US 17, then 1,000 ft. S on Hwy 162.

Description: A CAMPGROUND on a lake with open & shaded sites.

Rates: $$

Number of Sites: 113

Number of Full Hookups: 66

Number of Water/Electric Hookups: 21
Number of Sites with No Hookups: 26
Number of Pull-Thru Sites: 75
Services: Dump Station, LP Gas by Meter, LP Gas by Weight, Partial Handicap Access
Open All Year
Pets: Pet Restrictions
Hookup Information: 20 amps, 30 amps, 50 amps, 50 amps Fee
Amenities: A/C Allowed, Fire Rings, Heater Not Allowed, Ice, Laundry, Limited Groceries, Phone or Modem Hookup—Central Location, Phone or Modem Hookups at Site (need activ.), Public Phone, RV Supplies
Recreation: Basketball, Boating, Electric Motors Only, Fishing, Hiking Trails, Lake Fishing, Pavilion, Playground, Pool, Sports Field, Volleyball
Discounts: FMCA Discount
Credit Cards Accepted: Discover, MasterCard, Visa

Ocean Lakes Family Campground
MYRTLE BEACH (Horry)
Phone: 800-876-4306
Web site: *www.oceanlakescamping.com*
Directions: From jct. US 501 & Business US 17: Go 6¼ mi. S on Business US 17.
Description: Oceanfront, semi-wooded campground with shaded & open sites.
Rates: $$–$$$$
Number of Sites: 3,385
Seasonal Sites: Many Seasonal Sites
Number of Full Hookups: 3,385
Number of Pull-Thru Sites: 893
Typical Site Width: 40 Ft.
Services: LP Gas by Meter, LP Gas by Weight, Partial Handicap Access
Open All Year
Hookup Information: 20 amps, 30 amps, 50 amps
Amenities: A/C Allowed, Cable TV, Full-Service Store, Heater

Allowed, Ice, Laundry, Phone or Modem Hookup—Central Location, Phone or Modem Hookups at Site (on arrival), Public Phone, RV Supplies, Traffic Control Gate

Recreation: Basketball, Bike Rentals, Coin Games, Fishing, Fishing Supplies, Hiking Trails, Horseshoes, Lake Fishing, Local Tours, Mini-Golf, Mini-Golf Fee, Pavilion, Planned Activities, Playground, Pool, Recreation Hall, Recreation Room/Area, Saltwater Fishing, Saltwater. Swimming, Shuffleboard, Volleyball, Wading Pool

Credit Cards Accepted: ATM On site, Discover, MasterCard, Visa

---

Green Acres Family Campground
WALTERBORO (Colleton)
Phone: 800-474-3450

Directions: From jct. I-95 (exit 53) & Hwy 63: Go 100 ft. W on Hwy 63, then ½ mi. N on Frontage Rd.

Description: Semi-wooded CAMPGROUND near Interstate with shaded & open sites.

Rates: $
Number of Sites: 135
Number of Full Hookups: 80
Number of Water/Electric Hookups: 40
Number of Sites with No Hookups: 15
Number of Pull-Thru Sites: 105
Typical Site Width: 50 ft.
Services: Dump Station, LP Gas by Meter, LP Gas by Weight, Non-Guest Dumping, Non-Guest Dumping Fee
Open All Year
Hookup Information: 30 amps, 50 amps, 50 amps Fee
Amenities: A/C Allowed, Cable TV, Cable TV Fee, Heater Allowed, Ice, Laundry, Phone or Modem Hookup—Central Location, Phone or Modem Hookups at Site (need activ.), Public Phone, RV Supplies, Wood
Recreation: Basketball, Playground, Pool
Discounts: FMCA Discount
Credit Cards Accepted: MasterCard, Visa

SOUTH DAKOTA

Al's Oasis Campground
CHAMBERLAIN (Lyman)
Phone: 800-675-6959
Web site: *www.alsoasis.com*

Directions: From jct. I-90 (Exit 260-Oacoma) & Bus 90: Go 100 ft. N, then ¼ mi. E on US 90.

Description: Level, mostly gravel campsites overlooking the Missouri River.

Rates: $$
Number of Sites: 97
Number of Full Hookups: 50
Number of Water/Electric Hookups: 22
Number of Sites with No Hookups: 25
Open: April 15
Close: Oct. 31
Number of Pull-Thru Sites: 64
Typical Site Width: 25 ft.
Services: Dump Station, LP Gas by Weight, Partial Handicap Access
Hookup Information: 20 amps, 30 amps, 50 amps
Amenities: A/C Allowed, Cable TV, Fire Rings, Grills, Heater Allowed, Ice, Laundry, Limited Groceries, Phone or Modem Hookup—Central Location, Public Phone, RV Supplies
Recreation: Basketball, Pavilion, Playground, Pool, Recreation Room/Area
Credit Cards Accepted: Discover, MasterCard, Visa

KOA-Mount Rushmore
HILL CITY (Pennington)
Phone: 800-562-8503
Web site: *www.palmergulch.com*

Directions: From South city limits: Go 2¾ mi. S on US 16, then 3 mi. NE on Hwy 244.

Description: CAMPGROUND with shaded and open, level sites nestled in the heart of the Black Hills.

Rates: $$–$$$$

Number of Sites: 460

Number of Full Hookups: 135

Number of Water/Electric Hookups: 165

Number of Sites with No Hookups: 160

Open: May 1

Close: Oct. 1

Number of Pull-Thru Sites: 185

Typical Site Width: 35 ft.

Services: Dump Station, LP Gas by Meter, LP Gas by Weight, Partial Handicap Access

Hookup Information: 20 amps, 30 amps, 50 amps

Amenities: A/C Allowed, Cable TV, Fire Rings, Full-Service Store, Grills, Heater Allowed, Ice, Laundry, Phone or Modem Hookup—Central Location, Phone/Modem Hookups at Site (on arrival), Public Phone, RV Supplies, Wood

Recreation: Basketball, Bike Rentals, Boating, Coin Games, Equipped Pavilion, Fishing, Fishing Supplies, Hiking Trails, Horseshoes, Local Tours, Mini-Golf, Mini-Golf Fee, Pedal Boat Rentals, Planned Activities, Playground, Pond Fishing, Pond Swimming, Pool, Recreation Hall, Recreation Room/Area, Sports Field, Volleyball, Wading Pool, Whirlpool

Discounts: KOA 10% Value Card Discount

Credit Cards Accepted: ATM On site, Discover, MasterCard, Visa

Facility Fully Operational: Memorial Day through Labor Day

Yogi Bear of Sioux Falls

SIOUX FALLS (Minnehaha)

Phone: 605-332-2233

Web site: *www.jellystonesiouxfalls.com*

Directions: From jct. I-229 & I-90: Go 1½ mi. E on I-90 (exit 402), then 1 block N on CR 121.

Description: CAMPGROUND with spacious sites separated by trees on grassy, rolling terrain.

Rates: $$

Number of Sites: 111

Seasonal Sites: Some Seasonal Sites

Number of Full Hookups: 97

Number of Water/Electric Hookups: 14

Number of Pull-Thru Sites: 97

Typical Site Width: 35 ft.

Services: Dump Station, LP Gas by Meter, LP Gas by Weight

Open All Year

Hookup Information: 15 amps, 20 amps, 30 amps, 50 amps, 50 amps Fee

Amenities: A/C Allowed, Fire Rings, Groceries, Heater Allowed, Ice, Laundry, Phone or Modem Hookup—Central Location, Phone or Modem Hookups at Site (need activ.), Public Phone, RV Supplies, Wood

Recreation: Basketball, Bike Rentals, Coin Games, Mini-Golf, Mini-Golf Fee, Pavilion, Planned Activities, Playground, Pool, Recreation Hall, Recreation Room/Area, Sports Field, Volleyball, Whirlpool

Credit Cards Accepted: Discover, MasterCard, Visa

Facility Fully Operational: April 1 through Oct. 15.

TENNESSEE

Chattanooga's Raccoon Mtn. Caverns & Campground
CHATTANOOGA (Hamilton)
Phone: 423-821-9403

Directions: From jct. I-24 (exit 174) & US 41/64: Go 1¼ mi. N on US 41/64, then 600 yd. SW on West Hill Rd.

Description: Rolling, mountain view CAMPGROUND with level, open & shaded sites.

Rates: $–$$

Number of Sites: 130

Number of Full Hookups: 55

Number of Water/Electric Hookups: 44

Number of Sites with No Hookups: 31

Number of Pull-Thru Sites: 51

Typical Site Width: 22 ft.

Services: Dump Station, Non-Guest Dumping, Non-Guest Dumping Fee

Open All Year

Pets: Pet Restrictions

Hookup Information: 30 amps, 50 amps

Amenities: A/C Allowed, Cable TV, Groceries, Heater Allowed, Ice, Laundry, Phone or Modem Hookup—Central Location, Phone or Modem Hookups at Site (need activ.), Public Phone, RV Supplies, Wood

Recreation: Basketball, Coin Games, Equipped Pavilion, Horseshoes, Playground, Pool, Recreation Room/Area, Sports Field, Volleyball

Credit Cards Accepted: Discover, MasterCard, Visa

Smoky Bear Campground (formerly Huc A Bee)
GATLINBURG (Sevier)
Phone: 800-850-8372

Directions: From jct. I-40 (exit 435) & Hwy 32/US 321: Go 13 mi. S on Hwy 32/US 321, then 4½ mi. S on US 321.

Description: An RV PARK with level, shaded sites in a wooded setting.

Rates: $$–$$$

Number of Sites: 49

Number of Full Hookups: 49

Open: March 1

Close: Dec. 1

Number of Pull-Thru Sites: 9

Typical Site Width: 30 ft.

Services: Partial Handicap Access

Hookup Information: 20 amps, 30 amps, 50 amps

Amenities: A/C Allowed, Cable TV, Fire Rings, Heater Allowed, Ice, Laundry, Phone or Modem Hookup—Central Location, Public Phone, RV Supplies, Wood

Recreation: Basketball, Play Equipment, Pool, Whirlpool

Credit Cards Accepted: Discover, MasterCard

Holiday Nashville Travel Park
NASHVILLE (Davidson)
Phone: 800-547-4480

Directions: Westbound: From I-40E (exit 215-Briley Pkwy): Go 5½ mi. N on Briley Pkwy. Southbound: From I-65 N & Briley Pkwy

(Opryland exit): Go 4½ mi. S on Briley Pkwy. Both From Briley Pkwy: Go ¼ mi. W on McGavock Pike, then 1 mi. N on Music Valley Dr.

Description: A grassy CAMPGROUND with level open & shaded sites.

Rates: $$–$$$

Number of Sites: 256

Number of Full Hookups: 168

Number of Water/Electric Hookups: 62

Number of Sites with No Hookups: 26

Number of Pull-Thru Sites: 238

Typical Site Width: 35 ft.

Services: Dump Station, LP Gas by Meter, LP Gas by Weight, Non-Guest Dumping, Non-Guest Dumping Fee, Partial Handicap Access

Open All Year

Hookup Information: 20 amps, 30 amps, 50 amps, 50 amps Fee

Amenities: A/C Allowed, A/C Fee, Cable TV, Full-Service Store, Grills, Heater Allowed, Ice, Laundry, Phone or Modem Hookup—Central Location, Public Phone, RV Supplies

Recreation: Badminton, Basketball, Coin Games, Local Tours, Mini-Golf, Planned Activities, Playground, Pool, Recreation Room/Area, Shuffleboard, Volleyball

Discounts: FCRV 10% Discount, FMCA Discount

Credit Cards Accepted: MasterCard, Visa

TEXAS

Traveler's World RV Resort

SAN ANTONIO (Bexar)

Phone: 800-755-8310

Web site: *www.travelersworldrv.com*

Directions: From jct I-37 (exit 135) & SE Military Dr.: Go 3 mi. W on Military Dr., then 1¼ mi. N on Roosevelt.

Description: A level, shady RV PARK in town.

Rates: $$

Number of Sites: 165

Number of Full Hookups: 165
Number of Pull-Thru Sites: 30
Typical Site Width: 35 ft.
Services: Dump Station, LP Gas by Meter, LP Gas by Weight, Non-Guest Dumping, Non-Guest Dumping Fee, Partial Handicap Access
Hookup Information: 30 amps, 50 amps
Amenities: A/C Allowed, Cable TV, Cable TV Fee, Heater Allowed, Ice, Laundry, Limited Groceries, Phone or Modem Hookup—Central Location, Phone or Modem Hookups at Site (need activ.), Public Phone, RV Supplies
Recreation: Horseshoes, Local Tours, Planned Activities (winter only), Playground, Pool, Recreation Hall, Recreation Room/Area, Whirlpool
Discounts: FMCA Discount
Credit Cards Accepted: MasterCard, Visa

Amarillo RV Ranch
AMARILLO (Potter)
Phone: 806-373-4962

Directions: From jct I-40 & I-27: Go 5 mi. E on I-40 (exit 74), then ½ mi. W on N frontage road.
Description: Level, prepared sites in an RV PARK.
Rates: $$
Number of Sites: 90
Seasonal Sites: Some Seasonal Sites
Number of Full Hookups: 90
Number of Pull-Thru Sites: 70
Typical Site Width: 34 ft.
Services: LP Gas by Meter, LP Gas by Weight, Partial Handicap Access
Open All Year
Hookup Information: 30 amps, 50 amps
Amenities: A/C Allowed, Cable TV, Heater Allowed, Ice, Laundry, Limited Groceries, Phone or Modem Hookup—Central Location, Phone or Modem Hookups at Site (need activ.), Phone or Modem Hookups at Site (on arrival), Public Phone, RV Supplies
Recreation: Pavilion, Playground, Pool, Recreation Hall, Whirlpool
Discounts: FMCA Discount
Credit Cards Accepted: American Express, Discover, MasterCard, Visa

Padre Palms RV Park
CORPUS CHRISTI (Nueces)
Phone: 361-937-2125

Directions: From jct I-37 & Hwy 358 (S Padre Island Dr.): Go 15½ mi. SE on S Padre Island Dr., then ½ mi. NE on Hwy 358 (N.A.S. Dr.), then ½ mi. SE (R) on Skipper Lane.

Description: Sunny, grassy RV PARK close to Gulf.

Rates: $$

Number of Sites: 76

Seasonal Sites: Some Seasonal Sites

Number of Full Hookups: 76

Number of Pull-Thru Sites: 76

Typical Site Width: 25 ft.

Services: Dump Station, Non-Guest Dumping, Non-Guest Dumping Fee

Open All Year

Pets: Pet Restrictions

Hookup Information: 30 amps, 50 amps, 50 amps Fee

Amenities: A/C Allowed, Cable TV, Heater Allowed, Ice, Laundry, Phone or Modem Hookup—Central Location, Phone or Modem Hookups at Site (need activ.), Public Phone, RV Supplies

Recreation: Fishing Guides, Fishing Supplies, Horseshoes, Local Tours, Planned Activities, Pool, Recreation Hall, Shuffleboard, Wading Pool

Credit Cards Accepted: Discover, MasterCard, Visa

Season Exceptions: Planned activities in winter only.

Sandy Lake RV Park
DALLAS (Denton)
Phone: 972-242-6808

Directions: From jct I-35E & Loop I-635: Go 4 mi. N on I-35E (exit 444), then ½ mi. W on Sandy Lake Rd.

Description: Shaded, level sites with asphalt and concrete parking pads, in a metro area.

Rates: $$

Number of Sites: 260

Number of Full Hookups: 260
Number of Pull-Thru Sites: 200
Typical Site Width: 20 ft.
Services: LP Gas by Meter
Open All Year
Hookup Information: 30 amps, 50 amps
Amenities: A/C Allowed, Groceries, Heater Allowed, Ice, Laundry, Phone or Modem Hookup—Central Location, Phone or Modem Hookups at Site (need activ.), Public Phone, RV Supplies
Recreation: Pavilion, Pool, Recreation Hall, Recreation Room/Area
Credit Cards Accepted: MasterCard, Visa

UTAH

Ruby's Inn RV Park & Campground
BRYCE CANYON (Garfield)
Phone: 435-834-5301
Web site: *www.rubysinn.com*
Directions: From jct. Hwy 12 & Hwy 63: Go 2 mi S on Hwy 63.
Description: A CAMPGROUND in a scenic area with open & shaded sites.
Rates: $$
Number of Sites: 228
Number of Full Hookups: 114
Number of Water/Electric Hookups: 14
Number of Sites with No Hookups: 100
Open: April 1
Close: Oct. 31
Number of Pull-Thru Sites: 60
Typical Site Width: 27 ft.
Services: Dump Station, LP Gas by Meter, Non-Guest Dumping, Non-Guest Dumping Fee
Hookup Information: 20 amps, 30 amps, 50 amps
Amenities: A/C Allowed, Grills, Groceries, Heater Allowed, Ice, Laundry, Phone or Modem Hookup—Central Location, Public Phone, RV Supplies, Wood

Recreation: Fishing Supplies, Hiking Trails, Local Tours, Planned Activities, Pool, Whirlpool

Credit Cards Accepted: American Express, ATM Onsite, Diners Club, Discover, MasterCard, Visa

United Campground of Green River
GREEN RIVER (Emery)
Phone: 435-564-8195

Directions: Westbound from I-70 (exit 162): Go 1¾ mi. N & W on Business I-70. Entrance on left. Eastbound from I-70 (exit 158): Go 2¾ mi. N & E on Business I-70. Entrance on right.

Description: Level open and shaded sites with a mountain view.

Rates: $–$$

Number of Sites: 81

Number of Full Hookups: 65

Number of Sites with No Hookups: 16

Number of Pull-Thru Sites: 59

Typical Site Width: 22 ft.

Services: Dump Station, LP Gas by Meter, Non-Guest Dumping, Non-Guest Dumping Fee

Open All Year

Hookup Information: 30 amps, 50 amps, 50 amps Fee

Amenities: A/C Allowed, Cable TV, Cable TV Fee, Fire Rings, Grills, Heater Allowed, Ice, Laundry, Limited Groceries, Phone or Modem Hookup—Central Location, Phone or Modem Hookups at Site (need activ.), Public Phone, RV Supplies, Wood

Recreation: Basketball, Playground, Pool

Discounts: FMCA Discount

Credit Cards Accepted: American Express, Discover, MasterCard, Visa

Dinosaurland-KOA
VERNAL (Uintah)
Phone: 435-789-2148

Directions: From jct. US 40 & US 191: Go 9 blocks N on US 191.

Description: Grassy, shaded sites with a mountain view.

Rates: $–$$

Number of Sites: 65

Number of Full Hookups: 57

Number of Water/Electric Hookups: 8

Number of Pull-Thru Sites: 60

Typical Site Width: 20 ft.

Services: Dump Station, LP Gas by Meter, Non-Guest Dumping, Non-Guest Dumping Fee

Open All Year

Hookup Information: 20 amps, 30 amps, 50 amps

Amenities: A/C Allowed, A/C Fee, Cable TV, Cable TV Fee, Groceries, Heater Allowed, Ice, Laundry, Phone or Modem Hookup—Central Location, Public Phone, RV Supplies

Recreation: Badminton, Equipped Pavilion, Horseshoes, Mini-Golf, Mini-Golf Fee, Play Equipment, Pool, Recreation Room/Area, Sports Field, Volleyball

Discounts: KOA 10% Value Card Discount

Credit Cards Accepted: MasterCard, Visa

Facility Fully Operational: April 1 through Oct. 31

Season Exceptions: Self-service Nov. through March

VERMONT

Limehurst Lake Campground

BARRE (Orange)

Phone: 802-433-6662

Web site: *www.limehurstlake.com*

Directions: From jct. I-89 (exit 6) & Hwy 63: Go 4 mi. E on Hwy 63, then 6 mi. S on Hwy 14.

Description: Open partially shaded terrain, with grassy sites beside a lake.

Rates: $$

Number of Sites: 92

Number of Full Hookups: 27

Number of Water/Electric Hookups: 30

Number of Sites with No Hookups: 15

Open: April 15

Close: Nov. 1

Number of Pull-Thru Sites: 8

Average Site Width: 35 ft.

Services: Dump Station, LP Gas by Meter, Portable Dump

Amenities: A/C Allowed, A/C Fee, Cable TV, Fire Rings, Grills, Heater Allowed, Heater Fee, Hot Shower Fee, Ice, Laundry, Limited Groceries, Phone or Modem Hookup —Central Location, Phone or Modem Hookups at Site (need activ.), Public Phone, RV Supplies, Wood

Recreation: Basketball, Canoe Rentals, Canoeing, Coin Games, Equipped Pavilion, Fishing, Fishing Supplies, Hiking Trails, Horseshoes, Kayak Rentals, Kayaking, Lake Fishing, Lake Swimming, Pedal Boat Rentals, Planned Activities (Weekends Only), Playground, Recreation Room/Area, Rowboat Rentals, Shuffleboard, Sports Field, Volleyball

Discounts: FCRV 10% Discount, FMCA Discount

Credit Cards: MasterCard, Visa

Lake Bomoseen Campground

BOMOSEEN (Rutland)

Phone: 802-273-2061

Directions: From jct. US 4 & Hwy 30 (Exit 4): Go 5 mi. N on Hwy 30.

Description: A lakeside location with shaded sites on Lake Bomoseen.

Rates: $$$

Number of Sites: 120

Number of Full Hookups: 48

Number of Water/Electric Hookups: 50

Number of Sites with No Hookups: 22

Hookup Information: 20 amps, 30 amps, 50 amps, 50 amps Fee

Open: May 1

Close Oct. 15

Number of Pull-Thru Sites: 8

Average Site Width: 50 ft.

Services: Dump Station, LP Gas by Meter, LP Gas by Weight, Non-Guest Dumping, Non-Guest Dumping Fee

Amenities: A/C Allowed, Cable TV, Fire Rings, Full-Service Store, Heater Allowed, Hot Shower Fee, Ice, Laundry, Marine Gas, Phone or Modem Hookup—Central Location, Phone or Modem Hookups at Site (need activ.), Public Phone, RV Supplies, Traffic Control Gate, Wood

Recreation: Badminton, Basketball, Bike Rentals, Boating, Canoe Rentals, Canoeing, Coin Games, Dock, Fishing, Fishing Supplies, Hiking Trails, Horseshoes, Kayak Rentals, Kayaking, Lake Fishing, Mini-Golf, Mini-Golf Fee, Motorboat Rentals, Pavilion, Pedal Boat Rentals, Planned Activities (Weekends Only), Playground, Pontoon Rentals, Pool, Ramp, Recreation, Hall, Recreation Room/Area, Rowboat Rentals, Shuffleboard, Sports Field, Stream Fishing, Volleyball, Wading Pool, Whirlpool

Credit Cards: American Express, Discover, MasterCard, Visa

Breezy Meadows Campground
CONCORD (Essex)
Phone: 802-695-9949

Directions: From jct. I-91 & I-93: Go 2 mi. E on I-93 to exit 1 (Hwy 18), then ½ mi. N on Hwy 18, then 8 mi. E on US 2.

Description: A grassy, open & shaded CAMPGROUND beside the Moose River.

Rates: $$
Number of Sites: 61
Number of Full Hookups: 39
Number of Water/Electric Hookups: 22
Number of Sites with No Hookups: 0
Hookup Information: 20 amps, 30 amps, 50 amps, 50 amps Fee
Open: Mid-May
Close: Mid-Oct.
Number of Pull-Thru Sites: 13
Services: Dump Station, LP Gas by Meter, LP Gas By Weight, Portable Dump
Amenities: A/C Allowed, Cable TV, Fire Rings, Heater Allowed, Ice, Laundry, Limited Groceries, Phone or Modem Hookup—Central Location, Public Phone, RV Supplies, Wood
Recreation: Basketball, Boating, Canoe Rentals, Canoeing, Coin Games, Equipped Pavilion, Fishing, Fishing Supplies, Hiking Trails,

Horseshoes, Pedal Boat Rentals, Planned Activities (Weekends Only), Playground, Pool, Recreation Room/Area, River Fishing, Shuffleboard, Sports Field, Volleyball

Credit Cards: Discover, Visa, MasterCard

Sugar Ridge RV Village & Campground
DANVILLE (Caledonia)
Phone: 802-684-2550
Web site: *www.sugarridgervpark.com*

Directions: From jct. I-91 (exit 21) & US 2: Go 4½ mi. W on US 2.

Description: A luxury RV PARK located mountainside.

Rates: $$$

Number of Sites: 149

Number of Full Hookups: 132

Number of Water/Electric Hookups: 7

Number of Sites with No Hookups: 10

Hookup Information: 30 amps, 50 amps

Open: May 1

Close: Oct. 31

Number of Pull-Thru Sites: 4

Average Site Width: 50 ft.

Services: Dump Station, LP Gas by Meter, LP Gas by Weight, Partial Handicap Access

Amenities: A/C Allowed, Cable TV, Cable TV Fee, Fire Rings, Grills, Groceries, Heater Allowed, Ice, Laundry, Phone or Modem Hookup—Central Location, Phone or Modem Hookups at Site (need activ.), Public Phone, RV Supplies, Wood

Recreation: Basketball, Coin Games, Fishing, Fishing Supplies, Hiking Trails, Horseshoes, Mini-Golf, Mini-Golf Fee, Planned Activities, Playground, Pond Fishing, Pool, Recreation Hall, Shuffleboard, Sports Field, Tennis, Volleyball, Wading Pool, Whirlpool

Credit Cards: Discover, MasterCard, Visa

Pine Valley RV Resort
QUECHEE (Windsor)
Phone: 802-296-6711

Directions: From jct. I-89 (exit 1) & US 4: Go ½ mi. W on US 4.

Description: A resort RV PARK with open & wooded sites.

Rates: $$–$$$

Number of Sites: 92

Number of Full Hookups: 49

Number of Water/Electric Hookups: 43

Number of Sites with No Hookups: **0**

Hookup Information: 20 amp, 30 amp, 50 amp

Open: April 26

Close: Oct. 20

Number of Pull-Thru Sites: 17

Average Site Width: 30 ft.

Services: Dump station, LP Gas by Meter, LP Gas By Weight

Amenities: A/C Allowed, A/C Fee, Cable TV, Fire Rings, Heater Allowed, Heater Fee, Hot Shower Fee, Ice, Laundry, Limited Groceries, Phone or Modem Hookup—Central Location, Phone or Modem Hookups at Site (need activ.), Public Phone, RV Supplies, Wood

Recreation: Boating, Canoe Rentals, Canoeing, Fishing, Fishing Supplies, Pedal Boat, Rentals, Play Equipment, Pond Fishing, Pool, Recreation Hall, Recreation Room/Area

Discounts: FMCA Discount

Credit Cards Accepted: Discover, MasterCard, Visa

VIRGINIA

KOA-Charlottesville
CHARLOTTESVILLE (Albemarle)
Phone: 434-296-9881
Web site: *www.charlottesvillekoa.com*

Directions: From jct. I-64 (exit 121): Go 8½ mi. S on Hwy 20, then 1½ mi. W on SR 708.

Description: CAMPGROUND with wooded sites in a mountain setting.

Rates: $$

Number of Sites: 71

Number of Full Hookups: 34

Number of Water/Electric Hookups: 23

Number of Sites with No Hookups: 14

Open: Mid-March

Close: Mid-Nov.

Number of Pull-Thru Sites: 18

Typical Site Width: 25 ft.

Services: Dump Station, LP Gas by Meter, LP Gas by Weight

Hookup Information: 20 amps, 30 amps, 50 amps, 50 amps Fee

Amenities: A/C Allowed, Fire Rings, Heater Allowed, Ice, Laundry, Limited Groceries, Phone or Modem Hookup—Central Location, Public Phone, RV Supplies, Wood

Recreation: Basketball, Coin Games, Fishing, Hiking Trails, Pavilion, Playground, Pond Fishing, Pool, Recreation Room/Area, Volleyball

Discounts: KOA 10% Value Card Discount

Credit Cards Accepted: MasterCard, Visa

KOA-Fredericksburg/Washington D.C.

FREDERICKSBURG (Spotsylvania)

Phone: 540-898-7252

Directions: Southbound: From jct. I-95 (Massaponax exit 126) & US 1: Go 4 mi. S on US 1, then 2½ mi. E on Hwy 607. Northbound: From jct. I-95 (Thornburg exit 118) & US 1: Go 4 mi. N on US 1, then 2½ mi. E on Hwy 607.

Description: CAMPGROUND with spacious, semi-wooded sites.

Rates: $$-$$$

Number of Sites: 117

Number of Full Hookups: 48

Number of Water/Electric Hookups: 39

Number of Sites with No Hookups: 30

Number of Pull-Thru Sites: 49

Typical Site Width: 30 ft.

Services: Partial Handicap Access, Dump Station, LP Gas by Meter, LP Gas by Weight, Non-Guest Dumping, Non-Guest Dumping Fee

Open All Year

Hookup Information: 20 amps, 30 amps, 50 amps, 50 amps Fee

Amenities: A/C Allowed, Cable TV, Grills, Groceries, Heater Allowed, Ice, Laundry, Phone or Modem Hookup—Central Location, Public Phone, RV Supplies, Wood

Recreation: Bike Rentals, Coin Games, Fishing, Fishing Supplies, Hiking Trails, Horseshoes, Pavilion, Pedal Boat Rentals, Playground, Pond Fishing, Pool, Recreation Hall, Sports Field, Volleyball

Discounts: KOA 10% Value Card Discount

Credit Cards Accepted: Discover, MasterCard, Visa

Holiday Trav-L-Park of Virginia Beach
VIRGINIA BEACH (City of Virginia Beach)
Phone: 800-548-0223
Web site: *www.htpvabeach.com*

Directions: From Jct. I-264 (exit 22) & Birdneck Rd.: Go 3 mi. SE on Birdneck Rd., then ¼ mi. S on General Booth Blvd.

Description: An activity-oriented CAMPGROUND with semi-wooded sites.

Rates: $$–$$$$

Number of Sites: 900

Number of Full Hookups: 350

Number of Water/Electric Hookups: 300

Number of Sites with No Hookups: 250

Number of Pull-Thru Sites: 550

Typical Site Width: 30 ft.

Services: Dump Station, LP Gas by Meter, Portable Dump, Partial Handicap Access

Open All Year

Hookup Information: 20 amps, 30 amps, 50 amps

Amenities: A/C Allowed, Full-Service Store, Heater Allowed, Ice, Laundry, Phone or Modem Hookup—Central Location, Public Phone, RV Supplies, Wood

Recreation: Badminton, Basketball, Bike Rentals, Coin Games, Horseshoes, Mini-Golf, Mini-Golf Fee, Pavilion, Planned Activities, Playground, Pool, Recreation Hall, Shuffleboard, Sports, Field, Volleyball, Wading Pool, Whirlpool

Discounts: FCRV 10% Discount, FMCA Discount

Credit Cards Accepted: ATM Onsite, Discover, MasterCard, Visa

WASHINGTON

Trailer Inns
BELLEVUE (King)
Phone: 425-747-9181
Web site: *www.trailerinnsrv.com*

Directions: Eastbound: From jct I-405 & I-90: Go 1 mi. E on I-90 (exit 11A), then 5 blocks E on the frontage road SE 37th (follow signs). Westbound: From I-90 (exit 11 Eastgate): Go 1 block S on 150th Ave SE, then 5 blocks E on the frontage road SE 37th (follow signs).

Description: Metro area RV PARK with sites on blacktop.

Rates: $$–$$$$

Number of Sites: 76

Seasonal Sites: Many Seasonal Sites

Number of Full Hookups: 76

Number of Pull-Thru Sites: 26

Typical Site Width: 28 ft.

Services: LP Gas by Meter

Open All Year

Pets: Pet Restrictions

Hookup Information: 20 amps, 30 amps, 50 amps

Amenities: A/C Allowed, Cable TV, Grills, Heater Allowed, Ice, Laundry, Phone or Modem Hookup—Central Location, Phone or Modem Hookups at Site (need activ.), Public Phone, RV Supplies

Recreation: Coin Games, Playground, Pool, Recreation Room/Area, Whirlpool

Credit Cards Accepted: MasterCard, Visa

Alderwood RV Resort
SPOKANE (Spokane)
Phone: 888-847-0500

Directions: From I-90 (exit 287A): Go 8¼ mi. N on Argonne Rd, then 2¼ mi. W on Hwy 206 (Mt Spokane Rd), then cross intersection at Hwy 2 & follow Frontage Rd.

Description: A fully landscaped & paved destination resort.

Rates: $$–$$$

Number of Sites: 105

Number of Full Hookups: 105

Number of Pull-Thru Sites: 57

Typical Site Width: 20 ft.

Services: Dump Station, LP Gas by Meter, Non-Guest Dumping, Non-Guest Dumping Fee, Partial Handicap Access

Open All Year

Hookup Information: 20 amps, 30 amps, 50 amps

Amenities: A/C Allowed, Cable TV, Heater Allowed, Ice, Laundry, Limited Groceries, Phone or Modem Hookup—Central Location, Phone or Modem Hookups at Site (need activ.), Phone or Modem Hookups at Site (on arrival), Public Phone, RV Supplies

Recreation: Badminton, Basketball, Mini-Golf, Pavilion, Planned Activities, Playground, Pool, Putting Green, Recreation Hall, Recreation Room/Area, Volleyball

Discounts: FMCA Discount

Credit Cards Accepted: Discover, MasterCard, Visa

Yakima-KOA
YAKIMA (Yakima)
Phone: 800-562-5773

Directions: From jct I-82 (exit 34) & Hwy 24: Go 1 mi. E on Hwy 24, then ¼ mi. N on Keys Rd.

Description: Riverside CAMPGROUND with grassy sites.

Rates: $$

Number of Sites: 174

Seasonal Sites: Some Seasonal Sites

Number of Full Hookups: 60

Number of Water/Electric Hookups: 39

Number of Electric Hookups: 12

Number of Sites with No Hookups: 63

Number of Pull-Thru Sites: 66

Typical Site Width: 18 ft.

Services: Dump Station, LP Gas by Meter, Non-Guest Dumping, Non-Guest Dumping Fee, Partial Handicap Access

Open All Year

Hookup Information: 20 amps, 30 amps, 50 amps, 50 amps Fee

Amenities: A/C Allowed, Fire Rings, Heater Allowed, Ice, Laundry, Limited Groceries, Phone or Modem Hookup—Central Location, Phone or Modem Hookups at Site (need activ.), Public Phone, RV Supplies, Wood

Recreation: Basketball, Bike Rentals, Boating, Canoeing, Coin Games, Fishing, Fishing Supplies, Hiking Trails, Pedal Boat Rentals, Planned Activities (Weekends Only), Playground, Pond Fishing, Pool, River Fishing, Sports Field

Discounts: KOA 10% Value Card Discount

Credit Cards Accepted: Discover, MasterCard, Visa

Season Exceptions: Planned activities Memorial Day through Labor Day

Issaquah Village RV Park

ISSAQUAH (King)

Phone: 800-258-9233

Directions: From I-90 (exit 17): Go 1 block N to 229th Ave. SE, then 1 block E on 66th Ave. E, then ¼ mi. S on 1st St.

Description: Landscaped & treed with prepared sites.

Rates: $$–$$$

Number of Sites: 56

Seasonal Sites: Mostly Seasonal Sites

Number of Full Hookups: 56

Number of Pull-Thru Sites: 2

Typical Site Width: 25 ft.

Services: Dump Station, LP Gas by Meter, Non-Guest Dumping, Non-Guest Dumping Fee

Policies: Big Rigs Welcome, Open All Year, Partial Handicap Access

Hookup Information: 20 amps, 30 amps, 50 amps

Amenities: A/C Allowed, Cable TV, Heater Allowed, Laundry, Phone or Modem Hookup—Central Location, Phone or Modem Hookups at Site (need activ.), Public Phone, RV Supplies

Recreation: Playground

Credit Cards Accepted: MasterCard, Visa

WEST VIRGINIA

Harpers Ferry/Washington DC NW KOA

HARPERS FERRY (Jefferson)

Phone: 800-KOA-9497

Web site: *www.harpersferrykoa.com*

Directions: From jct. US 340 & Harpers Ferry Park entrance: Go 25 ft. S on Harpers Ferry entrance road, then ¼ mi. W on Campground Rd.

Description: A CAMPGROUND on a Civil War battlefield, located at the scenic confluence of the Potomac.

Rates: $$$–$$$$

Number of Sites: 311

Seasonal Sites: Some Seasonal Sites

Number of Full Hookups: 142

Number of Water/Electric Hookups: 67

Number of Sites with No Hookups: 102

Number of Pull-Thru Sites: 104

Typical Site Width: 35 ft.

Services: Dump Station, LP Gas by Meter, Non-Guest Dumping, Non-Guest Dumping Fee, Partial Handicap Access

Open All Year

Hookup Information: 20 amps, 30 amps, 50 amps

Amenities: A/C Allowed, Fire Rings, Grills, Groceries, Heater Allowed, Ice, Laundry, Phone or Modem Hookup—Central Location,

Phone or Modem Hookups at Site (need activ.), Public Phone, RV Supplies, Traffic Control Gate, Wood

Recreation: Basketball, Bike Rentals, Coin Games, Float Trips, Hiking Trails, Horseshoes, Local Tours, Pavilion, Planned Activities, Playground, Pool, Recreation Hall, Recreation Room/Area, Sports Field, Volleyball, Wading Pool

Discounts: KOA 10% Value Card Discount

Credit Cards Accepted: Discover, MasterCard, Visa

Season Exceptions: Off-Season Rates

Mountain Lake Campground
SUMMERSVILLE (Nicholas)
Phone: 304-872-4220

Directions: From town: Go 1 mi. S on US 19, then 2 mi. W on Airport Rd.

Description: Shaded or open sites near a large lake & recreational areas.

Rates: $

Number of Sites: 200

Number of Water/Electric Hookups: 132

Number of Sites with No Hookups: 68

Number of Pull-Thru Sites: 15

Typical Site Width: 50 ft.

Services: Dump Station, Non-Guest Dumping, Non-Guest Dumping Fee, Portable Dump

Open All Year

Pets: Pet Restrictions

Hookup Information: 30 amps, 50 amps

Amenities: A/C Allowed, Fire Rings, Groceries, Heater Allowed, Ice, Laundry, Phone or Modem Hookup—Central Location, Public Phone, RV Supplies, Wood

Recreation: Badminton, Basketball, Boating, Canoeing, Coin Games, Fishing, Hiking Trails, Horseshoes, Kayaking, Lake Fishing, Lake Swimming, Mini-Golf, Mini-Golf Fee, Play Equipment, Recreation Hall, Sports Field, Volleyball

Credit Cards Accepted: MasterCard, Visa

Fox Fire Camping Resort
MILTON (Cabell)
Phone: 304-743-5622

Directions: From jct. I-64 (exit 28) & US 60: Go 3 mi. W on US 60, then ¼ mi. NE on Fox Fire Rd.

Description: Open, grassy sites in a rustic area.

Rates: $$–$$$

Number of Sites: 117

Seasonal Sites: Some Seasonal Sites

Number of Full Hookups: 117

Number of Pull-Thru Sites: 34

Typical Site Width: 36 ft.

Services: LP Gas by Meter, LP Gas by Weight, Partial Handicap Access

Open All Year

Pets: Pet Restrictions

Hookup Information: 30 amps, 50 amps, 50 amps Fee

Amenities: A/C Allowed, Heater Allowed, Ice, Laundry, Limited Groceries, Phone or Modem Hookups at Site (need activ.), Public Phone, RV Supplies, Traffic Control Gate, Wood

Recreation: Badminton, Basketball, Canoe Rentals, Coin Games, Fishing, Hiking Trails, Horseshoes, Kayak Rentals, Kayaking, Lake Fishing, Lake Swimming, Mini-Golf, Mini-Golf Fee, Pavilion, Pedal Boat Rentals, Planned Activities (Weekends Only), Playground, Pool, Recreation Room/Area, Sports Field, Tennis, Volleyball, Whirlpool

Dallas Pike Campground
WHEELING (Ohio)
Phone: 304-547-0940

Directions: Westbound: From jct. I-70 (exit 11-Dallas Pike): Go 300 ft. S on Dallas Pike, then ½ mi. W on Jenkins McCutcheon Rd. Eastbound: From I-70 (exit 11 Dallas Pike): Go ¼ mi. W on McCutcheon Rd.

Description: A natural wooded area on rolling hills.

Rates: $$

Number of Sites: 159
Number of Full Hookups: 65
Number of Water/Electric Hookups: 15
Number of Electric Hookups: 16
Number of Sites with No Hookups: 63
Number of Pull-Thru Sites: 72
Typical Site Width: 50 ft.
Services: Dump Station, Non-Guest Dumping, Non-Guest Dumping Fee
Open All Year
Pets: Pet Restrictions
Hookup Information: 20 amps, 30 amps, 50 amps, 50 amps Fee
Amenities: A/C Allowed, A/C Fee, Cable TV, Fire Rings, Grills, Heater Allowed, Heater Fee, Ice, Laundry, Limited Groceries, Phone or Modem Hookup—Central Location, Phone or Modem Hookups at Site (need activ.), RV Supplies, Wood
Recreation: Basketball, Coin Games, Hiking Trails, Horseshoes, Pavilion, Play Equipment, Pool, Recreation Room/Area, Shuffleboard, Volleyball
Credit Cards Accepted: MasterCard, Visa

WISCONSIN

Yogi Bear Jellystone Park Camp-Resort
FREMONT (Waupaca)
Phone: 800-258-3315
Directions: From jct. CR H & US 10: Go 1½ mi. W on US 10.
Description: CAMPGROUND on Partridge Lake, & close to Wolf River.
Rates: $$$–$$$$
Number of Sites: 261
Seasonal Sites: Some Seasonal Sites
Number of Full Hookups: 65
Number of Water/Electric Hookups: 164
Number of Electric Hookups: 11
Number of Sites with No Hookups: 21
Open: April 15

Close: Oct. 15

Number of Pull-Thru Sites: 28

Typical Site Width: 50 ft.

Services: Dump Station, LP Gas by Meter, LP Gas by Weight, Non-Guest Dumping, Non-Guest Dumping Fee, Portable Dump

Hookup Information: 30 amps, 50 amps

Amenities: A/C Allowed, Fire Rings, Heater Allowed, Ice, Laundry, Limited Groceries, Phone or Modem Hookup—Central Location, Public Phone, RV Supplies, Wood

Recreation: Badminton, Basketball, Boating, Canoe Rentals, Canoeing, Coin Games, Dock, Fishing, Fishing Guides, Fishing Supplies, Hiking Trails, Horseshoes, Kayak Rentals, Kayaking, Lake Fishing, Mini-Golf, Mini-Golf Fee, Motorboat Rentals, Pavilion, Pedal Boat Rentals, Planned Activities, Playground, Pond Fishing, Pontoon Rentals, Pool, Ramp, Recreation Hall, Recreation Room/Area, River Fishing, Rowboat Rentals, Shuffleboard, Sports Field, Volleyball, Wading Pool

Credit Cards Accepted: MasterCard, Visa

Oakdale KOA
OAKDALE (Monroe)
Phone: 800-562-1737

Directions: From jct. I-90/94 (exit 48) & CR PP: Go 1 block N on CR PP, then 2 blocks E on Woody Dr., then 1 block S on Jay St.

Description: Level, mostly shaded CAMPGROUND.

Rates: $$

Number of Sites: 80

Number of Full Hookups: 48

Number of Water/Electric Hookups: 12

Number of Electric Hookups: 8

Number of Sites with No Hookups: 12

Open: Mid-May

Close: Mid-Oct.

Number of Pull-Thru Sites: 33

Typical Site Width: 40 ft.

Services: Dump Station, LP Gas by Meter, LP Gas by Weight

Hookup Information: 20 amps, 30 amps, 50 amps

Amenities: A/C Allowed, Cable TV, Fire Rings, Heater Allowed, Ice, Laundry, Limited, Groceries, Phone or Modem Hookup—Central Location, Phone/Modem Hookups at Site (on arrival), Public Phone, RV Supplies, Wood

Recreation: Basketball, Coin Games, Horseshoes, Pavilion, Playground, Pool, Recreation Hall, Recreation Room/Area, Sports Field, Volleyball

Discounts: KOA 10% Value Card Discount

Credit Cards Accepted: Discover, MasterCard, Visa

Rice Lake/Spooner KOA
RICE LAKE (Barron)
Phone: 800-KOA-3460
Web site: *www.ricelakekoa.com*

Directions: From jct. US 53 & Hwy 48: Go 10 mi. N on Hwy 53, then 1 mi. E on campground driveway.

Description: Lakeside, semi-wooded CAMPGROUND with open & shaded sites.

Rates: $$–$$$

Number of Sites: 103

Seasonal Sites: Some Seasonal Sites

Number of Full Hookups: 36

Number of Water/Electric Hookups: 53

Number of Electric Hookups: 6

Number of Sites with No Hookups: 8

Open: April 25

Close: Oct. 6

Number of Pull-Thru Sites: 20

Typical Site Width: 30 ft.

Services: Dump Station, LP Gas by Meter, LP Gas by Weight, Non-Guest Dumping, Non-Guest Dumping Fee, Partial Handicap Access

Hookup Information: 20 amps, 30 amps, 50 amps

Amenities: A/C Allowed, Fire Rings, Groceries, Heater Allowed, Ice, Laundry, Phone or Modem Hookup—Central Location, Public Phone, RV Supplies, Wood

Recreation: Basketball, Bike Rentals, Boating, Canoe Rentals, Canoeing, Coin Games, Dock, Fishing, Fishing Supplies, Hiking Trails, Kayak Rentals, Kayaking, Lake Fishing, Lake Swimming, Motorboat Rentals, Pedal Boat Rentals, Planned Activities (Weekends Only), Playground, Pontoon Rentals, Pool, Ramp, Recreation Room/Area, Rowboat Rentals, Sports Field, Volleyball

Discounts: KOA 10% Value Card Discount

Credit Cards Accepted: American Express, Discover, MasterCard, Visa

Season Exceptions: Heated pool open: May 25 through Sept. 2.

WYOMING

Casper KOA North
CASPER (Natrona)
Phone: 800-562-4704

Directions: From jct I-25 (exit 191) & Wardwell Rd.: Go 1 block W on Wardwell Rd., then 1 mi N on Salt Creek Hwy, then 1 block W on Sunset Dr.

Description: An RV PARK with open, level sites with a mountain view.

Rates: $–$$

Number of Sites: 66

Seasonal Sites: Some Seasonal Sites

Number of Full Hookups: 35

Number of Water/Electric Hookups: 29

Number of Sites with No Hookups: 2

Open: April 1

Close: Nov. 1

Number of Pull-Thru Sites: 34

Typical Site Width: 35 ft.

Services: Dump Station, LP Gas by Meter, Non-Guest Dumping, Non-Guest Dumping Fee, Partial Handicap Access

Hookup Information: 20 amps, 30 amps, 50 amps

Amenities: Laundry, Phone or Modem Hookup—Central Location, Public Phone

Recreation: Mini-Golf, Mini-Golf Fee, Planned Activities, Playground, Pool, Recreation Room/Area

Cheyenne-KOA
CHEYENNE (Laramie)
Phone: 307-638-8840
Directions: From jct I-80 (exit 367) & Campstool Rd.: Go 200 ft. N on Campstool Rd, then ½ mi. E on north frontage road.
Description: CAMPGROUND with open, surfaced sites outside of town.
Rates: $$
Number of Sites: 53
Number of Full Hookups: 12
Number of Water/Electric Hookups: 41
Number of Pull-Thru Sites: 42
Typical Site Width: 25 ft.
Services: Dump Station, LP Gas by Meter, Non-Guest Dumping, Non-Guest Dumping Fee, Partial Handicap Access
Open All Year
Hookup Information: 20 amps, 30 amps
Amenities: A/C Allowed, Cable TV, Cable TV Fee, Grills, Heater Allowed, Ice, Laundry, Limited Groceries, Phone or Modem Hookup—Central Location, Phone or Modem Hookups at Site (need activ.), Public Phone, RV Supplies, Wood
Recreation: Badminton, Basketball, Bike Rentals, Coin Games, Equipped Pavilion, Mini-Golf, Mini-Golf Fee, Playground, Pool, Recreation Room/Area, Sports Field, Volleyball
Discounts: FMCA Discount, KOA 10% Value Card Discount
Credit Cards Accepted: Discover, MasterCard, Visa
Season Exceptions: Pool Open June 1 through Sept. 15; Campground Open Year-Round.

The Virginian RV Resort
JACKSON (Teton)
Phone: 800-321-6982
Directions: From jct Hwy 22 & US 26/89/191: Go ¼ mi. NE on US 26/89/191, then 1 block S on Virginia Lane (1 mi. SW of Town Square off US 26/89/191).

Description: Level, grassy sites in an RV PARK with mountain views in a resort town.

Rates: $$$–$$$$

Number of Sites: 104

Number of Full Hookups: 104

Open: May 1

Close: Oct. 15

Number of Pull-Thru Sites: 68

Typical Site Width: 30 ft.

Services: Dump Station, Non-Guest Dumping, Non-Guest Dumping Fee

Hookup Information: 20 amps, 30 amps, 50 amps

Amenities: A/C Allowed, Cable TV, Grills, Heater Allowed, Ice, Laundry, Phone or Modem Hookup—Central Location, Public Phone

Recreation: Pool, Whirlpool

Discounts: FMCA Discount, KOA 10% Value Card Discount

Credit Cards Accepted: American Express, ATM On site, Diners Club, Discover, MasterCard, Visa

Southern Canada

ALBERTA

KOA-Calgary West
CALGARY
Phone: 403-288-0411

Directions: On Hwy 1, inside west city limits.

Description: A CAMPGROUND with tiered, level sites and gravel pads next to Canada Olympic Park.

Rates: $$–$$$

Number of Sites: 350

Number of Full Hookups: 121

umber of Water/Electric Hookups: 163

Number of Sites with No Hookups: 66

Open: April 15

Close: Oct. 14

Number of Pull-Thru Sites: 81

Typical Site Width: 20 ft.

Services: Dump Station, LP Gas by Weight, Partial Handicap Access

Hookup Information: 30 amps

Amenities: A/C Allowed, Groceries, Heater Allowed, Ice, Laundry, Phone or Modem Hookup—Central Location, Public Phone, RV Supplies, Traffic Control Gate

Recreation: Coin Games, Hiking Trails, Horseshoes, Local Tours, Mini-Golf, Mini-Golf Fee, Playground, Pool, Recreation Room/Area, Volleyball

Discounts: KOA 10% Value Card Discount

Credit Cards Accepted: MasterCard, Visa

Facility Fully Operational: June 21 through Sept. 1

McLean Creek Campground
BRAGG CREEK
Phone: 403-949-3132
Altitude: 5,000

Directions: From jct. Hwy 22 & Hwy 66: Go 14½ km/9 mi. SW on Hwy 66.

Rates: Call for information

Number of Sites: 170

Typical Site Width: 30 ft.

Number of Electric Hookups: 96

Number of Sites with No Hookups: 74

Number of Pull-Thru Sites: 12

Services: Dump Station, Partial Handicap Access

Open All Year

Amenities: A/C Allowed, Fire Rings, Groceries, Heater Allowed, Ice, Laundry, Public Phone, RV Supplies, Traffic Control Gate, Wood

Recreation: Fishing, Fishing Supplies, Hiking Trails, Playground, River Fishing

Credit Cards Accepted: MasterCard, Visa

Whitemud Creek Golf & RV Park
EDMONTON
Phone: 780-988-6800

Directions: From jct. Hwy 2 & Ellerslie Rd.: Go 3.2 km/2 mi. W on Ellerslie Rd., then 3.2 km/2 mi. S on 127 St., then 3.2 km/2 mi. W on 41st Ave., then 3.2 km/2 mi. N on 156 St.

Description: Large, grassy sites adjacent to a golf course in a rural setting.
Rates: $$$
Number of Sites: 125
Seasonal Sites: Some Seasonal Sites
Number of Full Hookups: 125
Typical Site Width: 45 ft.
Open All Year
Services: Partial Handicap Access
Hookup Information: 30 amps, 50 amps, 50 amps Fee
Accepts Full Hookup Units Only
Amenities: A/C Allowed, Heater Allowed, Hot Shower Fee, Ice, Laundry, Phone or Modem Hookups at Site (on arrival), Public Phone
Recreation: Dock, Fishing, Pond Fishing, Putting Green, Recreation Room/Area
Credit Cards Accepted: MasterCard, Visa

BRITISH COLUMBIA

Fort Victoria RV Park
VICTORIA
Phone: 250-479-8112

Directions: From jct. Hwy 1 & Helmicken Rd: Go 2 km/1¼ mi. S on Helmicken Rd, then 200 meters W on Hwy 1A.

Description: Metro RV park with gravel pads in open and shaded sites.
Rates: $$
Number of Sites: 300
Number of Full Hookups: 250

Number of Water/Electric Hookups: 50

Number of Pull-Thru Sites: 8

Typical Site Width: 30 ft.

Services: Dump Station, LP Gas by Meter, LP Gas by Weight

Open All Year

Hookup Information: 15 amps, 30 amps, 50 amps

Amenities: A/C Allowed, Cable TV, Heater Allowed, Ice, Laundry, Phone or Modem Hookup—Central Location, Phone or Modem Hookups at Site (need activ.), Public Phone, RV Supplies

Recreation: Fishing Guides, Local Tours, Playground

Discounts: FCRV 10% Discount, FMCA Discount

Credit Cards Accepted: MasterCard, Visa

Burnaby Cariboo RV Park

BURNABY

Phone: 604-420-1722

Directions: From Hwy 1 (exit 37—Gaglardi Way): Go 90 meters/100 yards N on Gaglardi to Cariboo Rd, then 60 meters/200 ft. E on Stormont Rd, then 270 meters/300 yards N on Cariboo Rd, then 60 meters/200 ft. E on Cariboo Pl.

Description: RV PARK in the heart of greater Vancouver with paved, patio landscaped sites.

Rates: $$–$$$$

Number of Sites: 241

Number of Full Hookups: 217

Number of Sites with No Hookups: 24

Typical Site Width: 35 ft.

Services: Dump Station, Partial Handicap Access

Open All Year

Hookup Information: 30 amps

Amenities: A/C Allowed, Cable TV, Cable TV Fee, Full-Service Store, Heater Allowed, Ice, Laundry, Phone or Modem Hookups at Site (on arrival), Public Phone, RV Supplies,

Recreation: Badminton, Coin Games, Equipped Pavilion, Fishing, Fishing Guides, Hiking Trails, Horseshoes, Local Tours, Planned

Activities, Playground, Pool, Recreation Hall, Recreation Room/Area, River Fishing, Sports Field, Volleyball, Whirlpool
Discounts: FMCA Discount
Credit Cards Accepted: ATM Onsite, MasterCard, Visa

MANITOBA

Meadowlark Campground
BRANDON
Phone: 204-728-7205
Directions: (E-bnd Hwy 1 or N-bnd Hwy 10) From W jct. of Hwys 1 & 10: Go E 0.3 mi. on N service road; or (W-bnd Hwy 1 or S-bnd Hwy 10) From E jct. of Hwy 1 & 10: Go W 0.5 mi. on Hwy 1 to N service road, then W 200 ft. to park entrance on right.
Description: Good paved interior roads, some shaded sites.
Rates: $$
Number of Sites: 76
Number of Full Hookups: 66
Number of Water/Electric Hookups: 10
Open: April 15
Close: Oct. 15
Number of Pull-Thru Sites: 35
Typical Site Width: 35 ft.
Services: Dump Station, Non-Guest Dumping, Non-Guest Dumping Fee
Hookup Information: 30 amps, 50 amps
Amenities: Laundry, Phone or Modem Hookup—Central Location, Public Phone
Recreation: Playground
Discounts: FMCA Discount

Traveller's RV Resort
WINNIPEG
Phone: 204-256-2186
Directions: From east jct. Trans Canada Hwy 1 & bypass Hwy 100: Go

1.6 km/1 mi. S on bypass Hwy 100, then .4 km/¼ mi. N on Murdock Rd.

Description: A level, grassy CAMPGROUND with prepared sites.

Rates: Call for information

Number of Sites: 264

Number of Full Hookups: 264

Open: Mid-April

Close: Early Oct.

Number of Pull-Thru Sites: 102

Typical Site Width: 40 ft.

Services: Dump Station, Non-Guest Dumping, Non-Guest Dumping Fee

Hookup Information: 15 amps, 30 amps, 50 amps, 50 amps Fee

Amenities: A/C Allowed, Fire Rings, Grills, Heater Allowed, Ice, Laundry, Limited Groceries, Phone or Modem Hookup—Central Location, Public Phone, RV Supplies, Wood

Recreation: Badminton, Basketball, Coin Games, Local Tours, Mini-Golf, Mini-Golf Fee, Playground, Pool, Recreation Hall, Recreation Room/Area, Shuffleboard, Sports Field, Volleyball

Credit Cards Accepted: MasterCard, Visa

Pine Tree Campground & Trailer Park
PRAWDA
Phone: 204-426-5413

Directions: From east jct. Trans Canada Hwy & Hwy 506: Go ½ km/³⁄₁₀ mi. E on Hwy 1, watch for signs.

Description: Riverside, wooded sites in scenic area.

Rates: $

Number of Sites: 47

Number of Full Hookups: 3

Number of Water/Electric Hookups: 28

Number of Sites with No Hookups: 16

Number of Pull-Thru Sites: 4

Typical Site Width: 25 ft.

Services: Dump Station, Non-Guest Dumping, Non-Guest Dumping Fee

Open All Year

Hookup Information: 15 amps, 30 amps

Amenities: Laundry, Phone or Modem Hookup—Central Location, Public Phone

Recreation: Boating, Canoeing, Equipped Pavilion, Fishing, Pavilion, Playground, Recreation Room/Area, River Fishing, River Swimming

NEW BRUNSWICK

Escuminac Beach & Family Park
BAIE SAINTE ANNE (North Umberland)
Phone: 506-228-4532

Directions: On Hwy 117 & jct. Escuminac Point: Go 3 km/2 mi. E on Escuminac Point.

Description: Open sites on ocean view.

Rates: $

Number of Sites: 25

Number of Water/Electric Hookups: 25

Open: May 15

Close: Oct. 14

Services: Dump Station, Non-Guest Dumping, Non-Guest Dumping Fee, Portable Dump

Hookup Information: 15 amps

Amenities: Fire Rings, Ice, Laundry, Public Phone, Traffic Gate, Wood

Recreation: Badminton, Canoeing, Fishing, Horseshoes, Kayaking, Play Equipment, River Swimming, Saltwater Fishing, Saltwater Swimming, Volleyball

Credit Cards Accepted: Visa

Camping Plage Gagnon Beach
CAP PELE (Westmorland)
Phone: 800-658-2828

Directions: From I-15 (exit 46) & Hwy 133: Go 4.9 km/3mi. E on Hwy 133.

Description: CAMPGROUND with open, grassy sites on a beach.

Rates: $$

Number of Sites: 282

Seasonal Sites: Some Seasonal Sites
Number of Full Hookups: 240
Number of Water/Electric Hookups: 32
Number of Sites with No Hookups: 10
Open: May 1
Close: Oct. 15
Number of Pull-Thru Sites: 76
Typical Site Width: 30 ft.
Services: Dump Station, Non-Guest Dumping, Non-Guest Dumping Fee
Hookup Information: 15 amps, 30 amps, 50 amps, 50 amps Fee
Amenities: Fire Rings, Hot Shower Fee, Ice, Laundry, Limited Groceries, Phone or Modem Hookup—Central Location, Public Phone, RV Supplies, Traffic Control Gate, Wood
Recreation: Coin Games, Local Tours, Planned Activities (Weekends Only), Play Equipment, Playground, Recreation Hall, Recreation Room/Area, Saltwater Swimming, Volleyball
Credit Cards Accepted: ATM Onsite
Facility Fully Operational: June 20 through Aug. 30
Season Exceptions: Some seasonal sites in summer.

Camping Panoramic 86
EDMUNDSTON (SAINT JACQUES) (Madawaska)
Phone: 506-739-6544
Directions: From Trans Canada Hwy 2 (exit 8): Go 8 km/½ mi E on Hwy 144 (rue Principale), then .04 km/⅓ mi. NE on Ch. St. Joseph, then follow signs S for 1.8 km/1 mi., then .05 km/⅓ mi. W on Chemin Albert.
Description: A CAMPGROUND along a river.
Rates: $$
Number of Sites: 177
Seasonal Sites: Many Seasonal Sites
Number of Full Hookups: 137
Number of Water/Electric Hookups: 30
Number of Sites with No Hookups: 10
Open: May 1
Close: Oct. 30

Number of Pull-Thru Sites: 3

Typical Site Width: 40 ft.

Services: Dump Station, Non-Guest Dumping, Non-Guest Dumping Fee

Hookup Information: 15 amps, 30 amps

Amenities: A/C Allowed, Fire Rings, Heater Allowed, Ice, Laundry, Limited Groceries, Phone or Modem Hookup—Central Location, Public Phone, Wood

Recreation: Boating, Canoeing, Horseshoes, Kayaking, Planned Activities (Weekends Only), Play Equipment, Pool, Ramp, Recreation Hall, Wading Pool

Credit Cards Accepted: ATM Onsite, MasterCard, Visa

Facility Fully Operational: June 1 through Sept. 1

ONTARIO

Yogi Bear's Jellystone Park Camp-Resort

NIAGARA FALLS

Phone: 905-354-1432

Web site: *www.jellystoneniagara.ca*

Directions: From jct. Hwy 420 & QEW: Go 3.2 km/2 mi. S on QEW, then 183 meters/200 yd. E on McLeod Rd., then 2.4 km/1½ mi. S on Oakwood Dr.

Description: Grassy, level CAMPGROUND with open & shaded sites.

Rates: $$–$$$

Number of Sites: 320

Number of Full Hookups: 224

Number of Water/Electric Hookups: 20

Number of Sites with No Hookups: 76

Open: April 26

Close: Oct. 15

Number of Pull-Thru Sites: 24

Typical Site Width: 35 ft.

Services: Dump Station, LP Gas by Weight

Hookup Information: 15 amps, 30 amps, 50 amps, 50 amps Fee

Amenities: A/C Allowed, A/C Fee, Fire Rings, Full-Service Store, Grills,

Heater Allowed, Heater Fee, Ice, Laundry, Phone or Modem Hookup—Central Location, Public Phone, RV Supplies, Traffic Control Gate, Wood

Recreation: Basketball, Bike Rentals, Coin Games, Equipped Pavilion, Hiking Trails, Local Tours, Mini-Golf, Planned Activities, Playground, Pool, Recreation Hall, Recreation Room/Area, Volleyball, Wading Pool

Credit Cards Accepted: Diners Club, MasterCard, Visa

Green Acre Park
WATERLOO (Waterloo)
Phone: 877-885-7275

Directions: From jct. Hwy 401 & Hwy 8: Go 8 km/5 mi. W on Hwy 8, then 10.4 km/6½ mi. N on Hwy 85 (formerly Hwy 86), then 3.2 km/2 mi. W on Northfield Dr., then .8 km/½ mi. N on Westmound Rd., then 1.6 km/1 mi. W on Conservation Dr., then 90m/100 yd. S on Beaver Creek Rd.

Description: An RV PARK with level, landscaped, fully serviced sites.

Rates: $$–$$$

Number of Sites: 364

Seasonal Sites: Many Seasonal Sites

Number of Full Hookups: 320

Number of Water/Electric Hookups: 44

Number of Pull-Thru Sites: 47

Typical Site Width: 30 ft.

Services: Dump Station, LP Gas by Meter, LP Gas by Weight, Non-Guest Dumping, Non-Guest Dumping Fee, Portable Dump, Partial Handicap Access

Open All Year

Hookup Information: 30 amps, 50 amps

Amenities: A/C Allowed, Fire Rings, Heater Allowed, Hot Shower Fee, Ice, Laundry, Limited Groceries, Phone or Modem Hookup—Central Location, Public Phone, RV Supplies, Traffic Control Gate, Wood

Recreation: Badminton, Basketball, Bike Rentals, Equipped Pavilion, Fishing, Hiking Trails, Horseshoes, Mini-Golf, Mini-Golf Fee, Planned Activities, Playground, Pond Fishing, Pool, Putting Green, Recreation Hall, Recreation Room/Area, Shuffleboard, Sports Field, Volleyball, Whirlpool

Discounts: FCRV 10% Discount

Credit Cards Accepted: MasterCard, Visa

Facility Fully Operational: April 1 through Nov. 30

Season Exceptions: Pool opens mid-May.

Our Ponderosa Family Campground & Golf Resort
FOREST (Lambton)
Phone: 888-786-CAMP

Directions: From town: Go 9.6 km/6 mi. N on Hwy 21, then 90 m/100 yd. W on Lambton CR 7, then 1.6 km/1 mi. N on West Ipperwash Rd.

Description: Grassy, level CAMPGROUND near Ipperwash Beach with open & shaded sites.

Rates: $$$

Number of Sites: 387

Seasonal Sites: Mostly Seasonal Sites

Number of Full Hookups: 358

Number of Water/Electric Hookups: 29

Number of Pull-Thru Sites: 5

Typical Site Width: 40 ft.

Services: Dump Station, LP Gas by Meter, LP Gas by Weight, Non-Guest Dumping, Non-Guest Dumping Fee Partial Handicap Access

Open All Year

Hookup Information: 30 amps, 50 amps

Amenities: A/C Allowed, Fire Rings, Groceries, Heater Allowed, Ice, Laundry, Phone or Modem Hookup—Central Location, Public Phone, RV Supplies, Traffic Control Gate, Wood

Recreation: Basketball, Boating, Coin Games, Dock, Hiking Trails, Mini-Golf, Mini-Golf Fee, Pedal Boat Rentals, Planned Activities, Playground, Pool, Putting Green, Recreation Hall, Recreation Room/Area, Shuffleboard, Sports Field, Volleyball, Whirlpool

Credit Cards Accepted: MasterCard, Visa

Facility Fully Operational: May 1 through Oct. 15

The Dunes Oakridge Park
GRAND BEND (Lambton)
Phone: 519-243-2500
Web site: *www.dunesoakridge.com*

Directions: From jct. Hwy 81 & Hwy 21: Go 11 km/7 mi. S on Hwy 21, then 0.4 km/¼ mi. W on Northville Crescent.

Description: Level, open and shaded sites in a CAMPGROUND.

Rates: $$–$$$

Number of Sites: 250

Seasonal Sites: Many Seasonal Sites

Number of Full Hookups: 150

Number of Water/Electric Hookups: 20

Number of Sites with No Hookups: 80

Number of Pull-Thru Sites: 6

Typical Site Width: 45 ft.

Services: Dump Station

Open All Year

Hookup Information: 15 amps, 30 amps

Amenities: A/C Allowed, Cable TV, Fire Rings, Heater Allowed, Ice, Laundry, Limited Groceries, Public Phone, Traffic Control Gate, Wood

Recreation: Badminton, Basketball, Coin Games, Hiking Trails, Horseshoes, Planned Activities, Playground, Pool, Recreation Hall, Recreation Room/Area, Shuffleboard, Volleyball, Wading Pool

Credit Cards Accepted: MasterCard, Visa

Facility Fully Operational: Mid-May through mid-Oct

Milton Heights Campground
MILTON
Phone: 800-308-9120
Web site: *www.miltonhgtscampgrd.com*

Directions: From jct. Hwy 401 (exit 320) & Hwy 25: Go 1.6 km/1 mi. N on Hwy 25, then 2.4 km/1½ mi. W on Campbellville Rd., then 90 meters/100 yd. S on Tremaine.

Description: Open & shaded grassy sites.

Rates: $$–$$$

Number of Sites: 206

Number of Full Hookups: 118

Number of Water/Electric Hookups: 48

Number of Sites with No Hookups: 40

Number of Pull-Thru Sites: 30

Typical Site Width: 40 ft.

Services: Dump Station, LP Gas by Weight, Non-Guest Dumping, Non-Guest Dumping Fee, Partial Handicap Access

Open All Year

Pets: Pet Restrictions

Hookup Information: 30 amps, 50 amps

Amenities: A/C Allowed, Fire Rings, Groceries, Heater Allowed, Ice, Laundry, Phone or Modem Hookup—Central Location, Public Phone, RV Supplies, Traffic Control Gate, Wood

Recreation: Badminton, Basketball, Coin Games, Equipped Pavilion, Horseshoes, Playground, Pool, Recreation Room/Area, Volleyball

Discounts: FMCA Discount

Credit Cards Accepted: Diners Club, MasterCard, Visa

Campers Cove

WHEATLEY (Essex)

Phone: 800-265-5833

Web site: *www.camperscove.ca*

Directions: From center of town (jct. Erie S. & Hwy 3): Go 3.6 km/2¼ mi. E on Hwy 3, then 0.8 km/½ mi. S on Campers Cove Rd.

Description: Semi-wooded, lakeside CAMPGROUND with many planned activities.

Rates: $$$

Number of Sites: 324

Seasonal Sites: Mostly Seasonal Sites

Number of Full Hookups: 306

Number of Water/Electric Hookups: 14

Number of Sites with No Hookups: 4

Open: May

Close: Sept. 30

Number of Pull-Thru Sites: 8

Typical Site Width: 50 ft.

Services: Dump Station, LP Gas by Weight, Non-Guest Dumping, Non-Guest Dumping Fee

Hookup Information: 20 amps, 30 amps, 50 amps,

Amenities: A/C Allowed, Fire Rings, Groceries, Ice, Laundry, Phone or Modem Hookup—Central Location, Public Phone, RV Supplies, Traffic Control Gate, Wood

Recreation: Badminton, Basketball, Bike Rentals, Boating, Canoeing, Coin Games, Equipped Pavilion, Fishing, Hiking Trails, Kayak Rentals, Kayaking, Lake Fishing, Lake Swimming, Planned Activities, Playground, Recreation Room/Area, Shuffleboard, Sports Field, Volleyball

Credit Cards Accepted: MasterCard, Visa

Woodland Park
SAUBLE BEACH (Bruce)
Phone: 519-422-1161
Web site: *www.woodlandpark.on.ca*

Directions: From north city limits: Go 0.4 km/¼ mi. N on CR 13 (Sauble Falls Rd).

Description: Semi-wooded CAMPGROUND with open & shaded sites.

Rates: $$–$$$

Number of Sites: 730

Seasonal Sites: Mostly Seasonal Sites

Number of Full Hookups: 720

Number of Sites with No Hookups: 10

Open: May 1

Close: Thanksgiving

Number of Pull-Thru Sites: 7

Typical Site Width: 40 ft.

Services: LP Gas by Weight. Partial Handicap Access

Hookup Information: 30 amps, 50 amps

Amenities: A/C Allowed, Cable TV, Cable TV Fee, Fire Rings, Groceries, Heater Allowed, Hot Shower Fee, Ice, Laundry, Phone or

Modem Hookup—Central Location, Public Phone, RV Supplies, Traffic Control Gate, Wood

Recreation: Badminton, Basketball, Coin Games, Hiking Trails, Horseshoes, Planned Activities, Playground, Pool, Recreation Hall, Recreation Room/Area, Sports Field, Volleyball, Whirlpool

Credit Cards Accepted: MasterCard, Visa

Season Exceptions: 100 overnight sites available.

QUEBEC

KOA-Quebec City
SAINT NICOLAS (Chaudiere/Apalaches)
Phone: 418-831-1813

Directions: 1 mi. W of I-73: Go W on I-20 (exit 311), then left at traffic light going E on I-20, (exit 311). Cross over I-20. Turn left at Oliver Rd. (service road).

Description: Rolling, semi-wooded CAMPGROUND.

Rates: $$–$$$

Number of Sites: 206

Number of Full Hookups: 96

Number of Water/Electric Hookups: 42

Number of Electric Hookups: 12

Number of Sites with No Hookups: 56

Open: May 1

Close: Oct. 12

Number of Pull-Thru Sites: 120

Services: Dump Station, LP Gas by Meter, LP Gas by Weight, Non-Guest Dumping, Non-Guest Dumping Fee

Hookup Information: 15 amps, 30 amps, 50 amps, 50 amps Fee

Amenities: A/C Allowed, Fire Rings, Groceries, Heater Allowed, Heater Fee, Ice, Laundry, Phone or Modem Hookup—Central Location, Phone or Modem Hookups at Site (need activ.), Public Phone, RV Supplies, Wood

Recreation: Badminton, Basketball, Coin Games, Horseshoes, Local Tours, Pavilion, Playground, Pool, Recreation Hall, Recreation Room/Area, Volleyball

Discounts: KOA 10% Value Card Discount
Credit Cards Accepted: ATM Onsite, MasterCard, Visa

KOA Montreal South
SAINT PHILIPPE DE LAPRAIRIE (Monteregie)
Phone: 450-659-8626

Directions: From I-15 (exit 38): Go 1.6 km/1 mi. E on Boul Monette.
Description: Treed, grassy sites with clear, level pull-thrus.
Rates: $$–$$$
Number of Sites: 222
Number of Full Hookups: 89
Number of Water/Electric Hookups: 103
Number of Sites with No Hookups: 30
Open: May 1
Close: Oct. 10
Number of Pull-Thru Sites: 200
Services: Dump Station, Non-Guest Dumping, Non-Guest Dumping Fee, Partial Handicap Access
Hookup Information: 20 amps, 30 amps, 50 amps, 50 amps Fee
Amenities: A/C Allowed, A/C Fee, Fire Rings, Groceries, Heater Allowed, Heater Fee, Ice, Laundry, Phone or Modem Hookup—Central Location, Public Phone, RV Supplies, Wood
Recreation: Badminton, Basketball, Horseshoes, Local Tours, Mini-Golf, Mini-Golf Fee, Playground, Pool, Recreation Room/Area, Volleyball, Wading Pool
Discounts: KOA 10% Value Card Discount
Credit Cards Accepted: MasterCard, Visa

Camping Alouette Inc.
SAINT MATHIEU DE BELOEIL (Monteregie)
Phone: 450-464-1661
Web site: *www.campingalouette.com*

Directions: From Hwy I-20 (exit 105): Go 1.6 km/1 mi. NE on service road (ch. de l'Industrie).
Description: Open sites CAMPGROUND.

Rates: $$–$$$

Number of Sites: 400

Seasonal Sites: Some Seasonal Sites

Number of Full Hookups: 335

Number of Water/Electric Hookups: 25

Number of Sites with No Hookups: 40

Number of Pull-Thru Sites: 140

Services: Dump Station, LP Gas by Meter, LP Gas by Weight, Non-Guest Dumping, Non-Guest Dumping Fee, Partial Handicap Access

Open All Year

Pets: Pet Restrictions

Hookup Information: 15 amps, 30 amps, 50 amps, 50 amps Fee

Amenities: A/C Allowed, Fire Rings, Groceries, Heater Allowed, Hot Shower Fee, Ice, Laundry, Phone or Modem Hookup—Central Location, Public Phone, RV Supplies, Traffic Control Gate, Wood

Recreation: Badminton, Basketball, Coin Games, Hiking Trails, Horseshoes, Local Tours, Planned Activities (Weekends Only), Playground, Pool, Recreation Hall, Recreation Room/Area, Shuffleboard, Volleyball, Wading Pool

Credit Cards Accepted: MasterCard, Visa

Facility Fully Operational: April 1 through Nov. 30

NOVA SCOTIA

Dunromin Campsites

ANNAPOLIS ROYAL (Annapolis)

Phone: 902-532-2808

Web site: *www.dunromincampsite.com*

Directions: From east town limits: Go 2.4 km/1½ mi. E on Hwy 1.

Description: CAMPGROUND with open or shaded grassy sites.

Rates: $$–$$$

Number of Sites: 210

Seasonal Sites: Some Seasonal Sites

Number of Full Hookups: 82

Number of Water/Electric Hookups: 83
Number of Sites with No Hookups: 45
Open: May 1
Close: Oct. 15
Number of Pull-Thru Sites: 30
Typical Site Width: 30 ft.
Services: Dump Station, LP Gas by Meter, LP Gas by Weight, Non-Guest Dumping, Non-Guest Dumping Fee
Hookup Information: 30 amps, 50 amps,
Amenities: Fire Rings, Ice, Laundry, Limited Groceries, Phone or Modem Hookup—Central Location, Public Phone, Wood
Recreation: Boating, Canoe Rentals, Canoeing, Coin Games, Dock, Fishing, Fishing Supplies, Hiking Trails, Horseshoes, Kayak Rentals, Kayaking, Pedal Boat Rentals, Play Equipment, Playground, Pool, Ramp, Recreation Hall, Saltwater Fishing, Saltwater Swimming, Sports Field, Volleyball, Whirlpool
Credit Cards Accepted: Diners Club, MasterCard, Visa

Baddeck Cabot Trail Campground
BADDECK (Victoria)
Phone: 902-295-2288
Web site: *www.baddeckcabottrailcampground.com*
Directions: Located 8 km/5 mi. W of Baddeck on Hwy 105, between exits 7 & 8.
Description: CAMPGROUND with semi-wooded or open sites and full-service restaurant.
Rates: $$
Number of Sites: 174
Number of Full Hookups: 66
Number of Water/Electric Hookups: 60
Number of Electric Hookups: 6
Number of Sites with No Hookups: 42
Open: May 15
Close: Oct. 15
Number of Pull-Thru Sites: 51
Typical Site Width: 24 ft.

Services: Dump Station, Non-Guest Dumping

Hookup Information: 15 amps, 30 amps, 50 amps, 50 amps Fee

Amenities: A/C Allowed, Fire Rings, Grills, Groceries, Heater Allowed, Ice, Laundry, Phone or Modem Hookup—Central Location, Public Phone, RV Supplies, Wood

Recreation: Badminton, Basketball, Boating, Canoe Rentals, Canoeing, Coin Games, Fishing, Hiking Trails, Horseshoes, Kayaking, Local Tours, Planned Activities (Weekends Only), Playground, Pool, Recreation Room/Area, River Fishing, Rowboat Rentals, Saltwater Fishing, Sports Field, Volleyball

Discounts: KOA 10% Value Card Discount

Credit Cards Accepted: ATM Onsite, Diners Club, MasterCard, Visa

Halifax West KOA

HALIFAX (Halifax)

Phone: 888-562-4705

Directions: From jct. Hwy 102 & Hwy 101 (exit 4B): Go 15.2 km/9½ mi. W on Hwy 101 (exit 3), then 2 km/1¼ mi. E on Hwy 1.

Description: Open and wooded campground on a river.

Rates: $$–$$$

Number of Sites: 86

Number of Full Hookups: 20

Number of Water/Electric Hookups: 46

Number of Sites with No Hookups: 20

Open: May 15

Close: Oct. 15

Number of Pull-Thru Sites: 15

Typical Site Width: 25 ft.

Services: Dump Station, Non-Guest Dumping, Non-Guest Dumping Fee, Partial Handicap Access

Hookup Information: 30 amps, 50 amps

Amenities: A/C Allowed, Fire Rings, Heater Allowed, Ice, Laundry, Limited Groceries, Phone or Modem Hookup—Central Location, Public Phone, Traffic Control Gate, Wood

Recreation: Basketball, Bike Rentals, Boating, Canoe Rentals,

Canoeing, Coin Games, Dock Fishing, Kayak Rentals, Kayaking, Pedal Boat Rentals, Planned Activities (Weekends Only), Playground, Pool, Recreation Hall, Recreation Room/Area, River Fishing, River Swimming, Volleyball
Discounts: KOA 10% Value Card Discount
Credit Cards Accepted: Diners Club, MasterCard, Visa

Index

Deceptive advertising, 208, 247–48
Depreciation, 20, 128
Destinations, suggested, 144–46,
183–86, 244–45
Disabled travelers, 11–12
Dispute resolution, 127–28
Driving safety
basic tips/skills, 137–38, 142
controlling speed, 135
medications and, 136
motorhomes, 50–51, 81–83
night driving, 136
scheduling time/distances and,
135, 143, 151–52
short learning trip for, 141–42
trailers, 62–63
Dry camping, 230

E

Earthquakes, 258–59
Electrical systems. *See* Power
Emergencies, 189–202
becoming lost, 197–98
cell phones for, 191–92, 198–99
emergency kits, 191–93
evacuation routes, 260
first aid, 197
medical, 187, 195–97
ready-to-eat meals, 192–93
sleep breaks/disorders, 199–201
tools for, 192
See also Safety
Entertainment systems, 111–12, 182,
237
Environment, protecting, 254–56
Estate auctions, 22
Extended warranties, 123–25

F

Factory buying, 19
Family challenges, 8–10

Fifth-wheel trailers, 57–59
Finances. *See* Budget
considerations; Buying RVs;
Upgrading RVs
Fire safety, 112–13, 188, 190–91, 261
Floods, 259
Floor plan options, 17
Florida destinations, 183–85,
244–45
Fluid levels, 78–79
Fold-down (foldup) trailers, 34–36
maintenance, 36–38
setting up, 41–42
Food, 165–78
buying while traveling, 176–77
cooking, 156, 174–75, 256
dishes/utensils for, 168, 177–78
planning ahead, 165–67
prepackaged meals, 171–73, 192–93
simple menus, 169–71
special occasion meals, 175–76
stocking galley, 168–69
storage, 168–69, 173–74, 256–57
wildlife and, 256–57
Forest fires, 261
Fresh water, 107, 154, 193
Front porch neighborhood, 5
Fuel costs, 26, 44, 81

G

Games/activities, 180–81, 238
Gas detectors, 132
GCWR (gross combined weight
rating), 61, 87, 88
Global Positioning System (GPS),
81, 150–51
Good Sam Club, 246–47
Gray water, 108
GVWR (gross vehicle weight
rating), 61, 87, 88

For Travel!

The Everything® Family Guide to New York City, 2nd Edition
Rich Mintzer

The Everything® Family Guide to New York City, 2nd Ed. features all of New York's best-loved attractions, from Battery Park to Museum Mile. Starting with the must-see landmarks—the Statue of Liberty and Empire State Building—to surprising secret treasures that are off the beaten path, this book includes information on where to stay and eat, neighborhood explorations, shows and attractions, New York after dark, and more.

1-59337-136-5

$14.95($19.95 CAN)

1-59337-137-3

14.95 ($19.95 CAN)

The Everything® Family Guide to Washington D.C., 2nd Edition
Lori Perkins

The Everything® Family Guide to Washington D.C., 2nd Ed. captures the spirit and excitement of this unique city, from important historical showpieces such as the White House and the Smithsonian, to the best museums, galleries, and family activities. You'll find up-to-date reviews for tons of hotels and restaurants, guided tours, loads of attractions and activities, museums for every interest, and more!

To order, call 800-872-5627 or visit www.everything.com

1-58062-742-0

$14.95 ($19.95 CAN)

Travel Guide to The Disneyland Resort®, California Adventure®, Universal Studios®, and the Anaheim Area

Jason Rich

With millions of visitors each year, it's easy to see why Disneyland® is one of America's favorite vacation spots for families. Containing the most up-to-date information, this brand-new expansive travel guide contains everything needed to plan the perfect getaway without missing any of the great new attractions. This book rates all the rides, shows, and attractions for each member of the family, allowing readers to plan the perfect itinerary for their trip.

Family Guide to The Walt Disney World Resort®, Universal Studios®, and Greater Orlando, Fourth Edition

Jason Rich

Packed with fun things to see and do, the Orlando area is the number one vacation destination in the country. In this newest edition, travel expert Jason Rich shares his latest tips on how the whole family can have a great time—without breaking the bank. In addition to the helpful ride, show, and attractions rating system, the revised fourth edition contains a fully updated hotel/motel resource guide, rated restaurant listings, and the inside scoop on all the new additions.

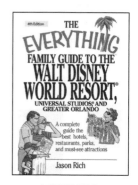

1-59337-179-9

$14.95 ($19.95 CAN)